Virtualization
FOR
DUMMIES®

by Bernard Golden

Wiley Publishing, Inc.

Virtualization For Dummies®

Published by
Wiley Publishing, Inc.
111 River Street
Hoboken, NJ 07030-5774

www.wiley.com

Copyright © 2008 by Wiley Publishing, Inc., Indianapolis, Indiana

Published by Wiley Publishing, Inc., Indianapolis, Indiana

Published simultaneously in Canada

For general information on our other products and services, please contact our Customer Care Department within the U.S. at 800-762-2974, outside the U.S. at 317-572-3993, or fax 317-572-4002.

For technical support, please visit www.wiley.com/techsupport.

Wiley also publishes its books in a variety of electronic formats. Some content that appears in print may not be available in electronic books.

Library of Congress Control Number: 2007940109

ISBN: 978-0-470-14831-0

10 9 8 7 6 5 4 3

WILEY

About the Author

Bernard Golden has been called "a renowned open source expert" (IT Business Edge) and "an open source guru" (SearchCRM.com) and is regularly featured in magazines like *Computerworld, InformationWeek,* and *Inc.* His blog "The Open Source" is one of the most popular features of CIO Magazine's Web site. Bernard is a frequent speaker at industry conferences like LinuxWorld, the Open Source Business Conference, and the Red Hat Summit. He is the author of *Succeeding with Open Source,* (Addison-Wesley, 2005, published in four languages), which is used in over a dozen university open source programs throughout the world. Bernard is the CEO of Navica, a Silicon Valley IT management consulting firm.

Dedication

To Sebastian and Oliver, the bright stars Kocab and Pherkad, Guardians of the Pole of the Golden family constellation. May your lives be blessed in the ways you've blessed mine.

Author's Acknowledgments

So many people have helped in the writing of this book that it would be justi-fied in calling it a collaboration of the willing. Their enthusiasm in sharing information and perspective has been invaluable. I'd like to thank everyone who offered help and encouragement and to especially thank the following:

Kyle Looper and Paul Levesque of Wiley Publishing, Inc., who gently yet irre-sistibly pushed me toward finishing the book. Kyle generously contracted for the book, and Paul affably helped shape it in the direct and comprehensible *For Dummies* style.

David Marshall, who performed the key duty of technical reviewer for the book, providing much valuable feedback. David is a real virtualization guru who writes the weekly virtualization newsletter for InfoWorld and also works at the virtualization startup Inovawave.

From HP: Andy Scholl helped me comprehend HP's myriad of virtualization technologies and products.

From IBM: Chris Almond, Greg Kelleher, Jerone Young, and Bob Zuber helped me comprehend this very large organization's various virtualization initiatives, and I appreciate their assistance.

From Novell: Jonathan Ervine, Kerry Kim, and Justin Steinman provided insight about Novell's virtualization objectives and technology.

From Platespin: Richard Azevedo and Bojan Dusevic were very generous and helpful with their time, much appreciated in helping me sort out the complex topic of P2V migration.

From Red Hat: Joel Berman, Nick Carr, Jan Mark Holzer, Rob Kenna, and Brian Stevens all very generously shared their time and expertise, especially aiding with the Fedora hands-on chapter.

From Sun: Joanne Kisling, Chris Ratcliffe, Paul Steeves, Joost Pronk van Hoogeveen, and Bob Wientzen described Sun's virtualization efforts and clari-fied Sun's future plans.

From VMware: Joe Andrews, Bogomil Balkansky, and Melinda Wilken were extremely helpful in understanding the different components and products that incorporate the VMware technology.

From XenSource: John Bara, Christof Berlin, Peter Blum, Simon Crosby, and Roger Klorese helped enabled me to describe the Xen architecture and technology.

Publisher's Acknowledgments

We're proud of this book; please send us your comments through our online registration form located at `www.dummies.com/register/`.

Some of the people who helped bring this book to market include the following:

Acquisitions and Editorial

Senior Project Editor: Paul Levesque

Acquisitions Editor: Kyle Looper

Copy Editor: Virginia Sanders

Technical Editors: David Marshall

Editorial Manager: Leah Cameron

Editorial Assistant: Amanda Foxworth

Sr. Editorial Assistant: Cherie Case

Cartoons: Rich Tennant
(`www.the5thwave.com`)

Composition Services

Project Coordinator: Kristie Rees

Layout and Graphics: Reuben W. Davis, Alissa Ellet, Melissa K. Jester, Barbara Moore, Christine Williams

Proofreaders: Laura L. Bowman, John Greenough

Indexer: Ty Koontz

Anniversary Logo Design: Richard Pacifico

Publishing and Editorial for Technology Dummies

Richard Swadley, Vice President and Executive Group Publisher

Andy Cummings, Vice President and Publisher

Mary Bednarek, Executive Acquisitions Director

Mary C. Corder, Editorial Director

Publishing for Consumer Dummies

Diane Graves Steele, Vice President and Publisher

Joyce Pepple, Acquisitions Director

Composition Services

Gerry Fahey, Vice President of Production Services

Debbie Stailey, Director of Composition Services

Contents at a Glance

Table of Contents

Foreword

*W*hen Bernard invited me to write an introduction to this book, I found myself reminded of a frequently repeated conversation with my father, who is a retired engineer. Typically, it goes like this: "Simon, what does virtualization do?" — followed by a lengthy reply from me and then a long pause from my father — "And why is that useful?" Now, I certainly don't think that my father really has much use for server virtualization, but a lot more people do need it — and need to understand it — than currently use it.

Although virtualization is all the rage in the tech industry press, and savvy market watchers have observed the exciting IPO of VMware, and Citrix's acquisition of my own company, XenSource, the market for virtualization software is largely unaddressed. Depending on whose research you read, only 7 percent or so of x86 servers are virtualized, and only a tiny fraction of desktop or mobile PCs are virtualized. But the virtualization market is white hot, and every day new announcements in storage, server, and network virtualization make the picture more complex and harder to understand.

Virtualization For Dummies is the perfect way to develop a complete understanding of both the technology and the benefits of virtualization. Arguably, virtualization is simply a consequence of Moore's Law — the guideline developed by Intel founder Gordon Moore that predicts a doubling in the number of transistors per unit area on a CPU every couple of years. With PCs and servers becoming so incredibly powerful, the typical software suites that most users would install on a single physical server a few years ago now consume only a few percent of the resources of a modern machine. Virtualization is simply a consequence of the obvious waste of resources — allowing a machine to run multiple virtualized servers or client operating systems simultaneously. But if that were all that were needed, there wouldn't be such a fuss about virtualization. Instead, virtualization is having a profound impact on data center architectures and growth, on software lifecycle management, on security and manageability of software, and the agility of IT departments to meet with new challenges. And it is these opportunities and challenges that urgently need to be articulated to technologists and business leaders alike in an accessible and understandable way.

Having spent many enjoyable hours with Bernard Golden, a recognized open source guru, President and CEO of Navica, and self-taught virtualization expert, I cannot think of a better-qualified author for a book whose objective is to cut through the hype and clearly and succinctly deal with virtualization and its effects on IT and users alike. I always look forward to reading

Bernard's frequently published commentaries on Xen, VMware, and Linux, which combine his hands-on experience with those products and a rare depth of insight into industry dynamics. I know firsthand that Bernard is a master of the subject of virtualization because he is one of the most persistent and demanding beta testers of XenEnterprise, XenSource's server virtualization product, where his feedback has provided us with terrific guidance on how to improve the product overall. This, together with Bernard's incisive, clear, and articulate style, makes this book a pleasure to read and a terrific contribution to the virtualization industry — a concise categorization of virtualization that will further the understanding of the technology and its benefits, driving uptake of virtualization generally. It is with great pleasure that I strongly recommend that you read this book.

Simon Crosby

CTO, XenSource, Inc.

Introduction

*I*f you work in tech, there's no way you haven't heard the term *virtualization*. Even if you don't work in tech, you might have been exposed to virtualization. In August 2007, virtualization's leading company, VMware, went public with the year's most highly anticipated IPO. Even people who confuse virtualization with visualization sit up and pay attention when a blockbuster IPO comes to market. To show how hot the sector is, VMware was bought by the storage company EMC for $625 million in 2004, but it has, as of this writing, a market capitalization of $25.6 *billion*.

The excitement and big dollars illustrate a fundamental reality about virtualization: It's transforming the way computing works. Virtualization is going to fundamentally change the way you implement and manage data centers, the way you obtain and install software, and the way you think about the speed with which you can respond to changing business conditions. The changes that virtualization will cause in your work environment will be so profound that, in ten years time, you'll look back on the traditional ways of managing hardware and software the way your grandparents looked back on operator-assisted telephone dialing after the introduction of direct dialing.

I wrote this book because I'm convinced that the world is on the cusp of an enormous change in the use of information technology, also known as IT. In the past, IT was expensive, so it was limited to must-have applications such as accounting and order tracking. In the past, IT was complex, so it had to be managed by a group of wizards with their own special language and incantations. That's all changing.

In the future, IT will be cheap, so applications will be ubiquitous, and low-priority applications will finally get their day in the sun. In the future, implementing IT will be simple, so groups outside of IT will shun the wizards' robes and arcane language and implement their own applications, which will, of course, make central IT's role even more important because it will have to create a robust yet malleable infrastructure.

Instead of IT being this special thing that supports only certain aspects of a business, it will become pervasive, suffusing throughout every business operation and every business interaction. It's an incredibly exciting time for IT; I compare it to the rise of mass production made possible by Henry Ford. Because of Henry Ford, automobiles went from playthings for the wealthy to everyday belongings of the masses, and society was transformed by mobility and speed. Virtualization is the mass production of IT.

Just as the automobile industry underwent rapid transformation after Ford invented mass production in 1913, the virtualization marketplace is transforming the IT industry today. One of the biggest challenges for this book is to present a coherent and unified view of the topic even though virtualization is evolving at an incredible pace. At times, I felt that writing this book was like trying to nail Jell-O to the wall. During just one week of the writing of this book, the IPO of VMware went from an event no one had even considered to the technology financial event of the year; in the same week, XenSource, the commercial sponsor of the open source Xen virtualization project, was purchased by Citrix for $500 million. Furthermore, myriads of virtualization technology and product announcements occurred, making me, at times, wish I could push a Pause button on the market so that I could have a hope of completing an up-to-date book. Alas, virtualization's fevered evolution shows no sign of diminishing — good for the virtualization user, challenging for the virtualization writer.

Why Buy This Book?

Even though virtualization is changing the face of technology, it is, unfortunately, still riddled with the complexities and — especially — the arcane language of tech. Two seconds into a conversation about virtualization, you'll start hearing terms like *hypervisor* and *bare metal,* which sound, respectively, like something from *Star Wars* and an auto shop class.

It's unfortunate that virtualization can be difficult to approach because of this specialized terminology. It's especially unfortunate because understanding and applying virtualization will be, in the near future, a fundamental skill for everyone in IT — and for many people working in other disciplines like marketing and finance. Consequently, having a strong grounding in virtualization is critical for people wanting to participate in the IT world of the future.

This book is designed to provide a thorough introduction to the subject. It assumes that you have no knowledge of virtualization and will leave you (I hope) with a good grasp of the topic. My objective is for you to be completely comfortable with virtualization and its many elements and to be able to participate and contribute to your organization's virtualization initiatives. The book also serves as a jumping-off point for deeper research and work in virtualization.

Foolish Assumptions

This book doesn't assume you know much about virtualization beyond having heard the term. You don't have to know any of the technical details of the topic, and you certainly don't need to have done hands-on work with virtualization. (The book provides the opportunity to do hands-on work with virtualization, with three chapters devoted to installing and implementing different virtualization products.)

I define every virtualization term you encounter. I also make it a point to thoroughly explain complex topics so that you can understand the connections between different virtualization elements.

The book *does* assume that you have a basic understanding of computers, operating systems, and applications and how they work together to enable computers to do useful work. Because virtualization shuffles the placement and interaction of existing system software and hardware layers, it's important to have a grasp of how things are traditionally done. However, if you've worked with computers, used an operating system, and installed applications, you should have the knowledge base to make use of the book's content.

How This Book Is Organized

As is the case with other *For Dummies* books, this book doesn't assume that you'll begin on page one and read straight through to the end. Each chapter is written to stand alone, with enough contextual information provided so that you can understand the chapter's content. Cross-references are provided to other chapters that go into more detail about topics lightly touched on in a given chapter.

You'll soon notice, though, that individual chapters are grouped together in a somewhat-less-than-random order. The organizing principle here is the *part,* and this book has five of them.

Part 1: Getting Started with a Virtualization Project

Getting a good grounding in a subject is critical to understanding it and, more important, to recognizing how you can best take advantage of it. Part I provides a whirlwind tour of the world of virtualization — from where it is today to beyond where it will be tomorrow.

Chapter 1 is where you get an overview of virtualization, including an introduction to why it's such a hot topic. Chapter 1 also discusses the basic philosophy of virtualization — the abstraction of computer functionality from physical resources. Chapter 2 describes the business reasons that are driving virtualization's explosive growth, and it discusses how you can make a business case for your virtualization project. If you want a deeper understanding of the different technologies that make up virtualization as well as the different ways virtualization is applied in everyday use, Chapter 3 is for you. Finally, if you want to get a sense of where virtualization is heading, Chapter 4 provides a glimpse of the exciting initiatives that are being made possible by virtualization.

Part II: Server Virtualization

Server virtualization is where the hottest action is in today's virtualization world. The most obvious use cases and the most immediate payoffs are available with server virtualization, and this part covers it all.

Chapter 5 gives you information for a litmus test to inform you whether server virtualization makes sense for you. The chapter lets you do a bit of self-testing to see whether your organization is ready to implement virtualization. Just as important, the chapter gives you the tools you'll need to find out whether it doesn't make sense for you to implement virtualization. Chapter 6 provides in-depth information on how to make a financial assessment of your virtualization project, including how to create a spreadsheet to calculate all the costs and benefits of a potential virtualization project. Chapter 7 discusses the all-important topic of how to manage a virtualization project; there's far more involved here than just installing a virtualization hypervisor. Finally, Chapter 8 discusses a very important topic — the hardware you'll use to run your virtualization software. There are many exciting developments in hardware with significant influence on the operational and financial benefits of virtualization.

Part III: Server Virtualization Software Options

Sometimes I see a movie with a happy ending and wonder "Yeah, but how did the rest of their lives turn out?" Virtualization can be something like that. If you listen to vendors, you just install their software and — presto! — instant virtualized infrastructure. Just like real life isn't like the movies, real infrastructure isn't like that, either, and Part III helps you have a true happy ending.

Chapter 9 deals with the critical issue of how to migrate an existing physical infrastructure to a virtualized one. (**Hint:** It's more complex than the vendors claim.) Chapter 10 addresses managing a virtualized infrastructure; there are a plethora of options, and this chapter provides help in deciding which option is a good choice for you. Chapter 11 addresses a topic that's often an afterthought in virtualization: storage. For many organizations, virtualization provides the impetus to move to shared (also known as *virtualized*) storage. It's important to know what your storage options are and how to select one.

Part IV: Implementing Virtualization

If you're like me, theoretical understanding goes just so far. Then I want to roll up my sleeves and get my hands dirty. If you're like that as well, rejoice! Part IV can feed your hands-on hunger. In this part, I present three different examples of how to install and use virtualization. Best of all, each of the products used for the examples is available at no cost, making it possible for you to work along with them with no financial commitment.

Chapter 12 illustrates how to implement VMware Server as well as how to install a guest virtual machine. Chapter 13 works through Xen virtualization via the open source Linux distribution Fedora. Chapter 14 also illustrates a Xen-based virtualization, but the chapter uses the free XenExpress product from XenSource to share a different way of applying Xen virtualization.

Part V: The Part of Tens

Every *For Dummies* book concludes with a few chapters that provide a final burst of valuable information delivered in a sleek, stripped-down format — the time-honored ten-point list.

In Chapter 15, you get a list of the ten must-do steps for your first virtualization project. Chapter 16 shares ten no-no's to avoid in a virtualization project. And Chapter 17 gives you ten great virtualization resources for you to use after you finish this book.

Icons Used in This Book

This icon flags useful, helpful tips, or shortcuts.

This icon marks something that might be good to store away for future reference.

Pay attention. The bother you save might be your own.

This icon highlights tidbits for the more technically inclined that I hope augment their understanding — but I won't be offended if less-technically inclined readers hurry through with eyes averted.

Where to Go from Here

Pick a page and start reading! You can use the Table of Contents as a guide, or my parts description in this introduction, or you can leaf through the index for a particular topic. If you're an accounting type, you might jump right into Chapter 6 — the chapter with all the lovely spreadsheets. If you're a hardcore techie type, you might want to check out Chapter 8 — yes, yes, the hardware chapter. Wherever you start, you'll soon find yourself immersed in one of the more exciting stories to come down the tech pipe in a long time.

Chapter 1

Wrapping Your Head around Virtualization

*I*t seems like everywhere you go these days, someone is talking about virtualization. Technical magazines trumpet the technology on their covers. Virtualization sessions are featured prominently at technology conferences. And, predictably enough, technology vendors are describing how *their* product is the latest word in virtualization.

If you have the feeling that everyone else in the world understands virtualization perfectly while you're still trying to understand just what it is and how you might take advantage of it, take heart. Virtualization *is* a new technology. (Actually, it's a pretty well-established technology, but a confluence of conditions happening just now has brought it into new prominence — more on that later in this chapter.) Virtualization *is* a technology being widely applied today with excellent operational and financial results, but it's by no means universally used or understood. That's the purpose of this book: to provide you with an introduction to the subject so that you can understand its promise and perils and create an action plan to decide whether virtualization is right for you, as well as move forward with implementing it should you decide it *is* right for you.

Sadly, not even this book can protect you from the overblown claims of vendors; there is no vaccine strong enough for that disease. This book helps you sort out the hope from the hype and gives you tools to feel confident in making your virtualization decisions.

Virtualization: A Definition

Virtualization refers to a concept in which access to a single underlying piece of hardware, like a server, is coordinated so that multiple guest operating systems can share that single piece of hardware, with no guest operating system being aware that it is actually sharing anything at all. (A *guest operating system* is an operating system that's hosted by the underlying virtualization software layer, which is often, you guessed it, called the *host system.*) A guest operating system appears to the applications running on it as a complete operating system (OS), and the guest OS itself is completely unaware that it's running on top of a layer of virtualization software rather than directly on the physical hardware.

Actually, you've had experience with something like this when you used a computer. When you interact with a particular application, the operating system "virtualizes" access to the underlying hardware so that only the application you're using has access to it — only your program is able to manipulate the files it accesses, write to the screen, and so on. Although this description oversimplifies the reality of how operating systems work, it captures a central reality: The operating system takes care of controlling how applications access the hardware so that each application can do its work without worrying about the state of the hardware. The operating system *encapsulates* the hardware, allowing multiple applications to use it.

In *server* virtualization — the most common type of virtualization — you can think of virtualization as inserting another layer of encapsulation so that multiple operating systems can operate on a single piece of hardware. In this scenario, each operating system believes it has sole control of the underlying hardware, but in reality, the virtualization software controls access to it in such a way that a number of operating systems can work without colliding with one another. The genius of virtualization is that it provides new capability without imposing the need for significant product or process change.

Actually, that last statement is a bit overbroad. A type of virtualization called paravirtualization does require some modification to the software that uses it. However, the resulting excellent performance can make up for the fact that it's a little less convenient to use. Get used to this exception business; the subject of virtualization is riddled with general truths that have specific exceptions. Although you have to take account of those exceptions in your particular project plans, don't let these exceptions deter you from the overarching circumstances. The big picture is what you need to focus on to understand how virtualization can help *you.*

Virtualization is actually a simple concept made complex by all the exceptions that arise in particular circumstances. It can be frustrating to find yourself stymied by what seems to be a niggling detail, but unfortunately, that's the reality of virtualization. If you stop to think about it, the complexity makes sense — you're moving multiple operating systems and applications onto a new piece of software called a *hypervisor,* which in turn talks to underlying hardware. Of course it's complex! But don't worry, if you hang in there, it usually comes out right in the end. Chapters 12 through 14 offer real examples of how to install several flavors of virtualization software and successfully put guest OSes onto the software. Work through the examples, and you'll be an expert in no time!

So, if you take nothing more away from this section than the fact that virtualization enables you to share a hardware resource among a number of other software systems, that's enough for you to understand the next topic — what's making virtualization so important *now.*

Why Virtualization Is Hot, Hot, Hot — The Four Drivers of Virtualization

Despite all the recent buzz about it, virtualization is by no means a new technology. Mainframe computers have offered the ability to host multiple operating systems for over 30 years. In fact, if you begin to discuss it, you might suffer the misfortune of having someone begin to regale you with tales of how *he* did virtualization in the old days.

The truth is that your old gaffer is right. Yeah, virtualization as a technology is nothing new, and yeah, it's been around for many years, but it was confined to "big iron" (that is, mainframes). Four trends have come together in just the past couple of years that have moved virtualization from the dusty mainframe backroom to a front-and-center position in today's computing environment.

When you take a look at these trends, you can immediately recognize why virtualization is much more than the latest technology fad from an industry that has brought you more fads than the fashion industry.

Trend #1: Hardware is underutilized

I recently had an opportunity to visit the Intel Museum located at the company's headquarters in Santa Clara, California. The museum contains a treasure trove of computing — from a giant design-it-yourself chip game to a set of sterile clothes (called a *bunny suit*) you can put on while viewing a live camera feed from a chip-manufacturing plant. It's well worth a visit. But tucked near the back of the museum, in a rather undistinguished case, is ensconced one of the critical documents of computing. This document, despite its humble presentation, contains an idea that has been key to the development of computing in our time.

I refer to the article by Intel cofounder Gordon Moore in the April 1965 issue of *Electronics Magazine,* in which he first offered his observation about the compounding power of processor computing power, which has come to be known as "Moore's Law."

In describing the increasing power of computing power, Moore stated: "The complexity for minimum component costs has increased at a rate of roughly a factor of two per year." Clearly, Moore wasn't in charge of marketing at Intel, but if you translate this into something the average human can understand, he means that each year (actually, most people estimate the timeframe at around 18 months), for a given size processor, twice as many individual components can be squeezed onto a similarly sized piece of silicon. Put another way, every new generation of chip delivers twice as much processing power as the previous generation — at the same price.

This rapid doubling of processing power has had a tremendous impact on daily life, to an extent that's difficult to comprehend for most people. Just over ten years ago, I ran the engineering group of a large enterprise software vendor. Everybody in the group knew that a major part of the hassles involved in getting a new release out the door involved trying to get acceptable performance out of the product on the then-latest generation of hardware. The hardware just wasn't that capable. Today's hardware, based upon the inexorable march of Moore's Law, is around 100,000 times as powerful — in ten short years!

What you need to keep in mind to understand Moore's Law is that the numbers that are continuing to double are themselves getting larger. So, if you take year one as a base, with, say, processing power of 100 million instructions per second (MIPS) available, then in year two, there will be 200; in year three, 400; and so on. Impressive, eh? When you get out to year seven or eight, the increase is from something like 6,400 to 12,800 in one generation. It has grown by 6,400. And the next year, it will grow by 12,800. It's mind boggling, really.

Moore's Law demonstrates increasing returns — the amount of improvement itself grows over time because there's an exponential increase in capacity for every generation of processor improvement. It's that exponential increase that's responsible for the mind-boggling improvements in computing — and the increasing need for virtualization.

And that brings me to the meaning of this trend. Unlike ten years ago, when folks had to sweat to get software to run on the puny hardware that was available at that time, today the hardware is so powerful that software typically uses only a small portion of the available processing power. And this causes a different type of problem.

Today, many data centers have machines running at only 10 or 15 percent of total processing capacity. In other words, 85 or 90 percent of the machine's power is unused. In a way, Moore's Law is no longer relevant to most companies because they aren't able to take advantage of the increased power available to them. After all, if you're hauling a 50-pound bag of cement, having a truck come out that can carry 20,000 pounds instead of this year's model that can only carry 10,000 pounds is pretty irrelevant for your purposes. However, a lightly loaded machine still takes up room and draws electricity, so the cost of today's underutilized machine is nearly the same as if it was running at full capacity.

It doesn't take a rocket scientist to recognize that this situation is a waste of computing resources. And, guess what? With the steady march of Moore's Law, next year's machine will have twice as much spare capacity as this year's — and so on, for the foreseeable future. Obviously, there ought to be a better way to match computing capacity with load. And that's what virtualization does — by enabling a single piece of hardware to seamlessly support multiple systems. By applying virtualization, organizations can raise their hardware use rates from 10 or 15 percent to 70 or 80 percent, thereby making much more efficient use of corporate capital.

Moore's Law not only enables virtualization, but effectively makes it mandatory. Otherwise, increasing amounts of computing power will go to waste each year.

So, the first trend that's causing virtualization to be a mainstream concern is the unending growth of computing power brought to you by the friendly folks of the chip industry. By the way, the same trend that's described in chips by Moore's Law can be observed in the data storage and networking arenas as well. They just don't have a fancy name for their exponential growth — so maybe Gordon Moore was a marketing genius after all. However, the rapid improvement in these other technology areas means that virtualization is being explored for them as well — and because I like being complete, I work in coverage of these areas later on in this book.

Trend #2: Data centers run out of space

The business world has undergone an enormous transformation over the past 20 years. In 1985, the vast majority of business processes were paper based. Computerized systems were confined to so-called backroom automation: payroll, accounting, and the like.

That has all changed, thanks to the steady march of Moore's Law. Business process after business process has been captured in software and automated, moving from paper to computers.

The rise of the Internet has exponentially increased this transformation. Companies want to communicate with customers and partners in real time, using the worldwide connectivity of the Internet. Naturally, this has accelerated the move to computerized business processes.

To offer a dramatic example, Boeing's latest airliner, the 787 Dreamliner, is being designed and built in a radically new way. Boeing and each of its suppliers use Computer-Aided Design (CAD) software to design their respective parts of the plane. All communication about the project uses these CAD designs as the basis for discussion. Use of CAD software enables testing to be done in computer models rather than the traditional method of building physical prototypes, thereby speeding completion of the plane by a year or more.

As you might imagine, the Dreamliner project generates enormous amounts of data. Just one piece of the project — a data warehouse containing project plans — runs to 19 terabytes of data.

Boeing's experience is common across all companies and all industries. How big is the explosion of data? In 2003, the world's computer users created and stored 5 exabytes (each exabyte is 1 million terabytes) of new data. A recent study by the Enterprise Strategy Group predicted that governments and corporations will store over 25 exabytes of data by the year 2010. Certainly, the trend of data growth within organizations is accelerating. The growth of data can be easily seen in one key statistic: In 2006, the storage industry shipped as much storage in one month as it did in the entire year of 2000. The research firm IDC estimates that total storage shipped will increase 50 percent per year for the next five years.

The net effect of all this is that huge numbers of servers have been put into use over the past decade, which is causing a real-estate problem for companies: They're running out of space in their data centers. And, by the way, that explosion of data calls for new methods of data storage, which I also address in this book. These methods go by the common moniker of *storage virtualization,* which, as you might predict, encapsulates storage and abstracts it from underlying network storage devices.

Virtualization, by offering the ability to host multiple guest systems on a single physical server, helps organizations to reclaim data center territory, thereby avoiding the expense of building out more data center space. This is an enormous benefit of virtualization because data centers cost in the tens of millions of dollars to construct. You can find out more about this in Chapter 4, where I discuss this trend, which is usually referred to as *consolidation* and is one of the major drivers for organizations to turn to virtualization.

Take a look at your data center to understand any capacity constraints you're operating with. If you're near capacity, you need virtualization — stat!

Trend #3: Energy costs go through the roof

In most companies' strategic thinking, budgeting power costs used to rank somewhere below deciding what brand of soda to keep in the vending machines. Companies could assume that electrical power was cheap and endlessly available.

Several events over the past few years have changed that mindset dramatically:

- ✔ The increasing march of computerization discussed in Trend #2, earlier in this chapter, means that every company is using more power as their computing processes expand.

- ✔ The assumption regarding availability of reliable power was challenged during the California power scares of a few years ago. Although later evidence caused some reevaluation about whether there was a true power shortage (can you say "Enron"?), the events caused companies to consider whether they should look for ways to be less power dependent.

- ✔ As a result of the power scares and Pacific Gas & Electric's resulting bankruptcy, power costs in California, home to Silicon Valley, have skyrocketed, making power a more significant part of every company's budget. In fact, for many companies, electricity now ranks as one of the top five costs in their operating budgets.

The cost of running computers, coupled with the fact that many of the machines filling up data centers are running at low utilization rates, means that virtualization's ability to reduce the total number of physical servers can significantly reduce the overall cost of energy for companies.

Data center power is such an issue that energy companies are putting virtualization programs into place to address it. See Chapter 5 to find out about an innovative virtualization rebate program Pacific Gas & Electric has put into place.

Trend #4: System administration costs mount

Computers don't operate on their own. Every server requires care and feeding by system administrators who, as part of the operations group, ensure that the server runs properly. Common system administration tasks include monitoring hardware status; replacing defective hardware components; installing operating system (OS) and application software; installing OS and application patches; monitoring critical server resources such as memory and disk use; and backing up server data to other storage mediums for security and redundancy purposes.

As you might imagine, this job is pretty labor intensive. System administrators don't come cheap. And, unlike programmers, who can be located in less expensive offshore locales, system administrators are usually located with the servers due to their need to access the physical hardware.

The steady increase in server numbers has meant that the job market for system administrators has been good — very good.

As part of an effort to rein in operations cost increases, virtualization offers the opportunity to reduce overall system administration costs by reducing the overall number of machines that need to be taken care of. Although many of the tasks associated with system administration (OS and application patching, doing backups) continue even in a virtualized environment, some of them disappear as physical servers are migrated to virtual instances. Overall, virtualization can reduce system administration requirements by 30 to 50 percent per virtualized server, making virtualization an excellent option to address the increasing cost of operations personnel.

Virtualization reduces the amount of system administration work necessary for hardware, but it doesn't reduce the amount of system administration required for guest OSes. Therefore, virtualization improves system administration, but doesn't make it vanish.

Four trends mean virtualization is hot

Looking at these four trends, you can see why virtualization is a technology whose time has come. The exponential power growth of computers, the substitution of automated processes for manual work, the increasing cost to power the multitude of computers, and the high personnel cost to manage that multitude all cry out for a less expensive way to run data centers. In fact, a newer, more efficient method of running data centers is critical because, given the four trends, the traditional methods of delivering computing are becoming cost prohibitive. Virtualization is the solution to the problems caused by the four trends I outline here.

Sorting Out the Types of Virtualization

If you've made it this far in this chapter, you (hopefully) have a rough idea of virtualization and why it's an important development. Your next step involves determining what your options are when it comes to virtualization. In other words, what are some common applications of the technology?

Virtualization has a number of common uses, all centered around the concept that virtualization represents an abstraction from physical resources. In fact, enough kinds of virtualization exist to make it a bit confusing to sort out how you might apply it in your organization.

I do what I can to sort out the virtualization mare's nest. If you're okay with gross generalizations, I can tell you that there are three main types of virtualization: client, server, and storage. Within each main type are different approaches or *flavors,* each of which has its benefits and drawbacks. The next few sections give brief descriptions of each of the three types of virtualization, along with examples of common implementations of them.

Client virtualization

Client virtualization refers to virtualization capabilities residing on a *client* (a desktop or laptop PC). Given that much of the earlier discussion of the driving forces behind virtualization focuses on the problems of the data center, you might wonder why virtualization is necessary for client machines at all.

The primary reason organizations are interested in pursuing client virtualization solutions has to do with the challenges they face in managing large numbers of computers controlled by end users. Although machines located in data centers typically have strict procedures about what software is loaded on them and when they're updated with new software releases, end user machines are a whole different story.

Because loading software is as easy as sticking a disc into the machine's CD drive (or a thumb drive into a USB slot), client machines can have endless amounts of non-IT-approved software installed. Each application can potentially cause problems with the machine's operating system as well as other approved applications. Beyond that, other nefarious software can get onto client machines in endless ways: via e-mail viruses, accidental spyware downloads, and so on. And, the hard truth is that Microsoft Windows, the dominant client operating system, is notorious for attracting attacks in the form of malware applications.

Added to the end user–caused problems are the problems inherent to client machines in general: keeping approved software applications up to date, ensuring the latest operating system patches are installed, and getting recent virus definitions downloaded to the machine's antivirus software.

Mixed together, this stew is a miserable recipe for IT. Anything that makes the management of client machines easier and more secure is of definite interest to IT. Client virtualization offers the potential to accomplish this.

Three main types — or flavors, if you will — of client virtualization exist: application packaging, application streaming, and hardware emulation.

Application packaging

Although the specifics of how application packaging is accomplished vary from one vendor to another, all the methods share a common approach: isolating an application that runs on a client machine from the underlying operating system. By isolating the application from the operating system, the application is unable to modify underlying critical operating system resources, making it much less likely that the OS will end up compromised by malware or viruses.

You can accomplish this application-packaging approach by executing the application on top of a software product that gives each application its own virtual set of system resources — stuff like files and registry entries. Another way to accomplish application packaging is by bundling the application and the virtualization software into a single executable program that is downloaded or installed; when the executable program is run, the application and the virtualization software cooperate and run in an isolated (or *sandboxed*) fashion, thereby separating the application from the underlying operating system.

Application packaging is a great way to isolate programs from one another and reduce virus transmission, but it doesn't solve the problem of end users installing nonpackaged software on client machines.

One thing to keep in mind with this approach is that it causes additional work as the IT folks prepare the application packages that are needed and then distribute them to client machines. And, of course, this approach does nothing to solve the problem of end users installing other software on the machine that bypasses the application packaging approach altogether. If you're loading a game onto your business laptop, you're hardly likely to go to IT and request that someone create a new application package so that you can run your game securely, are you?

Products that provide application packaging include SVS from Altiris, Thinstall's Virtualization Suite, and Microsoft's SoftGrid.

Application streaming

Application streaming solves the problem of how to keep client machines loaded with up-to-date software in a completely different fashion than application packaging. Because it's so difficult to keep the proper versions of applications installed on client machines, this approach avoids installing them altogether. Instead, it stores the proper versions of applications on servers in the data center, and when an end user wants to use a particular application, it's downloaded on the fly to the end user's machine, whereupon he or she uses it as though it were natively installed on the machine.

This approach to client virtualization can reduce the amount of IT work necessary to keep machines updated. Furthermore, it happens transparently to the end user because the updated application is automatically delivered to the end user, without any physical software installation on the client. It also has the virtue of possibly allowing client machines less capability to be deployed because less disk space is required to permanently store applications on the client hard drive. Furthermore, if this approach is taken to its logical conclusion and the client machine has no hard drive, it is possible that less memory is required because only the official IT applications can be executed on the machine. This result is because the end user can't execute any programs other than the ones available from the central server.

Although at first glance, this approach might seem like a useful form of virtualization, it is really appropriate only in certain circumstances — primarily situations in which end users have constant connectivity to enable application downloads when required. Examples of these situations include call centers and office environments where workers rarely leave the premises to perform work duties. In today's increasingly mobile workforce world, these circumstances apply to a small percentage of the total workforce. Perhaps the best way to think about this form of virtualization is as one that can be very useful in a restricted number of work environments.

This type of virtualization is offered by AppStream's Virtual Image Distribution, Softricity's Softgrid for Desktops, and Citrix's Presentation Server. Softricity has recently been acquired by Microsoft, and its SoftGrid product will soon be available as part of the Windows Server platform. SoftGrid will offer the capability of streaming applications to remote desktops.

Application streaming is best suited for static work environments where people don't move around much, such as call centers and form-processing centers, although some organizations are exploring using it for remote employees who have consistent network connectivity to ensure that applications can be streamed as necessary.

Hardware emulation

Hardware emulation is a very well-established form of virtualization in which the virtualization software presents a software representation of the underlying hardware that an operating system would typically interact with. (I discuss hardware emulation in more detail in the "Server virtualization" section, later in this chapter.) This is a very common type of virtualization used in data centers as part of a strategy to get higher utilization from the expensive servers that reside in them.

Because of the spread of *commodity hardware* (that's to say, hardware based on Intel's x86 chip architecture; these chips power everything from basic desktop machines to huge servers), the same hardware emulation type of virtualization that can be used in data centers can also be used on client machines. (The term *commodity* refers to the fact that the huge volumes of x86 processors sold make them so ubiquitous and inexpensive that they're almost like any other mass-produced, unspecialized product — almost as common as the canned goods you can get in any grocery store.)

In this form of client virtualization, the virtualization software is loaded onto a client machine that has a base operating system already loaded — typically Windows, but client hardware emulation virtualization is also available for systems running Mac and Linux operating systems.

After the hardware emulation software is loaded onto the machine, it's ready to support guest operating systems. Guest OSes are installed via the virtualization software; that is, rather than just sticking a CD into the machine's drive and rebooting it to install the operating system directly onto the hardware, you use the virtualization software's control panel to indicate your desire to install a guest OS (which can be either Windows or Linux). It sets up the container (often called the *virtual machine,* or VM for short) for the guest operating system and then directs you to put the CD in the drive, whereupon the normal installation procedure occurs.

After the installation completes, you control the virtual machine (which is a normal Windows or Linux system) through the virtualization software's control panel. You can start, stop, suspend, and destroy a VM from the control panel.

Interacting with the VM guest OS is just like interacting with it if it were the only OS on the machine. A guest OS displays graphics on the screen, the VM responds to keyboard and mouse commands, and so on. That's why it's called virtualization!

Products offering this type of virtualization are VMware's VMware Server and Microsoft's Virtual Server. On the Macintosh, SWsoft's Parallels product provides hardware emulation virtualization.

Server virtualization

When discussing trends driving virtualization, you'll soon discover that most of the examples that come up are focused on issues of the data center — the server farms that contain vast arrays of machines dedicated to running enterprise applications, databases, and Web sites.

That's not an accident. Most of the action in the virtualization world right now focuses on server virtualization — no surprise, then, if you see me spending most of my time in this book on precisely that topic.

IT organizations are avidly pursuing virtualization to gain more control of their sprawling server farms. Although client virtualization is interesting to them, server virtualization is critical because many IT organizations are running out of room in their data centers. Their inability to add more machines means they can't respond to important business initiatives, meaning they can't deliver necessary resources so that the other parts of the business can implement the company's strategy. Obviously, this inability to provide IT resources is unacceptable, and many, many IT organizations are turning to server virtualization to solve this problem.

Three main types of server virtualization exist:

- ✔ **Operating system virtualization:** Often referred to as *containers*
- ✔ **Hardware emulation:** Similar to the same type of virtualization described in the client virtualization section, earlier in the chapter

✔ **Paravirtualization:** A relatively new concept designed to deliver a lighter-weight (in terms of virtualization application size), higher-performance approach to virtualization

Check out the next few sections for an in-depth treatment of each of these three types.

Each type of server virtualization has its pros and cons. It's important to evaluate your likely use of virtualization to understand which virtualization technology is best suited for your needs. See Chapter 7 for a discussion of how to evaluate virtualization use.

Operating system virtualization (containers)

In the preceding "Client virtualization" section, I talk about hardware emulation being a virtualization architecture that installs a piece of software onto a machine. Guest operating systems are subsequently installed using the hardware emulation software. Many times, this approach to virtualization, in which the virtualization software is installed directly onto the machine, is described as a *bare-metal* approach, meaning there is no software between the virtualization software and the underlying hardware.

Operating system virtualization, by contrast, is installed on top of an existing operating system. It doesn't enable installation of virtual machines, each of which is isolated from any other virtualization machine. Rather, operating system virtualization runs on top of an existing host operating system and provides a set of libraries that applications interact with, giving each application the illusion that it is running on a machine dedicated to its use.

If this seems a bit confusing, take a look at Figure 1-1, which illustrates the concept. Here you can see a server running a host operating system. *That* operating system is running software that provides operating system virtualization, and a number of virtual OSes are running within the operating system virtualization software. Each of the virtual OSes has one or more applications running within it. The key thing to understand is that, from the application's execution perspective, it sees and interacts only with those applications running within its virtual OS, and it interacts with its virtual OS as though it has sole control of the resources of the virtual OS. Crucially, it can't see the applications or the OS resources located in another virtual OS. It's as though multiple operating systems are running on top of the real host OS. You can see why this approach to virtualization is often referred to as *containers:* Each set of applications is contained within its assigned virtual OS and cannot interact with other virtual OSes or the applications running in those virtual OSes.

You might wonder what use this approach to virtualization is. It can be extremely useful if you want to offer a similar set of operating system functionalities to a number of different user populations while using only a single machine. This is an ideal approach for Web-hosting companies: They use operating system virtualization to allow a hosted Web site to believe it has complete control of a machine, but in fact each hosted Web site shares the machine with many other Web sites, each of which is provided its own container. Every container has its own file system that looks like a complete operating system, but in fact the file system is mapped to the underlying host OS file system in such a way that it isolates each Web site's file system from the others. Another common use for operating system virtualization is when different organizations within a company each need to be provided with their own server, each of which is identical to the others.

The benefit of operating system virtualization is its efficiency. Rather than running a number of complete guest OSes so that applications can each have access to dedicated operating resources, operating system virtualization uses a set of libraries to provide operating system functionality and file-mapping services; consequently, much less software is required to enable the applications to be isolated. Therefore, operating system virtualization is quite efficient, enabling high performance for the overall system. Put another way, operating system virtualization imposes little overhead for the virtualization capability achieved, thereby ensuring most of the machine's resources are available to the applications running in the containers. This has the effect of allowing more containers to run on a given piece of hardware than would be possible with the more heavyweight hardware emulation virtualization approach.

Also, rather than having to license separate instances of guest OSes, operating system virtualization requires only one copy of the underlying OS while providing OS services via the virtualization software. The reduction in licensing costs for the guest OSes can be quite significant.

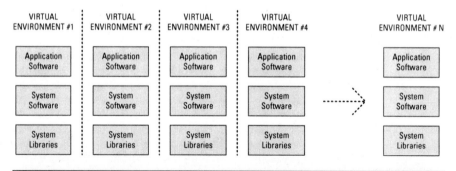

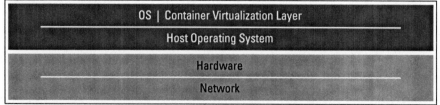

Figure1-1:
Operating
system
virtualiza-
tion.

Operating system virtualization has some limitations, though. First and foremost, this approach typically limits operating system choice. Containerization usually means that the containers offer the same operating system as the host OS. In other words, if the host OS is Linux, only Linux containers are available.

For many application profiles, having to stick with the same OS isn't really a problem. If you're supporting multiple Web sites, it's usually okay — or even ideal — that every guest OS is the same. However, for certain application profiles, it's not enough to just stick with the same general OS; the containers also have to be consistent with the host OS in terms of version number and even patch level. This need for an exact match can cause problems if you want to run different applications in the containers because applications are often certified for only a certain OS version and patch level; if you have different applications that require different certified OS and patch levels, you have a problem. Consequently, operating system virtualization is best suited for homogeneous configurations — for those arrangements, going the operating system virtualization route is an excellent choice.

Operating system virtualization is well suited when an organization requires large numbers of homogeneous operating environments. It's not such a good choice when different environments are required due to application requirements or operating system differences in version or patch level.

Companies offering operating system virtualization include Sun (as part of the Solaris operating system) and SWsoft, which offers the commercial product Virtuozzo and sponsors the open source operating system virtualization project called OpenVZ.

Hardware emulation

In hardware emulation (see Figure 1-2), the virtualization software (usually referred to as a *hypervisor*) presents an emulated hardware environment that guest operating systems operate upon. This emulated hardware environment is typically referred to as a *virtual machine monitor* (VMM). The guest OSes are installed in a *virtual machine* (VM) that interacts with the VMM rather than to the physical hardware upon which the virtualization software runs. In other words, rather than an operating system being installed on a physical machine, it's installed on a virtual machine that emulates the hardware that the OS would usually interact with. The VMM coordinates access between the guest VMs and the actual underlying hardware.

Because the guest OS and the VM are both stored in files that together form a complete system image, the image can be migrated from one hypervisor to another even though the hypervisors reside on different physical machines. This virtual machine portability offers great flexibility for system deployment and forms the basis for most of the advanced applications of virtualization, which are described in Chapter 3.

Virtualization enables operating systems that have been designed and delivered to run directly on hardware to run on an intervening layer of software known as a hypervisor. In order for a guest operating system to interact with the hypervisor, those parts of it that make hardware calls must be modified to make calls to the hypervisor instead. The hypervisor takes those guest OS calls and passes them along to the underlying physical hardware. In short, the guest OS must be modified in order to take advantage of virtualization.

Hardware emulation is a powerful virtualization technology because it performs the guest OS modifications at runtime through a technique known as Binary Translation; essentially, when the guest OS is installed, the virtualization software cleverly rearranges the internal guest OS software so that the calls that originally attempted to access physical hardware resources are now directed to resources within the VMM. Consequently, it is quite easy to use hardware emulation, because you install unmodified guest OSes, and the hardware emulation transparently takes care of modifying the various bits so that the entire virtualization assemblage works properly.

Hardware emulation takes advantage of the well-known technical architecture of the x86 chip to create a software emulation of the chip. Because the commodity x86 chip is so widely used, there's a large enough installed base to make hardware emulation virtualization economically viable.

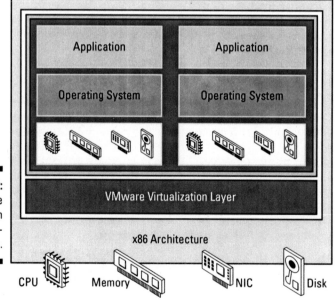

Figure 1-2:
Hardware emulation virtualization.

Because the hardware emulation hypervisor presents a consistent interface to guest OSes and takes responsibility for figuring out how to interact with the underlying hardware, this form of virtualization is quite flexible because it allows a guest OS installed and run on one hypervisor to be moved and run on a second hypervisor.

This approach to virtualization means that, rather than running in containers as happens with operating system virtualization (see the previous section), applications run in a truly isolated guest OS with one or more guest OSes running, one per VMM. The VMMs all reside on the virtualization hypervisor, no matter how many happen to be running at any given time. Not only does this approach support multiple OSes, it can support dissimilar OSes, differing in minor ways (such as version and patch level) or in major ways (for example, completely different OSes like Windows and Linux can simultaneously be run in hardware emulation virtualization software).

Common applications for hardware emulation are software development and quality assurance because they allow a number of different OSes to be run simultaneously, thereby facilitating parallel development or testing of software in a number of different operating system environments. Hardware emulation is also used in server consolidation, where a number of operating system and/or application environments are moved from separate physical servers to a single physical server running virtualization software.

If all this makes it sound as though hardware emulation is just what the IT doctor ordered, you need to know that the technology has a couple of drawbacks:

- ✔ **Performance penalty:** One drawback is that the virtualization software hurts performance, which is to say that applications often run somewhat slower on virtualized systems than they would if they were running on unvirtualized systems. This makes sense if you think about it. After all, you've piled things on pretty thick, what with the application you're working with, the operating system it runs on, and the VMM/hypervisor layer you've inserted below the operating system. Getting through that VMM/hypervisor layer is bound to take some machine cycles and thereby reduce performance somewhat. In practice, the benefits of virtualization usually outweigh performance concerns.

- ✔ **Device driver availability:** Another drawback to hardware emulation is that the virtualization software presents a standardized hardware interface to the guest operating system. The hypervisor translates requests for hardware resources by the guest OS into calls to the actual physical resources on the machine. This means that the hypervisor must contain the interfaces to the resources of the machine; these resources are referred to as *device drivers*. If you've ever installed new hardware in a PC, you know that you often have to install a device driver into the operating system so that the new hardware and the operating system can communicate. If there is hardware present on the machine that the hypervisor does not have drivers for, the guest OSes cannot access the capabilities of the underlying hardware. This can be a problem if an organization wants to, for example, connect a new type of storage to the hardware; if the hypervisor does not contain a driver for that new storage device, it cannot be used.

✔ **Device driver inflexibility:** If you install new hardware for a typical operating system and it does not contain a driver for it, the OS will ask you to load a new driver. This dynamic driver capability makes it possible to update the OS to reflect hardware additions. Hardware emulation hypevisors, by contrast, do not have the ability to dynamically load device drivers; hardware support is limited to those products that the hypervisor could support at time of shipment. This can cause problems, especially for organizations that want to take advantage of new hardware developments. For example, organizations that want move to the latest storage options can find that they're blocked from doing so because their virtualization software doesn't yet support a particular storage hardware device. Depending upon your organization's computing infrastructure, this might or might not be a problem, but it's definitely something to check out before embarking upon your virtualization journey.

Before committing to hardware emulation, be sure to survey your hardware environment to evaluate whether your potential hardware emulation virtualization product can fully support your needs.

Companies offering hardware emulation virtualization software include VMware (in two versions, VMware Server and ESX Server) and Microsoft, which offers a product called Virtual Server. VMware is the undisputed leader in the virtualization marketplace, and I discuss it extensively throughout this book. Microsoft's Virtual Server has much less presence in the marketplace and will be superseded by the virtualization functionality contained in Microsoft Server 2008, which is referred to as Microsoft Server virtualization. It turns out that Microsoft Server virtualization takes more of a paravirtualization approach to virtualization, which I get to discuss in the next section.

I show you how to install and use VMware Server, one of the VMware products, in Chapter 12.

Paravirtualization

Paravirtualization is the name for another approach to server virtualization. In this approach, rather than emulate a complete hardware environment, the virtualization software is a thin layer that *multiplexes* (that is, coordinates) access by guest operating systems to the underlying physical machine resources; in other words, paravirtualization doesn't create an entire virtual machine to host the guest OS, but rather enables the guest OS to interact directly with the hypervisor (see Figure 1-3). (By the way, the "para" in paravirtualization doesn't really mean anything. It's actually just a smart-alec term used to sneer at hardware emulation virtualization.)

This approach has two advantages: First, it imposes less performance overhead because it uses a very small amount of code. Hardware emulation (see the previous section) inserts an entire hardware emulation layer between the guest operating system and the physical hardware. By contrast, paravirtualization's thin software layer acts more like a traffic cop, allowing one guest OS access to the physical resources of the hardware while stopping all other guest OSes from accessing the same resources at the same time.

The second advantage of the paravirtualization approach when compared to hardware emulation is that paravirtualization doesn't limit you to the device drivers contained in the virtualization software. In fact, paravirtualization doesn't include any device drivers at all. Instead, it uses the device drivers contained in one of the guest operating systems — the one that's referred to as the *privileged guest* (Microsoft uses the term root partition to refer to the same thing). Without going into too much detail about this architecture here, suffice it to say that this is an advantage because it enables organizations to take advantage of all the capabilities of the hardware in the server, rather than being limited to hardware for which drivers are available in the virtualization software, as with hardware emulation virtualization.

Paravirtualization uses an operating system capability called *shared memory* to achieve high performance. Shared memory is memory that can be accessed by two different programs. Paravirtualization uses shared memory to send data back and forth between guest OSes and the hypervisor, thereby achieving high performance levels.

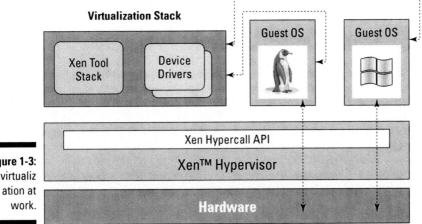

Figure 1-3: Paravirtualization at work.

Okay, so you clearly have a winner with the paravirtualization approach, right? Not so fast, cowpoke. There's one significant drawback to this approach to virtualization: Because it's so lightweight and yet still has to multiplex access to the underlying hardware, paravirtualization needs some help with the heavy lifting. In other words, it requires that the guest operating systems be modified prior to being run to interact with the paravirtualization interfaces. This can be accomplished only by having access to the source code of the guest OS. This access is possible for open source operating systems such as Linux or any of the BSD (Berkeley Software Distribution, a Unix-like open source operating system) flavors, but — crucially — it isn't possible for any Microsoft product. As you might imagine, the inability to virtualize Microsoft OSes is a significant drawback for many organizations. The good news is that the latest generation of chips from Intel and AMD provide functionality (called Intel VT and AMD-V, respectively) that enables unmodified operating systems, particularly Microsoft Windows, to be hosted by a paravirtualized hypervisor. Consequently, this drawback to paravirtualization will diminish as servers with these new chips take their place in production infrastructures.

The new chips from Intel and AMD are usually called *virtualization-enabled,* indicating that they have additional capability that allows some functionality that formerly was provided by the hypervisor to be moved to the chip. Because silicon (the chip) is ordinarily vastly faster than software, virtualization-enabled chips offer better virtualization performance.

The best-known product with the paravirtualization approach is a relatively new open source offering called Xen, which is sponsored by a commercial company called XenSource. Xen is included in the recent Linux distributions from Red Hat and Novell, as well as being available for many community Linux distributions like Debian and Ubuntu. XenSource itself sells Xen-based products as well. The forthcoming Microsoft Server virtualization is based on a paravirtualization approach to virtualization, and is scheduled to be available shortly after Microsoft Server 2008 is released.

Storage virtualization

The amount of data that organizations are creating and storing is exploding. Due to the increasing shift of business processes to Web-based digital applications, every company is being inundated with data.

This explosion of data is causing the following problems for many such companies:

- ✔ From a sheer storage capacity, many applications generate more data than can be stored physically on a single server.

✔ Many applications — particularly Internet-based ones — have multiple machines that need to access the same data. Having all the data sitting on one physical machine creates a bottleneck, not to mention the potential risk of a situation where many virtual machines might be made inoperable if a single physical machine containing all the application's data crashes.

✔ The explosion of machines mentioned earlier in the chapter causes backup problems; in other words, trying to create safe copies of data is a Herculean task when hundreds or even thousands of machines need data backup.

For these reasons, data has moved into virtualization as well. Moving data from many physical servers to a central location enables backups to be performed more efficiently. Furthermore, the central data repository can be configured with multiple physical storage devices to ensure that no hardware crash will ever make the organization's data unavailable. (For more information on data virtualization, see Chapter 11.) The three basic approaches to data storage are

✔ Direct-Attached Storage

✔ Network-Attached Storage

✔ Storage Area Network

I cover each of these options in the following sections.

Direct-Attached Storage

Direct-Attached Storage (DAS) is the traditional mode of data storage: hard drives attached to whatever physical server is running the application. DAS is easy to use but can be hard to manage. I talk in later chapters about why virtualization tends to cause organizations to reconsider sticking with a DAS architecture and think about moving to more sophisticated methods of data storage.

Network-Attached Storage

Network-Attached Storage (NAS) is a machine that sits on your network and offers storage to other machines. If you've ever used a remote drive in Windows, you've experienced NAS. However, NAS can be much more sophisticated than remote Windows drives; you can find specialized hardware appliances that can be filled with many hard drives and thereby provide multiple terabytes of storage.

You might think of NAS as the first step toward storage virtualization. NAS provides a single source of data, facilitating data backup. By collecting your data in one place, it also avoids the problem of multiple servers needing to access data located on another server.

NAS uses standard data communication protocols to send data back and forth between a server and the NAS device. This makes things simple but puts data traffic that's limited to the server in DAS usage onto the corporate network, which often causes a ripple effect as additional network capacity and hardware are required to support the NAS data traffic. See, I told you virtualization is a journey!

Although NAS helps with some of the problems associated with DAS, it carries its own set of issues. The network traffic caused by moving data back and forth from the NAS to individual servers can be considerable, stressing network capacity. The traffic can also interfere with other work carried on the network. And, of course, moving all data to a single NAS appliance just moves your risk because all your servers now depend on the NAS being available; if it goes down, everything goes down. For that reason, production environments that require absolute data availability typically use the Storage Area Network approach to data storage.

One advantage of NAS is that it's very cost effective. Some NAS appliances out on the market cost less than $1,000, which, when measured against the cost of labor to back up numerous machines, is a small drop in the budget bucket.

Storage Area Network

What if you have rapidly growing data storage needs and also need the assurance that your data is effectively backed up and that, more important, you're protected from data outages due to hardware failure? In that case, a Storage Area Network (SAN) is for you. Naturally, this being the technology industry, they had to choose an acronym that's easy to confuse with a similar solution — NAS, described in the preceding bullet.

SANs use highly specialized hardware and software to transform mere disk drives into a data storage solution that transfers data on its own high-performance network. SANs provide the ability to add additional storage capacity as data storage requirements grow; also, SANs can be configured to use multiple, redundant pieces of storage hardware so that data is always available, even if one or more pieces of storage hardware fail.

Within a SAN architecture, servers don't bother with transferring data across the standard corporate network — the standard Network Interface Card (NIC) to Ethernet cable to corporate network route. Instead, they usually use their own SAN interface device called a Host Bus Adapter (HBA) to connect to their SAN.

SANs use a specialized network protocol — either something called Fibre Channel or the alternative choice, iSCSI — for SAN network communication. At the other end of the SAN network is a hardware device that holds drives. This SAN device makes it easy to shift physical data storage, increase it, back it up, and even ship copies of the data to other locations to ensure business continuity in case of a natural disaster.

Companies move to SAN storage when they recognize that corporate data is a key resource that must be available 24/7 and needs to be conveniently managed. As you might expect, the price tag for that capability is large — very large. SANs can cost upwards of several million dollars, but when you consider the value of data, that level of investment is warranted for many companies.

Fibre Channel SANs use specialized data communication protocols to send data back and forth between a server and the data storage device on a separate network. Because the protocols are different, SANs require specialized hardware to be present on the server. By contrast, iSCSI-based SANs are able to use the standard corporate network for their data traffic, although this can raise the same kind of network congestion issues posed by NAS storage.

Creating the Virtualized Enterprise

If you're convinced that virtualization deserves a closer look and you want to know how to implement it in your organization, this book is for you. The purpose of the entire book is to give you information about how to evaluate virtualization, figure out which type of virtualization (and virtualization product) is right for you, and spell out the different ways you can migrate to (and manage) a virtualized environment. However, I'll give you the one-page preview right here. Here goes.

Most of the energy about virtualization in the industry focuses on server virtualization, and that's what this book primarily focuses on.

A typical first step in virtualization is a so-called server-consolidation project. This is a fancy term for moving the operating system and applications from a number of physical servers to a single server running virtualization software so that you can then run all the operating system/application configurations on a single physical server. (All of the pre-existing physical servers have been *consolidated* onto a single box — get it?)

Server consolidation provides a great payoff. Many organizations then decide to go further and create a pool of virtualized servers to enable load balancing and failover (that is, the ability to bring a new application up if a previous one crashed). Of course, after you move beyond server consolidation, you pretty much have to begin virtualizing your storage.

Although moving to virtualization might seem exciting (and, if not exciting, it can certainly be financially rewarding), it's not entirely painless. There's new software to obtain, people who have to be trained to use it, and project work that needs to be done to migrate all your existing physical servers to the new virtualized environment. All these things are necessary; failing to do any one of them raises the probability that you won't have a good outcome for your virtualization project. Fortunately, I address these topics in this book and provide tools for you to better find virtualization happiness.

In this book, I introduce the concept of the *virtualization life cycle,* the overall process of successfully introducing virtualization to your organization. Many people feel that all they need to do to be successful is buy some virtualization software and install it. That might get them started on the virtualization life cycle, but doesn't complete it. You'll be more successful if you address all the steps in the life cycle.

Okay, the whirlwind tour of virtualization has concluded. Time to move on to the real thing.

Chapter 2

Making a Business Case for Virtualization

*I*f you're reading this book, you're probably pretty excited about — or at least interested in — implementing virtualization in your organization. After all, who wouldn't be interested in solving the following problems?

✔ **You're drowning in servers.** With the proliferation of cheap hardware and the increasing move to digitization of business processes, IT organizations have increased the overall number of servers in their data centers. Because most organizations follow the "one application, one server" guideline, this means many, many more machines to keep track of. Many organizations find that they're out of room in their data centers, and the cost of increasing the amount of space available isn't anything remotely like the cost of buying a new server; data centers start at millions of dollars and can run upwards of hundreds of millions of dollars. Virtualization, by breaking the bounds of "one application, one server" and enabling multiple servers to run on a single piece of server hardware, reduces server sprawl.

✔ **You need to use your hardware more efficiently.** The overall percentage of applied processing capacity — called the *utilization* rate — in many data centers runs as low as 10 to 15 percent. This means that 85 to 90 percent of the capabilities of servers go unused. However, even if most of the capacity goes unused, the server still requires power and air conditioning, meaning that a lot of money is being wasted. By enabling multiple guest OSes to be run on servers, the utilization rate of servers can be brought up to 70 or 80 percent, a far more cost-effective use of the organization's hardware.

✔ **You need to reduce energy costs.** Having lots of servers loafing along at 10 or 15 percent utilization while paying full energy costs to power and cool them is a recipe for a large energy bill. By using virtualization software to migrate existing systems to fewer physical servers, you can save lots of energy — and energy costs.

✔ **You need to make IT operations in general more efficient.** Running servers take more than energy and air conditioning. Every server requires care and feeding by the operations staff. By reducing the overall number of servers, virtualization can reduce overall operations costs — and make IT more responsive to business needs.

"But," I hear you asking, "how do I know virtualization isn't like a hundred other technologies unleashed (or, in some cases, unloaded) on the market?" You know, the It-Solves-All-Problems technology that, when put into service, seems to create more problems than it solves.

For sure, no technology, including virtualization, is right for everyone. But virtualization appears to hold enormous promise — which I must believe in, or I wouldn't have written a book on it, right? — evidenced by the near-universal endorsement of the technology by companies as widely varying as IBM, HP, Sun, Microsoft, EMC, and Dell. If that cast of characters can agree on something, it must have some real potential. All the major analyst firms like Gartner and IDC agree, citing virtualization growth rates of over 50 percent.

To help you understand why virtualization is important as a business decision in addition to a technical decision, I highlight some of the areas where virtualization can (potentially) help your business financially. I cite examples, but keep this in mind: Virtualization is a relatively new technology, and there aren't that many case studies available. Moreover, organizations that have achieved excellent business results with virtualization often refuse to make their information public because they don't want competitors to know about what they're achieving with virtualization.

This chapter describes the major business benefits of virtualization to give you some background and ammunition as you pursue your virtualization efforts. For every benefit, I provide examples to illustrate the financial impact of the benefit, as well as a pointer to where in this book you can look for more detailed information on the particular topic.

Virtualization Lowers Hardware Costs

It's no secret that hardware costs have dropped dramatically over the past few years. My own journey through hardware acquisition is an example of this. My first PC, purchased about ten years ago, ran about $4,500. I replaced it four years later with one that cost only $1,900. I am writing this book on my most recent acquisition, a laptop that cost only $600. Of course, thanks to the magic of Moore's Law, the performance has only been getting better.

The laptop I'm typing on is a powerhouse compared to that first PC. As I recall, that first PC had a Pentium II chip running at 175 MHz. My laptop contains a dual-core chip running at 1.6 GHz, offering hundreds of times the performance of that first PC at a fraction of the cost.

And it's no secret that this steep price/performance curve holds true for server hardware as well. A four-processor machine, purchased for $50,000 or $60,000 in the year 1999, can be replaced by a dual-core single or dual-processor machine that costs less than $5,000 — and today's cheaper server far outstrips its 1999 counterpart in terms of performance.

When servers just coast along

As noted in Chapter 1, the increasing power of servers poses a different challenge to IT organizations: keeping their servers busy. The 1999 four-way processor box strained mightily to keep up with its processing workload; by contrast, today's dual-core (soon to be quad-core) machine loafs along with the same workload. Consequently, it sits idle much of the time, waiting for more work to use its full capacity. It wastes its potential, much like an Oscar-winning actor performing in a dreary dinner theater somewhere in the Midwest. However, the server still uses a full complement of expensive energy for power and air conditioning. It's like that Oscar-winning actor getting his or her full $20 million paycheck for performing Thornton Wilder's *Our Town* for a 100-person audience in Dubuque. Obviously, that would be a waste of talent (although a real opportunity for the audience); similarly, running a server at 15 percent utilization is a tremendous waste of computing potential.

And, by the way, that 15 percent estimate may be generous. I recently spoke to a company that did an evaluation of its server load factors preparatory to a virtualization implementation, and they found that many of their servers were running at 1 percent utilization or less! What they discovered was that someone at sometime threw together an application, installed it on a box in the data center, and then forgot about it, and as long as the server kept running, nobody paid any attention to it. There were many, many of these "orphan" applications in the data center; if you looked at your organization's data center, you might find an analogous situation.

When you start to look at server loads, you may run into resistance due to turf issues. Many people, both in IT and in end user organizations, take a proprietary attitude toward "their" servers, and are reluctant to let go of them, even if the load factor is quite low and moving to virtualization would make better economic sense. Approach this server utilization evaluation with tact in order to avoid conflict. See Chapters 6 and 7 for more information about how to manage the interpersonal aspects of a virtualization project.

Virtualization enables IT organizations to retire many of their low-performing servers and then migrate the applications to new hardware much better suited to supporting virtualization. (This is often referred to as *server consolidation* and is typically the initial step on the virtualization journey for IT organizations.) Although it's possible to use existing hardware to support virtualization, the ratio of retired to continuing servers is typically no more than four or five to one. Using the new generation of hardware, the ratios can be more like 10 or even 20 to one; in fact, the limiting factor of how many servers to host on a single physical server is likely to be your comfort level of having so many applications residing on a single box, rather than the pure processing capacity of the machine.

Chapter 8 goes into much more detail about selecting virtualization hardware and how to mitigate the single point of failure (SPOF) risk inherent in supporting so many virtual servers on a single piece of hardware.

A handy (if anonymous) real-world example

What kind of financial benefits are available through server consolidation? Here's one example, which sadly must remain anonymous as to the true identity of the company.

A large financial institution faced an unpalatable decision. To its current complement of branch-based servers, it needed to add encryption software to each one in order to comply with regulatory requirements regarding customer data privacy. To implement the software (an expensive item in its own right) at each branch, an additional server would need to be installed as well. Total cost: $35 million.

Even for a large financial institution, $35 million is more than chump change. Consequently, it decided to explore other options. It reviewed virtualization, and after due consideration, decided to migrate all the existing servers onto virtualized servers running in its data center, replacing the old servers with new, more powerful, virtualization-ready machines. It also decided to virtualize the data storage at the same time.

Because it was able to centralize its servers (and because they were so much more powerful), the financial institution no longer needed to purchase multiple copies of the encryption software, not to mention no longer needing to buy additional machines to run it.

The overall cost of the company's virtualization project? Only $3.5 million. It saved 90 percent of the expected cost of complying with the data privacy regulations. Definitely not chump change.

The company attained several other benefits, which I discuss as I address other virtualization benefits in this chapter.

As this example shows, the financial benefit of reduced hardware needs can be substantial indeed. Consequently, one of the main drivers for IT organizations to pursue virtualization is saving on overall hardware investment. Virtualization serves extremely well as a key part of a budget belt-tightening strategy.

Virtualization Increases IT Operational Flexibility

You live in a world of rapid change. The continuing transformation of the global economy makes change almost inevitable for every company. Beyond the macroeconomic events of the world, every company faces unique business circumstances within its industry. For example, many companies experience periods of peak demand brought on by holidays or the change of seasons. Some retail companies sell 75 percent of their total revenues during the Christmas season, whereas sports-oriented retailers often see summer as a heavy demand period.

Beyond the vagaries of external demand, IT organizations must deal with the day-in and day-out complications of running a sophisticated infrastructure. Machine components fail; operating systems get overloaded; applications crash, necessitating restart. IT operations can be a repetitive, even Sisyphean, job.

In the world of "one application, one server," all these challenges are extremely difficult to manage. Responding to seasonal demand causes IT organizations to provision additional machines, which can — from initial hardware order to actual startup of the machine — take days or even weeks. Ordering machines requires a lengthy budget approval process. After you acquire the machine, installing hardware, an operating system, and application software can consume days. If your company has been fortunate enough to receive ten times the usual daily traffic because someone in a blog raved about your whizzo product, taking weeks to be ready to respond to every visitor quickly is unacceptable.

"One application, one server" is the dominant reality in most data centers, driven in many cases by the application's need for a specified set of helper applications (Apache Web server, for example) for particular versions. It's critical to keep track of the entire application software infrastructure when you move a system from physical to virtual to ensure you re-create the necessary software environment for the application to work properly. An alternative to this painstaking tracking is to use migration software to move systems in an automated fashion. See Chapter 9 for more information on migration.

Responding to hardware failures can be even more difficult. If a key server loses a critical hardware resource, it can take hours or days to replace the hardware and bring the machine back online. In the worst case, when parts aren't readily available, servers can be offline for an extended period, which is an IT organization's nightmare.

Virtualization's promise

Virtualization can offer real IT operational flexibility benefits and address the critical IT risk exposures just mentioned.

It can help you deal with hardware failures or application/operating system crashes. Virtualization software can be configured to keep track of virtual machines and, if one goes down, immediately restart another instance on the same machine or even a different machine. This means that hardware crashes, rather than meaning a lengthy outage period, can be remedied in minutes.

Calculate the amount of time it takes to perform the outage recovery steps that follow. Then track how long it takes to perform the analogous recovery in a virtualized environment, and calculate the time and money savings from virtualization, including the financial advantages of increased application availability. You can use the resulting information in discussions with IT management and end users; it's amazing how much enthusiasm can be generated with a significant business case attached to a virtualization initiative. See Chapter 6 to find out how to form a virtualization business case.

Just think about what usually happens during an outage:

1. IT needs to be alerted to the situation.

2. IT studies the reason for the outage to determine the cause.

3. IT perhaps concludes that the failure of a hardware component necessitates moving the application to another machine.

4. IT must then locate an available machine and load the correct operating system and application.

5. IT must then configure the OS and application.

6. IT then has to restore the data from the most recent backup.

7. IT must then bring the machine online, perhaps updating network configuration tables to ensure the machine can be communicated with across the network.

8. Finally, recovery from the machine outage is over. Duration of the outage can run from hours to days or even weeks. For many mission-critical applications, every minute of downtime carries a significant cost in terms of revenue loss.

Experiencing an outage while running virtualization is much different. The virtualization software recognizes that the application is no longer working and automatically *fails over* (that is, starts another instance of the operating system and application) to a new virtual machine, which can be up and running in literally seconds.

 Virtualization software can even be smart enough to deal with the failure of an entire physical server hosting a number of virtual machines (VMs). If you've implemented a type of virtualization known as *server pooling,* the virtualization software can immediately start another virtual machine instance on another server should the original server be unavailable due to hardware failure. Server pooling is using virtualization to treat several individual servers as one seamless virtualization resource. If one server gets bogged down due to load, another virtual machine instance can be started on another server to spread the work across multiple machines. This is also known as *load balancing* because it divides the overall workload among two or more machines. (See Chapter 3 for a more complete description of server pooling and load balancing.)

 While server consolidation (moving a number of physical servers to a single server supporting a number of virtual machines) is the first step for many IT organizations, the ultimate benefit of virtualization may be much more focused on making IT more efficient and able to reduce operational costs. Many IT organizations report that virtualization has made their lives much easier because it frees them from the daily slog of managing a huge collection of temperamental physical servers.

Server pooling can also provide real benefits in helping IT organizations deal with the challenges of seasonal demand variation or company restructuring due to changing business conditions.

A handy (named) example

To illustrate the IT operational flexibility virtualization offers, consider art.com. This Web site makes fine art, from a wide range of artists, available for online purchase. The company, founded during the boom years (or bubble, if you prefer) of the Internet, has gone through tough times and emerged as a success. In fact, it's fulfilling its original mission of making art available to a new audience that previously never participated in the fine art market.

art.com's business has changed substantially as it has perfected its approach to the market. Part of its strategy has been to acquire other complementary companies in order to broaden the offerings of art.com.

And here is the IT operational flexibility challenge: As you might expect, changing your business offerings and merging companies means you face doing an IT infrastructure mashup. (Having lived through a couple of these situations, I assure you that it can be extremely challenging.)

The folks at art.com wanted to consolidate the acquired company's data center into art.com's facility. Ordinarily, that would be a protracted exercise in juggling hardware, doing backups, reinstalling systems, and so on. Instead, art.com took a different tack. First, the IT folks installed hardware at the art.com data center to support virtualized servers. Then, with that task out of the way, they used virtualization technology from VMware to migrate the systems from the acquired company's data center to art.com's new (and improved) data center.

The company now has taken its virtualization efforts a step further. Using VMware's Virtual Infrastructure 3 (VI3) product, art.com operates a pool of virtualized servers. When business initiatives require a new server instance, here's what happens:

1. IT instantiates an instance based on an existing image template.

   In other words, the IT staff has preconfigured virtualized servers ready for immediate use.

2. IT installs the necessary application into the virtual server.

3. IT brings up the new virtual server by making it available through the network.

This three-step setup dramatically reduces the time necessary to get a new server up and running. Think about it: Instead of ordering a new server, waiting for it to arrive, installing it into a rack, getting it connected to the data center network, and then finally installing and configuring an application — a process that can take weeks — art.com can get a server up in just a few hours. (I heard art.com's CTO claim that his group could bring up a new server in minutes.) And here's the really striking thing: art.com doesn't keep track of where the new virtualized server goes. VI3 decides which physical server is best suited to support the new virtual machine, and VI3 decides where to put it. Instead of IT worrying about physical installation, it can focus on monitoring and tuning the running infrastructure.

As the art.com example illustrates, virtualization can help IT organizations achieve much better operational flexibility, enabling them to support business initiatives better and more quickly.

Virtualization Reduces IT Operations Costs

Another aspect of virtualization is the way it can help IT reduce the cost of operations. Because virtualization encapsulates servers in a software image, it's possible to shift the image from one machine to another. I discuss this in the context of failover and load balancing in the "Virtualization's promise" section, earlier in the chapter. In the present context, what's important is virtualization's ability to migrate a running virtual server from one physical server to another.

One of the biggest challenges for an IT organization involves managing hardware. Obviously, hardware failures cause immediate problems. However, even in the absence of failures, IT has to maintain equipment. In addition, IT often has to modify equipment; for example, it might have to upgrade a Host Bus Adapter (essentially, a computer card that can communicate to a Storage Area Network) to ensure a server can talk to the newly upgraded storage network.

Virtualization makes hardware maintenance and upgrades easier and cheaper

Previrtualization, any kind of hardware maintenance work was a pain. Because production servers couldn't be taken out of service, maintenance and upgrades were typically scheduled for off-hours — evenings, nights, and weekends. In fact, important maintenance activities were often skipped due to the difficulty of scheduling the work, which, naturally enough, led to hardware failures and the type of service outage described in the "Virtualization's promise" section of this chapter.

However, even conscientious IT organizations find maintenance and upgrades difficult to accomplish. For starters, it's expensive to do this work in off-hours. Bringing staff in late at night or on weekends means overtime pay, making the work at least 50 percent more expensive than doing it during normal hours.

The organization might not pay overtime because its staff might be exempt from overtime pay conditions. Although not incurring extra payroll costs, there is still a cost to the organization as staff is forced to work additional, inconvenient hours. Making people work longer hours doesn't lead to satisfied employees. In fact, the cost of a dissatisfied employee might be higher than paying overtime, because the pocketbook hit you get when replacing an employee who quits is far higher than any overtime expense might be.

Job dissatisfaction is one of the major reasons IT personnel leave jobs. Using virtualization to reduce off-hours work can help raise job satisfaction and reduce turnover. Keep this in mind when making your case for virtualization.

The alternative to doing work off-hours is to perform it during normal business hours. This approach presents its own challenges, however. Because taking production systems down during working hours is a no-no, working on a production server means that another server has to be ready to take on the workload while IT tinkers with the production server. Bringing up a new server and migrating an application to it in the physical world is a task with many steps and lots of work; furthermore, it's easy to make a mistake during one of those steps, leading to additional complications.

All in all, none of the options available for server maintenance and upgrades are very attractive, which probably accounts for the work being put off by so many IT organizations. Certainly, no matter which option you choose, it's likely to be a significant expense, which, in these times of lean IT budgets, is unpleasant indeed.

Virtualization can make server maintenance and upgrades significantly easier and less expensive.

Instead of following a lengthy provision and application migration process, virtualization enables a running virtual machine to be migrated to another server very quickly, freeing up the original server to be worked on during normal business hours. The migration typically takes no more than a few minutes and can be done with no production outage. After the work is complete, the virtual machine can be migrated back to the original server, now fully fit after its maintenance session.

This kind of seamless migration might, depending on the virtualization software you're using, require a more capable (and more expensive, naturally) version of the software. And migration between machines will definitely require off-machine storage — in other words, using Network-Attached Storage (NAS) or a Storage Area Network (SAN). You need to assess whether the benefits of being able to perform maintenance and upgrades without the drama of off-hours, unhappy staff outweigh the cost of additional virtualization capability. However, given the rapid adoption of the more capable virtualization software as well as virtualized storage, it seems clear that many IT organizations have concluded that lower operations costs are an important aim and worth the necessary virtualization investment.

Virtualization means fewer servers and lower IT costs

Virtualization also reduces IT operational costs in a direct way. As the previous sections have indicated, keeping hardware performing at its peak requires continual care and feeding. And what does virtualization enable you to do? Use fewer physical machines. By allowing software virtual machines to take the place of physical machines, operational costs related to hardware maintenance might be cut by 60 percent or more, depending on the ratio of virtual servers to physical servers. In other words, by getting rid of four machines by virtualizing their operating systems and applications and moving them to a fifth machine, you reduce the total number of physical machines you're managing by 80 percent. Clearly, slashing the amount of work IT has to do in hardware maintenance means much lower operations costs.

Virtualization can also reduce operational costs when you consider the challenges of data management. Data is increasingly vital to organizations, and the sprawl of servers has made managing data an enormous challenge for most IT organizations.

Using Direct-Attached Storage (DAS) is easy — every server comes with it. However, with a couple of thousand servers sitting in your data center, managing the data becomes incredibly complex. Every server needs to be backed up, either by a time-consuming manual process or by a complex automated system that needs to coordinate every server in the data center. So, even though using DAS is easy, when looked at in aggregate, it's a real data management drawback.

Another drawback with regard to DAS is the fact that the total amount of data available on a single server is limited by the number of drive bays (a 1U pizza-box server — the squat, rack-mounted machines found in 90 percent of all data centers — typically has only two bays) and the size of the drives themselves. And, if you ever hit the limit of the local DAS, you're back to the maintenance and upgrade nightmare described earlier in this section.

The solution many IT organizations are moving to is storage virtualization. By moving all data to a centralized system, IT organizations can manage their total data as one item, rather than piecemeal, spread across hundreds or thousands of individual servers.

Storage virtualization can take many forms and be based on a number of different technologies. Ranging from straightforward to extremely complex, storage virtualization is a valuable addition to a virtualized environment. Depending on the technology base of the storage virtualization solution, there can be ramifications for networking and system administration, which should be kept in mind when you consider a move to storage virtualization.

By using storage virtualization, data backup is simplified. Most storage virtualization solutions come with a backup capability, enabling the same storage management system to handle the entire life cycle of data, from allocation to offline storage. By collapsing the number of tasks related to managing storage, storage virtualization reduces IT operations costs.

Virtualization Lowers Energy Costs

In Chapter 1, I discuss the cost of energy as being one of the four main motivations causing companies to implement virtualization.

Concern with the cost of power is a recent development for companies. The move to digitized business processes, both internal and Internet based, has been so dramatic that organizations often have used historic assumptions about energy use in their business planning. However, companies have implemented so many more systems recently that those historic assumptions are sadly out of date.

The lack of insight into just how much energy was costing companies has been exacerbated by the traditional split in how data centers are managed. Many companies assign the responsibility (and costs) for computer hardware like servers and network switches to IT, but assign the responsibility (and costs) for data center infrastructure services like power and air conditioning to . . . facilities. After all, a data center is a building, right? So facilities should manage it.

Unfortunately, that split in responsibility has meant that no single organization really kept track of how the growth in the number of servers was affecting other costs like power and air conditioning. As server sprawl has occurred, the consequence of running thousands of servers hasn't been clear.

That's all changed now. Skyrocketing energy costs have raised the issue of IT power costs well beyond the backwaters of facilities. Depending on how much of a company's business is digitized and runs across the Internet, energy might be one of the top-line items in terms of its overall cost structure. For many "Web 2.0" companies (Internet-powered companies like MySpace and Facebook), power is the second- or third-highest cost for the company overall.

Clearly, reducing overall energy consumption is important for companies, and the amount of energy use in running data centers is an obvious target. Beyond the bottom-line issue of energy cost, the rising concern with global warming is likely to make itself felt in increasing pressure upon companies to reduce energy consumption.

Virtualization is ideally suited for companies wanting to reduce energy use. Rather than powering thousands of machines, most of which are running at very low utilization rates, virtualization enables IT organizations to reduce the total number of machines in use by up to 90 percent.

Virtualization's potential for reducing energy costs is obvious. Organizations report slashing their energy bills by 50 percent or more, when compared to the cost of running a nonvirtualized infrastructure.

The cost of energy is likely to continue to rise for the foreseeable future. Build your business case with an expectation that energy costs will be even higher than they are today. In many scenarios, the energy savings are the single biggest benefit of moving to virtualization, so be sure to incorporate energy into your virtualization planning.

Additional savings are possible if you use the new power-sipping servers. Both AMD and Intel have delivered new chips that draw far fewer watts. The new mantra for both companies is "processing power per watt" rather than the old "processing power at any cost" approach.

Even higher energy savings are possible if you look at using the new generation of machines that are designed to serve as virtualization platforms. These machines, from companies like Sun and IBM, are built from the ground up for virtualization duties. This makes them much more suitable for a virtualized infrastructure than repurposed general-use servers pressed into virtualization duty.

You can find out more about your hardware choices in Chapter 8.

Make no mistake about it: You'll be hearing more and more about energy use in data centers, and companies will be coming under increasing pressure to run their data centers more efficiently. But take heart! You have resources to draw upon that can help you in your quest to save energy in your data center. Chapter 5 contains a description of an innovative new program from PG&E, the power company for Silicon Valley. The program offers a rebate for virtualization projects, based on the energy savings achieved during the first year of running virtualization in a company's data center.

Software Licensing Costs: A Challenge for Virtualization

Although hardware manufacturers have embraced virtualization wholeheartedly, enthusiasm for it among software vendors is much less consistent. As you begin to consider migrating your systems to a virtualized infrastructure, you'll undoubtedly find software licensing to be one of the most vexing problems you face.

General software licensing practices

I don't want to make it sound like software licensing isn't already a complicated subject. In fact, sometimes it seems like software vendors seek the most convoluted ways to set the pricing for their licenses. Some cynics might think that vendors deliberately make their licensing and pricing policies cryptic in order to allow them to arbitrarily overprice their products — and there might be some truth in that.

In the old days, software licensing was a bit more transparent. Software licenses were often priced according to the power of the chip inside the computer the software ran on. The notion, apparently, was that if the software could do more because the hardware was more powerful, you should pay more to use it.

That neat way of pricing began to get more complex as the hardware designs of servers got more complex. First came multiprocessor machines. The standard licensing response was to charge more, typically for each additional processor.

Things have gotten more complex with the advent of multicore processors. Multicore processors are single processors that contain more than one piece of silicon inside. Chip manufacturers pursued this multicore approach to address the problem that they faced when trying to cram more components onto single pieces of silicon: packing more processors in a tiny amount of space generates increasing amounts of heat and wastes energy. Today's state-of-the-art multicore chips have two cores inside them, but quad-core processors (containing, as you might expect, four cores) are on the horizon, and just over it lie 8- and 16-core processors.

One might say that multicore processors are a hardware manufacturer's choice of design to deliver incremental performance in an existing chip form factor. In other words, Intel and AMD choose to configure the internals of their chips to perform better in terms of energy use and heat generation, but overall, a multicore chip is still an individual chip.

Another way one could look at the situation would be to say that the multicore approach is more like jamming a multiprocessor design into a single processor, and that these new chips are really a different class of processor, rather than an improved version of an existing processor.

Some software vendors have taken the latter argument to heart and begun to charge multiprocessor prices for machines with multicore chips, seemingly transforming a lower-class machine into a more powerful system and, magically, thereby increasing the price of the vendors' software. This "magic" comes as a surprise to the customer, who learns the meaning of the term "sticker shock" as it finds that the software for its new $10,000 machine may run upwards of $250,000 instead of the expected $25,000 — all because the machine contains a quad-core processor.

However, I don't want to make it sound like software licensing revolves around only the hardware the software runs on. A number of other permutations of licensing approaches are used in the industry. Among them are

- ✔ **Named user:** Charging a licensing fee for every person that has a user account in the software. Needless to say, this can add up because even people who rarely use the software have to have a fully paid account.

- ✔ **Concurrent user:** Charging a licensing fee for the number of users actually using the product at any given time. Typically, this is handled by estimating the maximum number of users who might be using the software at any given time, and charging according to that number.

- ✔ **Base fee and user fee:** Charging a certain amount for a piece of software (for instance, some amount just to gain access to the software and have it running in your infrastructure) plus an incremental fee per user; the user fee can be of the named or concurrent user variant.

- ✔ **Transaction count:** Instead of focusing on who uses the software, this licensing approach charges for execution of business transactions (for example, adding a new account or processing an invoice). IBM, in particular, has explored this approach. It hasn't got much traction, but it's an attempt to better match the price of the software license to the value the customer gets from using it. Using the transaction count method is an attempt to address the resentment many companies feel due to paying per-user fees when, after all, the business value of the software is what they're interested in, not how many people are interacting with it.

Software licensing meets virtualization

Virtualization promises to add new layers of complexity to the software licensing mix.

For operating system software, questions arise as to whether a licensing fee is necessary for every virtual machine instance. For applications, questions arise as to how to assess license fees in a situation where the resources used by the application don't correspond to the actual resources of the underlying hardware.

For example, Oracle has taken the position that its fee should be based on the total number of processors in the server, whether or not all of them are actually used by a virtual machine that is running the Oracle software. Because virtualization products allow you to define how many of the machine's physical processors should be available for a specific virtual machine, it's easy to see that you might have a virtual machine running the Oracle software using only two of a machine's eight processors. Oracle's position is that you should pay a license fee based on an eight-processor box. However, many people, quite reasonably, feel that position is unreasonable and that they should pay for only a two-processor license. In fact, Oracle's license pricing is even more complex because it charges a premium for customers running the software on multicore processors.

At the time of this writing, a spat was going on between VMware and Microsoft about the latter's virtualization licensing policies. VMware states that Microsoft's licensing inhibits customer flexibility in deploying Microsoft-based virtual machines. I expect this bickering to continue for the foreseeable future, because Microsoft is gearing up to compete with VMware when Microsoft Server virtualization is released. The details of the conflict keep changing as Microsoft adjusts its position, but the impact is clear: End users are confused about their licensing rights and responsibilities in a virtualized environment, and the situation appears to be driven more by vendor business needs rather than by customer satisfaction.

Whether or not you agree with these vendors' approaches to software licensing in a virtualized world, one thing is clear: When it comes to virtualization, software licensing is a mess.

What this means for you, as you embark on your virtualization journey, is that you need to carefully check the conditions of your software licenses if you decide to migrate physical systems to virtualized ones.

Take a look at the total number of licenses you have from your software vendors. If you're having trouble with a vendor about moving some of your licenses to a virtualized environment, it's amazing how much more supportive they end up being about your virtualization plans once you inform them how many licenses you actually have from them.

What might you expect to find as you interact with vendors regarding their virtualization licensing policies? You'll probably find that vendors who are leaders in their category will be the most unyielding with regard to pricing. After all, if you're the lead dog, you have the most to lose with any change in the market. Vendors that have lower market shares will be the most flexible about working with you in your virtualization efforts. Again, that makes sense: They're much less threatened by market changes and might even see embracing virtualization as a strategy to improve their market position.

Here's one other thing to remain aware of as you consider vendor policies with regard to virtualization: Although every vendor is aware of the momentum of virtualization, some of them are less enthusiastic about supporting their products running in a virtualized environment. Chapter 5 contains some information about evaluating your vendors' support policies, and it presents a few strategies for mitigating a lack of enthusiasm on their part.

Chapter 3

Understanding Virtualization: Technologies and Applications

*Y*ou can easily appreciate the business benefits of virtualization: better use of corporate capital by reducing investment in hardware; reduced energy costs through server consolidation; lower operations costs through more efficient infrastructure administration; and freeing up space in over-crowded data centers. (Sounds like an MBA's idea of heaven, doesn't it?)

So, virtualization as a concept is definitely a good idea. Going from concept to reality, however, isn't a walk in the park. For example, a number of different server virtualization technologies are out there: operating system virtualization, hardware emulation, and paravirtualization, to be more precise. And you need to know what technologies the commercial virtualization products use, so that you can make an informed selection when it comes to choosing the product you'll use for your virtualization project. If that wasn't bad enough, you also have to use (or to be more precise, apply) virtualization itself a number of different ways. (You can stress server consolidation, failover, load balancing, or server pooling, for example.)

This chapter explores virtualization technologies and applications in more depth to provide a deeper understanding of the subject. This context makes it easier for you to select the right combination of technology and application for your server virtualization plans.

To get things off on the right foot, I walk you through the various virtualization technology choices that are available to you.

Virtualization Technologies

Keep in mind what virtualization is intended to provide: A way for multiple software products to share a single resource so that each software product can operate as though it has complete control of the underlying resource.

It's also important to have a basic understanding of the way computers operate In a nonvirtualized environment, you have your hardware, a physical resource containing its own set of resources: one or more processor(s), memory, a network interface, and a storage interface. Access to these resources is available only to software with the right level of privileges.

Residing on top of the hardware is an operating system. This operating system can access the underlying hardware resources because it operates with the right level of privileges. The operating system allows software applications, which have reduced privileges, to use operating system interfaces to access hardware resources. The applications are often referred to as user-level applications to distinguish them from operating system–level software. (Check out Figure 1-1 back in Chapter 1 for a graphical representation of my verbiage here.)

Keep in mind that virtualization isn't a new technology — in fact, virtualization has been around for many years. The key difference is that virtualization is now available for widely used, and extremely inexpensive, x86-based systems, rather than being limited to mainframes, as in the past.

By the way, the reasons they're called x86-based systems is that they use chips based on a design of Intel's which originated in chips ending in the designation 86 (for example, 386 and 486). This chip design was originally used in IBM's PC and has achieved near ubiquity, so much so that the tremendous volume of chips manufactured and the resulting low prices have resulted in x86 chips being referred to as *commodities.* Consequently, you'll often hear this new wave of virtualization being referred to as "virtualization on commodity hardware," meaning virtualization software running on systems that are powered by x86 chips. Overall, what this means is that virtualization has descended from the lofty pricing of mainframes and entered the low pricing of PC-based technology.

Another key factor about x86-based virtualization is the fact that, because it's based on commodity hardware, it must be built for (or, to use a fancier term, *architected* for) the x86 chip architecture. And that architecture has been fixed in its general characteristics since the IBM PC first saw the light of day more than 25 years ago. That fact causes some challenges for x86-based virtualization. Specifically, the chip was designed with no notion that multiple operating systems would need to share its resources; consequently, it makes no provision for the elegant sharing of a computer's resources. That has significant implications for how virtualization is implemented and how you, as an end user, can run applications in a virtualized environment. After all, running applications more efficiently is the point of the entire virtualization exercise. If virtualization doesn't help with that, there's no point in implementing it, is there? So, if implementation is the key, it makes sense to see what the different implementations actually look like (so much sense that I do precisely that in the next couple of sections).

Operating system virtualization

Operating system virtualization is perhaps the least known solution for virtualization, but under the right circumstances, it's the best solution there is.

Operating system virtualization (which I call OS virtualization from here on out) loads a virtualization layer of software on top of the base operating system running on the physical server. Unlike hardware emulation and para-virtualization (discussed in the following sections), OS virtualization provides a set of software interfaces that represent the OS interfaces available to applications; in other words, OS virtualization creates self-contained virtual environments that look (to the application) like an entire OS. Each of these self-contained virtual environments has its own file system (referred to as a *root* file system), a process table that contains individual applications, separate user populations, networking configuration, and system libraries. Because each of the virtual environments is self contained, another term for OS virtualization is *containers*. This "containerization" enables OS virtualization to provide many different virtual OS environments to different collections of applications, isolating each collection from the others and giving each collection the illusion of owning the entire OS.

In simpler terms, each virtual environment looks like a separate instance of an operating system.

You might find the preceding description of OS virtualization a bit confusing. What does a root file system mean? How about a process table? Let me shed some light on a few points:

- ✔ Every operating system has a **file structure.** For Windows, it usually includes the C: drive as the primary file storage mechanism; for Unix and Linux, the file system is hierarchical, with the top of the file system referred to as *root*. (Don't ask why the root is at the top, it just is.)

- ✔ Programs that run in the operating system are processes, and every one is represented in the **process table,** which keeps track of all the processes.

- ✔ Every operating system uses **networking** to talk to other machines, and each one has its own set of approved users, which is the machine's user population.

✔ **System libraries** are the system resources that applications call upon to interact with the operating system, and through the operating system, to the underlying hardware.

So, OS virtualization provides a software emulation of a complete operating system environment. You can load applications into a virtual environment and run them as though they were on a completely different machine from another application that's running in a separate virtual environment on the same physical server. And each virtual container can be assigned its own IP address and have that mapped to a domain name (such as the amazon.com in www.amazon.com), which means that each virtual environment can be treated as a separate system.

OS virtualization does clever things to reduce the amount of processing necessary to provide containerization. It maps the virtual file system to the underlying operating system's file system very cleanly, so little processing overhead is necessary for applications to read and write to physical drives. Files that are used by multiple virtual environments are held in a single copy to reduce unnecessary duplication.

One benefit of OS virtualization is that it imposes the least overhead of any virtualization solution. Consequently, it achieves the highest performance of all the virtualization solutions (although other solutions, particularly paravirtualization, achieve near-native performance as well). Also, because OS virtualization imposes the least overhead of any virtualization approach, it can support the highest *density* (that is, the highest number) of virtual environments for a given piece of hardware. Many OS virtualization environments support dozens and even hundreds of containers on a single machine.

Of course, every story has two sides, and OS virtualization has some drawbacks as well. Although containers are great for isolating applications, each container reflects the configuration of the underlying base operating system. In particular, that means that each container must be the same type, version, and patch level of the base operating system. Furthermore, each container is limited to the device drivers present in the base OS, which limits hardware flexibility, because hardware can't be put in place for just one container that requires it. And, of course, the entire collection of containers is dependent on the base OS: If it crashes, all of the containers will go down. (Please note that operating system virtualization providers are working hard to address the version and patch level limitations and may be able to address this issue in the future; for today, however, the limitations are present and inflexible.)

Consequently, OS virtualization supports only one operating system environment, which means that you can't mix guest operating systems. Depending on your desired virtualization architecture, this limitation might present a problem. On the other hand, many organizations find that they end up segregating their virtualized operating systems: Some virtualization servers run only Windows guests, and others run only Linux guests. So the single OS limitation of OS virtualization isn't a fatal drawback for these organizations.

What can be a bit more troublesome is the fact that all the virtual environments have to be the same version and patch level. Many applications are certified to run only on certain OS versions and patch levels. Therefore, you might not be able to achieve high-density virtualization on an OS virtualization server, because the applications require different virtual environments, which implies a different underlying OS. You can mitigate this problem by running multiple servers, each with a different OS version and patch level, but such a solution clearly isn't desirable, not to mention the difficulty of tracking and managing the different servers, each with its particular version and patch level.

Operating system virtualization can be obtained from Sun, which provides it as part of its Solaris operating system. A commercial provider of OS virtualization is SWsoft, whose Virtuozzo product is available for both Linux and Windows.

OS virtualization works best in data centers where IT can control the components in the software stack. For example, OS virtualization is a good choice for Web hosting. Companies that provide Web hosting can use OS virtualization to give each hosted Web site the illusion that it has a complete machine dedicated to its use, even though in reality it might be one of a couple of dozen Web sites, all of which are hosted on that single machine.

OS virtualization is also a good solution for Software as a Service (SaaS) environments. In SaaS environments, applications are run on a server and accessed by remote users via the Internet. If that sounds a lot like a Web site, you're not far off. The difference here is that instead of a set of content pages, the pages served up by a SaaS system provide application functionality. A large number of applications are being offered as SaaS, including Salesforce.com's Customer Relationship Management (CRM) application; Google's Docs and Spreadsheets (located at `http://docs.google.com` at the time of this writing), which provides Web-based word processing and spreadsheet functionality; and NetSuite, which offers a full Enterprise Resource Planning (ERP) application over the Web. OS virtualization can allow these companies to offer many instances of their products from a single server. Furthermore, any changes to the base operating system (for example, a new patch applied to the OS) are immediately propagated to all the virtual environments; in short, you patch the underlying OS instance and it is immediately propagated to all containers, vastly reducing the work typically required to push a patch out to a number of different servers.

Operating system virtualization is also well suited for training environments, in which a large number of students need to be given identical systems to work in. Traditionally, training is a very challenging type of application due to the need to provide each student an isolated environment; in the past this meant a "one student, one machine" environment, which is expensive, but also complex to manage because at the end of every class, each machine would need to be restored to an original state, ready for the next student. By using operating system virtualization, each student can have a separate environment while only requiring one physical machine. Even better is the fact that it's easy to restore the original system state by merely regenerating new containers from system definition files — much easier than reinstalling applications and so on.

Hardware emulation

One major downside of so-called x86 chips (see the intro to this section) is that that they don't provide any convenient way for multiple operating systems to share the resources of the computer. So if you want to run multiple operating systems (in contrast to running virtualization within a single copy of an operating system, discussed in the previous section), you need to implement a method whereby every time a virtualized operating system attempts to call upon system resources, you intercept the call and redirect it in such a way that the virtualization software can manage multiple instances of operating systems.

This interception and redirection of operating system calls requires clever software because it operates at a very low level — at the interface between the OS and the physical hardware. Not only does the software need to reliably catch (called trap) these calls, it must also do it very fast; otherwise, the performance hit of running virtualization would outweigh the benefits of hardware multiplexing. This specialized virtualization software even has its own name: hypervisor. (The term *hypervisor* is a bit of a play on words. An operating system is sometimes referred to as a supervisor, so the virtualization software acts as a supervisor of the supervisors and is therefore dubbed a hypervisor. This is what passes for humor in the computer science world.)

The best-established method of virtualizing access to system resources is called *hardware emulation*. In this method, the hypervisor creates a virtual machine by emulating an entire hardware environment. The operating system that's loaded into a virtual machine is a standard, unmodified product. As it makes calls for system resources, the hardware emulation software catches the system call and redirects it to manipulate data structures provided by the hypervisor. The hypervisor itself makes calls to the actual physical hardware underlying all the software.

Now, you might ask, how does the unmodified operating system end up making calls into the hypervisor when it's actually using calls that should go straight to the hardware?

Hardware emulation addresses that problem by cleverly substituting pieces of code within the operating system at runtime in a process called *binary translation*. What that means is that when the guest operating system is running (thus the use of the term *runtime*), the hardware emulation hypervisor goes in and changes part of the operating system. Because the operating system is an executable program, it's in a format of 1s and 0s (zeroes), which are required to interact with computer hardware, also known as a *binary* (thus the phrase *binary translation*). The hypervisor translates the native binary format of the OS to the binary format of the hypervisor in the areas of the OS that makes calls to hardware resources. And, by the way, hardware emulation can support both Windows and Linux guests.

Binary translation occurs in parts of the operating system that interact with the four key resources of the hardware: processor, memory, network, and storage. The hypervisor replaces key sections of operating system code, such as network device drivers, with code that talks to the *emulated hardware layer* (essentially, a virtualized motherboard, containing virtual representations of a processor, memory, and so on), which is implemented in the hypervisor. The hypervisor then arranges to forward the calls from the emulated hardware to the actual physical hardware on the server.

As you might imagine, this is complex stuff, worthy of rocket scientists. However, it does allow you to run unmodified operating systems (unmodified by you, that is; remember, the hardware emulation virtualization software modifies the operating system at runtime to enable it to cooperate with the hypervisor).

This approach has several strengths. Running unmodified operating systems simplifies your job — all you have to do is load operating systems into virtual machines. Furthermore, it lets you run unmodified applications within the guest operating systems, enabling you to use applications certified to run only on certain versions of operating systems: Because you don't modify the OS, your application should continue to be supported by its vendor. (Although that can be a bit tricky; see Chapter 5 for further discussion about vendor support in virtualized environments.) Furthermore, the hypervisor's provider takes care of coordinating access to the physical hardware resources, making it easy to use virtualization.

You can take a couple of different approaches to hardware emulation virtualization. One is that the hypervisor is installed on top of an existing operating system that resides on the physical server. In this approach, the hypervisor essentially acts as a user application that knows how to coordinate calls into the underlying existing operating system so that the hypervisor can coordinate access to the host operating system for a number of guest virtual machines. You might suspect that all the coordinating might take a lot of processor cycles and would therefore reduce overall system performance. You'd be right in that suspicion, too.

Another approach to hardware emulation is to install the hypervisor directly on the server without an intervening already-installed operating system. Because this approach installs directly on the server, it is often called *bare-metal* virtualization, to symbolize the fact that no software sits between the hypervisor and the "metal" of the server. In this approach to hardware emulation, the hypervisor intercepts system calls from the guest virtual machines and coordinates access to the underlying hardware directly. As you might also suspect, this approach provides much higher performance than the version of hardware emulation described in the previous paragraph.

Hardware emulation is the type of virtualization implemented by VMware, the category leader in x86 virtualization. (Microsoft's Virtual Server also implements hardware emulation.)

VMware provides products that implement both approaches to hardware emulation. VMware's VMware Server is installed atop an existing operating system (which can be Windows or one of several flavors of Linux), whereas its ESX Server implements bare-metal hardware emulation. Although VMware Server's approach to hardware emulation — the Install-it-on-top-of-the-OS path — imposes a significant performance hit, it can be usefully applied where performance isn't critical. For example, lightly loaded servers can usefully apply this approach to hardware emulation. It's also useful for virtualizing client machines like a desktop or notebook PC.

Hardware emulation does have some drawbacks:

✔ **It imposes a performance penalty, even for the bare-metal approach.** This problem occurs because translation is still going on, eating up some machine cycles as the hypervisor executes the translation. VMware does clever optimizations on this translation, caching data that is repeatedly accessed, and so on, but some performance penalty still exists. On the other hand, if you're moving from a Pentium III–based server that's running at only 15 percent utilization to a virtualized dual-core machine that offers 100 times the performance of the old machine and can thereby support six virtual machines, you might not be too worried that you're not getting 100 percent of the potential performance of the new server. You'd be happy just taking advantage of what's available from the new machine.

✔ **The idealized image of the hardware provided offers idealized device drivers.** The hypervisor contains real device drivers that talk to the underlying hardware. In other words, the hypervisor drives the underlying hardware, and as an end user, you must depend on the hypervisor to include the appropriate drivers for your hardware. Consequently, you're somewhat limited in your choice of hardware because you need the hypervisor to include drivers to interact with your hardware. Although VMware does a very good job of trying to keep up with new hardware releases and their accompanying device drivers, you might find your hardware is unsupported. So checking the hardware compatibility list for ESX Server support is critical if you go down this path. Note that VMware Server, while imposing a performance penalty, actually suffers less from the device driver issue because it is able to leverage the device drivers present in the underlying OS.

Paravirtualization

Paravirtualization is an alternative approach to virtualization. Instead of attempting to emulate the x86 hardware environment in software, a paravirtualization hypervisor coordinates (or *multiplexes*) access to the underlying hardware resources of the server. The best-known example of paravirtualization is the open source product called Xen. Microsoft Server virtualization to be released in the future also uses the paravirtualization approach.

This raises the question of how paravirtualization actually manages the coordination to the underlying hardware, because the guest operating systems contain code that expects to be able to interact directly with the hardware.

As part of the first faint glimmer of an answer to this question, let me paint you a picture of the architecture of paravirtualization. (Okay, if you think a picture is worth a thousand words, check out Figure 1-3 back in Chapter 1.) Visualize, if you will, a hypervisor residing on the hardware, meaning that paravirtualization is a bare-metal virtualization architecture. (If the term *bare metal* doesn't ring a bell or you think it involves playing loud rock music in the nude, check out how I define the term in the preceding section.) Instead of the virtual machine approach of hardware emulation, paravirtualization installs a guest OS — called *DomainU* in Xen parlance and *child partition* in Microsoft parlance — directly on the hypervisor. Paravirtualization also adds a wrinkle in that the hypervisor does not contain device drivers for network and storage resources; instead it has a *privileged guest,* called Domain0 in Xen parlance and the root partition in Microsoft parlance. Domain0 runs as a guest but has privileges that allow it to directly access resources on the underlying hardware, whereas regular guest OSes access those resources through Domain0. It's something like a bucket brigade: The guest OS sends a message to Domain0 to request access to a hardware resource. Domain0 accesses the hardware resource on behalf of the guest OS. When data returns to the hardware, Domain0 reads the information and then passes it back to the guest OS.

Domain0 is a standard operating system (like Red Hat Enterprise Linux) that has been modified to coordinate with the hypervisor to control access to hardware resources. In practice, from a user's perspective, the privileged guest looks just like a vanilla-version operating system; the required modifications reside in the kernel, far below what a user experiences while interacting with the OS.

Rather than modify the guest operating system at runtime via binary translation, paravirtualization requires that guest operating systems be modified prior to execution to include code that can interact with the paravirtualization hypervisor. After modification, when a guest operating system accesses the processor or memory, the modified code interacts with the hypervisor, which then coordinates access to those resources.

Paravirtualization also handles access to storage and network resources differently than hardware emulation virtualization. Whereas hardware emulation virtualization includes device drivers directly in the hypervisor, paravirtualization uses the native device drivers included in Domain0. Other guest operating systems have special *stub drivers* (called back-end drivers) that communicate with stub drivers in the privileged guest (called front-end drivers). A stub driver is one that allows the guest operating system to make a call to what looks like a regular device driver, but instead of making a hardware call, the stub driver communicates with its counterpart in Domain0. (Why the funny name? Because it removes all the code necessary to talk to a device driver, it's been effectively whittled down in size — a stub, in other words.)

After the privileged guest receives data from the guest OS's stub driver, it then forwards the data on to the real device driver on behalf of the guest OS. So, for example, a guest OS call to send data through the network would go through its stub network driver to the privileged guest, which would receive the network request in its stub driver and then pass the data on to its physical network card via a device driver. Communication between the two stub drivers is extremely fast because it makes use of a system resource called *shared memory* — essentially memory that can be accessed by more than one software process. Because the memory is written by one process and read by a second with no need to copy the data in the memory, shared memory can offer extremely fast data throughput.

A major benefit of this approach to device access is that the hypervisor doesn't need to contain any device drivers. It merely uses the shared memory communication to give the data to the privileged guest (remember, the privileged guest is a regular operating system that contains a whole set of device drivers for the underlying hardware), which can reuse the native device drivers for access to hardware resources. This means that end users don't depend on the virtualization software provider to support the hardware they own; instead, the privileged guest, which contains the drivers necessary to work with the hardware, provides hardware support. So, for example, if the Domain0 is Red Hat Enterprise Linux, then during installation, part of the process ensures all necessary device drivers are present. When a guest OS needs to access storage or the network, the hypervisor uses those drivers. This avoids a problem alluded to in the hardware emulation discussion earlier, where end users can find that their virtualization software doesn't support their hardware.

A second benefit of this approach to virtualization is that it offers very good performance because there is less runtime translation of operating system calls as in hardware emulation. I have heard Xen users state that they experience no more than a 2 to 3 percent performance hit running applications in virtualized operating systems compared to running the same applications in nonvirtualized operating systems.

However, paravirtualization has a major drawback: the requirement to modify guest operating systems prior to execution to include code to interact with the hypervisor. The guest operating system cannot be installed as-is; rather, you have to modify the OS kernel prior to installation. Modifying a kernel to enable it to be virtualized is no picnic — something I can attest to from personal experience. Moreover, modifying the kernel requires access to the source code. Although this modification is possible for open source operating systems like Linux or OpenSolaris, it isn't possible for proprietary operating systems, particularly Windows. So Xen users have been stuck being able to virtualize Linux operating systems, but not Windows. As you can imagine, this isn't a desirable situation. This state of affairs has essentially limited paravirtualization's uptake to technically savvy Linux users — admittedly a rather small subset of the computing universe.

Operating system vendors have instituted the following changes to mitigate this unappealing situation:

✔ Some Linux distributions have been modified to include both regular and paravirtualized hardware interfaces in their kernels so that they're capable at runtime of discerning which type of environment they're executing in and using the correct interface for the environment. This solution means you wouldn't need to hand-modify the kernel on that particular distribution to get it to run on the paravirtualized hypervisor.

✔ Some Linux distributions have been modified to serve as Dom0 privileged guests. This change means that no kernel modification is necessary to enable them to communicate with the hypervisor via back-end stub drivers and coordinate access from the stub drivers to the native drivers Dom0 already contains. Both Red Hat and Novell have included this capability in their most recent releases.

✔ The new generation of chips that has been released by both AMD and Intel provides virtualization support in hardware. The effect of this chip upgrade is that Xen can support non-paravirtualized operating systems, thereby removing one of the most significant barriers to adoption, particularly with respect to supporting Windows guests. For more information on this new generation of chips and further hardware advances, please see Chapter 8.

Paravirtualization may be obtained from any operating system that provides it as part of the native OS. Xen is included in most popular Linux distributions, XenSource (the commercial sponsor of Xen) sells an enhanced version of Xen as a commercial product called XenEnterprise, and Microsoft will include paravirtualization in its next Microsoft Server release.

To make the subject of virtualization technology easier to grasp, Table 3-1 summarizes the different types of virtualization, offers some comments on their strengths and weaknesses, and lists the different products available for each type.

Table 3-1	Virtualization Technologies	
Virtualization Type	**Comments**	**Products**
Operating System Virtualization	Provides an abstracted view of OS resources (root file system, process table, and so on); useful for homogeneous operating environments where consistent OS version is desirable (such as Web hosting); very scalable.	SWsoft OpenVZ (open source) and Virtuozzo (commercial); Sun OpenSolaris (open source) and Solaris (commercial)
Hardware Emulation	Provides an abstracted view of underlying hardware (that is, the emulated motherboard); based on binary translation of runtime guest OSes; offers support for guest OSes that might be heterogeneous; market-leading approach to virtualization	Microsoft Virtual Server (commercial); VMware VM server (commercial, but free); VMware ESX Server (commercial, leading virtualization product in market)
Paravirtualization	Light-weight virtualization approach multiplexes access to underlying hardware resources; high performance; requires guest OS modification prior to deployment, therefore somewhat more complex than hardware emulation; native guest OS support on latest generation of processor chips; available bundled with commercial operating systems	Xen (open source) available or free download; Xen also bundled with Linux distributions from Red Hat and Novell as well as other community distributions; XenSource (sponsor of Xen open source product) offers a commercial version of Xen with additional functionality; upcoming Microsoft Server product will include paravirtualization

This table will help you decide which virtualization technology is best suited for your environment; of course, your ultimate decision will be affected by the use you'll make of virtualization. If you look at the next chapter, you'll find a discussion of all the different ways virtualization can be applied to provide a more efficient and cost-effective computing infrastructure.

Assessing the implications of virtualization technology

As mentioned earlier, Microsoft is implementing paravirtualization in its upcoming Microsoft Server virtualization functionality. Microsoft is working closely with Novell and XenSource (the commercial sponsor of the Xen project) to ensure Microsoft Server virtualization can work well with Linux. Major Linux distributors like Red Hat and Novell are including virtualization as a feature in their current product releases.

The net effect of these initiatives is that the dominant operating systems in data centers will all include virtualization as a built-in feature. (By the way, Sun Microsystems is also planning to support Xen in a future Solaris release.) This means that you will have a number of virtualization options in the near future. You will be able to

✔ **Purchase a virtualization solution from virtualization software companies like VMware, SWsoft, Virtual Iron, or XenSource.** VMware is the clear leader in virtualization deployment and provides lots of resources to help you be successful. Should you be focused on a commercial operating system virtualization solution, you can use Virtuozzo from SWsoft (Virtuozzo). XenSource distributes a version of Xen with XenSource-specific functionality extensions.

✔ **Download a virtualization product for free.** You can select from operating system virtualization (OpenVZ from SWsoft and OpenSolaris from Sun) and paravirtualization (Xen) products, both of which include source code because they are open source products. If you don't demand source code access, there is also the free VMware Server available.

✔ **Use the virtualization functionality that is included in the operating system.** Many current and all future major operating systems will include paravirtualization as a built-in feature that can be used at no cost, assuming you have legal access to the operating system itself. Also, OpenSolaris and Solaris both offer operating system virtualization functionality.

Using a free product or the one included with the operating system might seem like a slam dunk. And that may be the right choice for you. On the other hand, the OS-included products may not be the right virtualization solution for you, whereas the established commercial products have a long track record, a robust ecosystem of service providers, and certified application software products, as well as a plethora of add-on helper applications to make them work even better.

More important, your choice of technology is likely to be affected by the way you'll apply it. It's just as important to know what you want to do as it is to know what tool you'll use. So I'd be remiss is I didn't immediately turn to a discussion of typical application profiles so that you have the entire picture in front of you.

Virtualization Applications

Virtualization as a technology has a general description: the abstraction of hardware resources so that multiple software products can share in the use of the hardware without conflicting with one another.

Just as critical as knowing how virtualization works is understanding how you can apply it. And this is where it gets fun. Virtualization can be useful in a number of scenarios. They range from simple and straightforward to complex and transformational. Understanding how you want to use virtualization is critical because that will dictate which virtualization solution is most appropriate for you. What are the most common applications of virtualization? In the following sections, I review the most common uses of virtualization and make recommendations about which products would be best suited for each use.

Want the general overview first? Okay, here's a list of the most common applications of virtualization:

- Development and testing
- Training
- Server consolidation
- Failover/high availability
- Load balancing
- Server pooling
- Disaster recovery

With that out of the way, it's time to examine each application in a bit more detail.

Development and testing

Imagine, if you will, the typical process of creating and releasing software. An engineer builds some software to implement certain functionality. Depending on the type of software, it might need to run on more than one operating system (say, on Linux and Solaris). And, of course, it might need to run on more than one version of each operating system, because the software might be used by organizations with different software environments. If the software is intended to run in a distributed environment (a fancy way of saying it might need to interact with two or more separate systems), it's important to engineer it so that it can operate in a mixed environment — with one part running on a Solaris operating system of a certain version and another part running on Windows of a certain version. Furthermore, it's important to develop on different patch levels of each operating system, not to mention multitier application environments with complex networking configurations.

After the engineer has built the software to run in those environment(s), the software is handed off to a testing group to ensure quality. Testing groups exist to exercise the software to make sure it operates as it's supposed to in all its supported configurations. A testing group assigned to test the distributed software described in the preceding paragraph would set up a configuration with a Solaris server and a Windows server, and then the group would do various tests to see whether the software really worked in that environment. Part of a test group's responsibility is to ensure that the software not only works correctly, but that it can handle being used incorrectly (known as *negative testing*). Test groups often do things like inputting data of the wrong type or feeding in a data file of the wrong format, all to see whether the software is likely to work in real-world usage conditions. One consequence of this kind of destructive testing is that it tends to crash machines and often wipes out the operating system, necessitating a fresh install of the OS and application before any additional testing can be done. (Of course, crashes can also happen in regular functionality testing, with the same effect: A lengthy reinstall is required before any further work can be accomplished.)

So, looking over the software development life cycle, there are many requirements for multiple systems. Failing to build and test in an environment that reflects real-world deployment scenarios means that end users are likely to be dissatisfied when the software is finally deployed in production. Consequently, software engineers and test personnel must have access to multiple systems.

There are a few problems with this situation, however:

- ✔ Only a portion of the development and test cycle requires multiple systems. After all, much of the time an engineer or tester is doing work that can easily be accomplished on a single machine.

- ✔ Most development and test work that is done on multiple machines is done only to ascertain basic functionality; therefore, many of the machines are lightly loaded and lightly exercised.

- ✔ When development or testing causes a system crash, it can take time and labor to reinstall everything to get ready for the next task.

- ✔ Keeping a bunch of machines sitting around for occasional development or test work requires space and ties up a lot of money; even in a time of cheap servers, dedicating several machines that are used only occasionally is wasteful.

Given these drawbacks, you can see why it would make sense to apply virtualization to development and testing efforts.

Even a developer's laptop is plenty powerful enough to support several guest machines. By using virtualization, a developer or tester can replicate a distributed environment containing several machines on a single piece of hardware. This setup negates the need to have a bunch of servers sitting around for the occasional use of developers or testers. It also avoids the inevitable conflict that occurs when an organization attempts to have its members share machines for distributed use. Just when one person wants to test some distributed functionality, someone else is already using the machines. Even worse, the machines are incorrectly configured, so the first thing a new user has to do is remove all the software on the machine and reinstall new software to get the right configuration for his or her purposes. As you can imagine, this repetitive teardown and reinstallation is a real drag on productivity.

Virtualization is also useful in testing and development in another way. One of the side effects of exercising software is that early versions often crash and damage not only the application, but also the underlying operating system as well as other applications in the software stack. To recover, it's necessary to reinstall all the software. Again, this is a real drag on productivity.

One of the great things about virtualization is that guest machines can be captured in a file. That is, an image of the complete virtualized machine — operating system, software stack, and applications — can be saved to a file. This makes sense when you consider that the virtualization software is running software virtual machines, so it has to have a standard format for the machines. Virtualization software can save these images onto a disk file and then load the file at a later time, ready to run.

This capability is a boon to developers and testers. Rather than having to repeatedly rebuild test instances, they can just save a complete virtual machine image and load it each time they trash a virtual machine instance. In terms of recovery time, the consequences of a machine crash go from hours to minutes (or even seconds).

This ability to save and restore virtual machine instances is an incredibly useful aspect of virtualization. The usefulness of virtualization for development was brought home to me in a recent conversation with a friend who works in development for a chip company. He noted that he was using virtualization on his laptop and running development applications in a virtual machine. The inevitable happened (that's why it's inevitable, right?), and the base operating system got corrupted, necessitating a complete OS reinstall. Dreading the extended reinstallation of numerous applications, he decided to take a chance on reloading the virtual machine image from a backup: two minutes later he was up and running with his entire tool set and data files available. He estimated he saved at least six hours of boring software loading. This is why virtualization is being widely adopted in development and testing.

Common virtualization products for use in development and test work are

- **VMware ESX Server:** This is a highly scalable, bare-metal hardware emulation virtualization product and is well suited for load testing. It is relatively expensive, so many testing and development organizations find that it's out of their price range.

- **VMware Server:** This is a hardware emulation virtualization product that installs on top of an existing operating system, and for that reason, it's less scalable than VMware's ESX Server. On the other hand, it's free, which makes it more attractive for budget-limited testing and development groups. Also, because much development and testing work requires lightly loaded machines, the limited scalability of VMware Server isn't much of a drawback.

- **Microsoft Virtual Server:** This is also a hardware emulation virtualization product that installs on top of an existing operating system and shares the performance limitations of VMware Server. However, given Microsoft's ubiquity, it is widely used in development and testing environments.

- **Xen:** This is an open source, highly scalable paravirtualization product that's provided with a number of Linux distributions. It can support Windows guests only on machines that contain the latest virtualization-enabled chips from AMD or Intel. Xen is very attractive for Linux-focused shops. Xen is included in flagship Linux distributions from Red Hat and Novell, as well as the free community Linux distributions from Fedora and OpenSUSE. Xen is also available in other community Linux distributions such as Debian and Ubuntu (and, of course, the list is continually growing).

- **XenSource:** XenSource is the commercial sponsor of Xen. It has several commercial products that offer paravirtualization and also are tuned to support Windows well. The products are priced from free up to a few hundred dollars per year. The free version is well suited for testing and development environments.

- **Sun:** Both the open source OpenSolaris and the commercial Solaris operating systems provide containers which are ideally suited for creating multiple virtual systems on a single piece of hardware. Note that these containers are homogeneous, making Sun's products poorly suited for development and testing of mixed environments (for example, a distributed system that includes both Linux and Windows).

Training

As briefly described earlier in the chapter, training is a common application of virtualization. Because technical training requires that students have a computer system available to experiment and perform exercises on, the management of a training environment has traditionally been very challenging and labor intensive.

Training typically tracks the following scenario:

1. The student begins with a basic technology setup. If the course is a database administration class, the basic setup has the operating system, the database software itself, a demo set of data in the database, and one or more applications.

2. The student performs set exercises involving more and more complex operations, each of which extends or modifies the basic technology setup.

3. At class end, the student leaves the course having successfully completed all exercises and having significantly modified the basic technology setup.

The challenge then faced is the need to restore the environments back to the basic setup.

With virtualization, the restoration process is quite simple. If operating system virtualization is being used, the modified containers are removed and new containers created, using an existing basic setting as a template for the new containers. If hardware emulation or paravirtualization is being used, the virtual machines used by the last batch of students are deleted and new virtual machines are created from images that represent the desired starting point. Presto — setting up training environments has gone from hours or days to minutes.

Common virtualization products for use in training are

- **VMware ESX Server:** This is a highly scalable, bare-metal hardware emulation virtualization product and may be used for training. It is quite scalable and relatively expensive, so it only makes sense in training environments where there are a large number of students to be hosted on a powerful server.

- **VMware Server:** Even though VMware Server is less scalable than ESX Server, it can be a good choice for training because training programs often don't impose very large processing requirements on systems. Therefore, the lower scalability of VMware Server isn't a drawback in that environment.

- **Microsoft Virtual Server:** Microsoft Virtual Server also doesn't scale that well; however, given the light loads often associated with training, Virtual Server might be well suited for training.

- **Xen:** Because Xen is free and available on many Linux distributions, it is very appropriate for training. Xen's paravirtualization architecture means high performance, so it is well suited for heavily loaded training programs.

✔ **XenSource:** XenSource's commercial products provide paravirtualization performance along with high-quality Windows support. XenSource can be a good choice for training — its XenExpress product, available at no cost, is an especially good choice.

✔ **SWsoft:** In the case of SWsoft, both its open source OpenVZ and its commercial Virtuozzo product provide operating system virtualization, which can easily provide the standardized systems necessary for training programs.

✔ **Sun:** In Sun's case, both its open source OpenSolaris and its commercial Solaris operating systems include containers (operating system virtualization) as part of the product. Containers can easily provide standardized environments for training programs.

Server consolidation

Server consolidation is what most people think of when they consider virtualization. *Consolidation* is the act of taking separate things and creating a union that contains all of them. So, for example, you might consider that 50 separate states are consolidated into the United States.

With respect to virtualization, consolidation refers to taking separate server instances and migrating them into virtual machines running on a single server. To be technically correct, consolidation would also be the act of taking a number of separate servers and migrating them onto fewer servers, with multiple virtual machines running on each server.

This is perhaps the easiest, most obvious application of virtualization. It addresses the problems most folks desperately want virtualization to address: underutilization of servers in the data center; server sprawl that threatens to overwhelm data center capacity; sky-high energy costs from running all those underutilized servers; and escalating operations costs as more system administrators are required to keep all those underutilized servers humming.

A typical server consolidation project accomplishes the following:

1. Identifies a number of underutilized systems in the data center.

2. Selects one or more servers to be the new virtualization servers; these might be existing or newly purchased.

3. Installs virtualization software on the new virtualization servers.

4. Creates new virtual machines from the existing servers.

5. Installs the new virtual machines on the new virtualization servers.

6. Begins running the virtual machines as the production servers for the applications inside the virtual machines.

The outcome is much more dramatic than this simple list would seem to indicate. Companies implementing server consolidation often move from running 150 physical servers to running 150 virtual machines on only 15 servers, with an understandable reduction in power, hardware investment, and employee time.

Naturally, the process of migrating systems requires many smaller tasks that aren't listed here. For example, each virtual machine must have a network address assigned and storage allotted (or have the existing virtualized storage the physical server is using assigned to the new virtual machine). The backup process for the new setup must be modified when it is no longer a question of just sticking a tape into a lot of separate servers. And, of course, the virtual machines must still be managed after the server consolidation project is complete.

Conceptually, however, the list captures the steps. And, in the overall scheme of things, migrating 150 servers to new virtual machines is much, much easier than migrating 150 systems to new physical servers — now that's a lot of work!

Many organizations are surprised at how pain-free the implementation of a server consolidation project can actually be. You can find more information about migration and virtualization management in Chapters 9 and 10, as well as more about the virtualization life cycle and all the elements of a virtualization project.

If you're in the market for a virtualization product for a server consolidation project, check out the following (commercial and open source) options:

- ✔ **SWsoft Virtuozzo:** This is a commercial operating system virtualization (also called *container*) product that is very well suited to support large numbers of virtualized systems. It's especially suited for consolidating environments that have large numbers of identical systems. For example, if an organization wants to centralize an environment in which a large number of branch offices all have their own on-premises servers, each of which is identically configured, then container virtualization is ideal. Unfortunately, this kind of homogeneous environment is pretty rare. SWsoft also sponsors the free open source container virtualization product OpenVZ, which you can use for the same server consolidation purposes.

- ✔ **Sun Solaris containers:** Similar to SWsoft's Virtuozzo, you can use Sun Solaris containers for server consolidation projects with a significant degree of homogeneity. Solaris is a commercial product that is also available in open source form as OpenSolaris. Sun also sells physical servers that are architected to support containers with better isolation between individual container instances.

- ✔ **VMware ESX Server:** The most widely deployed commercial server consolidation virtualization product today, VMware ESX Server is very scalable and therefore able to support high numbers of virtual machines per physical server. ESX Server's noncommercial counterpart VMware Server isn't a good candidate for server consolidation projects because it's installed on top of an existing base operating system. The extra layers of software affect its scalability as well as performance. On the other hand, VMware Server is free, which may neutralize some of its limitations for many users.

✔ **Xen:** The open source Xen product, available in a number of Linux distributions such as Red Hat Enterprise Linux and Novell's SUSE Linux Enterprise Server, is well suited for server consolidation projects that plan to migrate a number of disparate Linux servers to a smaller number of physical servers. Although Xen can support Windows guest machines, this support requires physical servers with the latest generation of chips from AMD and Intel. Moreover, Windows support has become available only recently at the time of this writing, so no one has much experience with it. Novell and Microsoft have announced a technical collaboration on virtualization; as a result, Xen might offer better support of Windows as this collaboration moves forward. You can find out more about virtualization hardware options in Chapter 8.

✔ **XenExpress, XenServer, and XenEnterprise:** These commercial products from XenSource, the commercial sponsor of Xen, are designed for mixed server consolidation projects. XenSource and Microsoft have collaborated to enhance Xen's ability to support Windows. In particular, XenSource offers Windows drivers to improve performance, as well as to enhance the hypervisor scheduler to run Windows guest machines more efficiently. XenExpress is free, but somewhat limited in functionality, whereas the other products offer more functionality but carry a price tag.

✔ **Virtual Iron:** Here you have a commercial company whose virtualization product incorporates the Xen hypervisor. Virtual Iron provides more-sophisticated management capabilities than the native Xen hypervisor. It offers a free, unlimited-use product for use on a single server while also offering a version that can span multiple servers on a fee basis.

Server consolidation is very likely going to be your first virtualization project — but I'm pretty sure you're not going to stop there. I like to say that virtualization is a journey, not a product, by which I mean that virtualization isn't something you buy and install; rather, it's a technology application that you're likely to find additional uses for after you begin applying it. And the first application of virtualization is usually server consolidation.

Failover/high availability/load balancing

Okay, time to consolidate my own discussion a bit and deal with a couple of topics in one fell swoop. Failover, high availability, and load balancing are often the next steps on your virtualization journey. Each one draws on the virtualization software's ability to efficiently manage virtual machine instances. A virtualization hypervisor constantly checks the status of individual virtual machines and is very good at the whole scheduling shtick — bringing virtual machines to active status if they aren't currently running and *quiescing* them (that is, taking an active virtual machine and putting it into a hibernate mode) when they're no longer needed.

This section discusses how virtualization enables failover, high availability, and load balancing. Be aware that every vendor describes these topics differently, and what one vendor calls high availability, another vendor will call failover, which makes it difficult to sort out what functionality a vendor really provides. I've used these terms to describe logical functionality and analyzed the different virtualization products in light of that logical arrangement, but don't be surprised if any specific vendor (or, indeed, any specific person whether vendor representative or co-worker) uses the terms differently.

Because the hypervisor is always aware of each virtual machine's status, you can configure the hypervisor to take certain actions if something untoward occurs with a virtual machine. So, for example, you can configure a hypervisor to automatically restart a new instance of a virtual machine should an existing instance crash. In contrast to the typical recovery times for crashed servers (anywhere from minutes to weeks), virtualization recovery times can be seconds. (Remember, the image of a complete virtual machine can be stored in a file and started very quickly by the hypervisor.)

This use of virtualization to quickly restart a new virtual machine instance upon noticing that a previous executing instance has crashed is known as *failover,* because work moves over to a new virtual machine when the old one fails. Clever, eh?

Why failover is important

Companies run many applications that they consider *mission critical,* which is a fancy term meaning that companies rely on these applications for a fundamental part of their business. If you're an insurance company, the systems that allow you to assess risk and accept new policies (known as underwriting) are vital; if they aren't working, the company can't generate any revenue.

Consequently, running applications on a single server exposes the company to a single point of failure (often referred to as SPOF). In other words, if the server goes down, the company can't run its mission-critical application until it gets the server up and running on a new piece of hardware. The duration of the outage can run from minutes to weeks, depending on the complexity of the application architecture and the availability of hardware. Obviously, the potential for application outage and the uncertainty of recovery time is unacceptable for mission-critical applications.

Beyond the vagaries of hardware malfunction, other issues affect application availability. Primarily, these issues relate to the application and its software components. So, to extend the underwriting example for a moment, the company faces risk if the application itself (or some underlying software component it relies on) crashes.

To address the risk of application unavailability, application vendors have offered technology to make their products more robust. Going by various names like clustering or high availability, this technology essentially mirrors one copy of the application to a second machine, and it keeps them consistent by constantly sending messages back and forth between the copies. If the secondary machine notices that the primary machine is no longer responding, it steps up to the plate and takes on the workload — when one system goes down, the application does a failover to the secondary system.

Although this functionality is clearly critical, it's important to note some less-than-desirable aspects to it:

- ✔ **It's application specific.** If every mission-critical application provides its own method of achieving failover, the IT operations staff has to know as many different technologies as there are applications. This is a recipe for complexity and high cost.

- ✔ **It's wasteful of resources.** Keeping a mirrored system up for every mission-critical application requires a lot of extra machines, each of which imposes its own operations costs, not to mention being wasteful of a lot of extra hardware. Furthermore, because one of the factors driving the move to virtualization is that data centers are overfilled with machines, a solution that requires even more machines seems undesirable.

- ✔ **It's expensive.** Every vendor recognizes that failover is mission critical, so it charges an arm and a leg for the functionality. And, because you need to purchase a failover solution for every application, pretty soon you're out of arms and legs.

Fortunately, virtualization provides a way to achieve failover much more conveniently and cost effectively. Instead of requiring a lot of spare equipment, virtualization can use additional virtual machines to provide failover capability. Moreover, virtualization actually provides some significant advantages in terms of how it delivers failover capability, making it a much more satisfactory solution for the vast majority of users.

Understanding the components of failover

Before looking at the various flavors of failover, it's important to understand the key resources that make up a virtual machine. In other words, if a machine needs to be restarted, what does it take to successfully do so? Put in computer science terms, what is its state?

What is *state?* Imagine if you will that you're playing a game of chess. At any point in time, the pieces are located on the chessboard, it is one player's turn to move, and if the game is going on in a competition, a certain amount of time is left on the clock for whichever player is due to move. That is the state of that chess game. For virtual machines, the state refers to the current context of the following key resources.

✔ The hardware representation of the virtual machine, including what resources are available to it. These include networking and storage adapters (that is, cards).

✔ External connections that the virtual machine uses, including IP addresses and storage locations and identifiers.

✔ The amount and settings of all memory the virtual machine is using. (Remember, this memory is used by the virtual machine but is actually controlled by the hypervisor.)

Every virtual machine, even one that has just been started and, as yet, has not done any work on behalf of a user, has a state. As applications execute on behalf of users, the state changes constantly. As you can see, failover, while simple conceptually, can be quite difficult to execute properly.

Failover: The simple case

The role of the hypervisor is to start, run, suspend, restore, and delete virtual machines. Part of doing that work is to constantly monitor the state of each virtual machine and react to requests by the virtual machine for hardware resources.

Because the hypervisor is constantly monitoring each virtual machine's status, it's relatively straightforward to configure the hypervisor to start a new instance of a virtual machine should it notice a previously running virtual machine is no longer present.

Because all the hypervisor has to do is start a new virtual machine based on the machine's image, the outage duration of a machine might be mere seconds. Obviously, this is a huge improvement over the minutes-to-days durations typical of nonvirtualized system restores.

However, this approach has a shortcoming. Although simple failover can restart a virtual machine, it can't restore the state of the original virtual machine's memory at the time of the crash. Instead, it brings up a new VM, ready to begin work. Any work in process at the time of the VM crash is lost.

Although losing memory state might seem like a fatal flaw, don't sell simple failover short. Just being able to recover systems in seconds instead of hours is an enormous improvement for most IT organizations because very few of them have any kind of failover mechanism in place today. For them, simple failover represents a huge improvement over the status quo.

A more serious issue is that simple failover deals with a virtual machine crash but does nothing to protect against hardware failure. In other words, if the virtual machine continues to operate but the underlying virtualization hardware fails, suddenly you have no hardware for the simple failover to execute upon. You can, however, address this hardware issue, as I discuss in the following section.

High availability

To insulate yourself from hardware failure as well as virtual machine failure, more comprehensive failover protection is necessary. It is to this end that *high availability* (typically referred to as HA) is used.

High availability extends the concept of simple failover to incorporate an additional hardware server. Instead of a crashed virtual machine being started on the same piece of hardware, it is started on a different server, thereby avoiding the problem of a hardware failure negating the use of virtualization failover.

But how does HA work? After all, how can a hypervisor on one physical server start a virtual machine on another hypervisor? The answer is that it can't.

High availability relies on an overarching piece of virtualization software that coordinates the efforts of multiple hypervisors. When a virtual machine on one hardware server crashes, the coordinating software starts another virtual machine on a separate hardware server.

Actually, it's a bit more complex than that. The coordinating virtualization software is constantly monitoring all the hypervisors and their virtual machines. If the coordinating software sees that the hypervisor on one server is no longer responding, the software then arranges to start any virtual machines that were on the failed hardware on other hardware.

So HA addresses the issue of hardware failure by using higher-level virtualization software to coordinate the hypervisors on two or more machines, constantly monitoring them and restarting virtual machines on other machines if necessary.

This setup certainly addresses the issue of hardware failure and makes the failover solution more robust. Note that moving to this multimachine virtualization is significantly more complicated than the single-machine situation. Remember, part of the state of a virtual machine is its network address and its storage resources. If you move a virtual machine to another piece of hardware, these bits of its state need to move as well or the new virtual machine won't be able to locate its storage or connect to the networks. So HA requires that virtualization software be able to migrate these parts of the virtual machine's state to another physical server and configure that server's hypervisor to use the machine's state from the original, failed hardware.

High availability provides an extra layer of failover protection at the cost of additional virtualization software complexity. Even though HA creates a new virtual machine on a second machine to replace the virtual machine that is no longer available on the original, crashed server, users working on the original virtual machine still lose the state of their work (in other words, HA replicates the virtual machine's state but does not replicate the user application's state).

Load balancing

The virtualization techniques I've described thus far in this section all address the issue of making a single virtual machine less subject to failure, whether by doing simple failover on a single machine or implementing clustering, which keeps a hot backup virtual machine at the ready on a second server.

Although all these approaches clearly have virtues, they also clearly have drawbacks. In the case of simple failover, you're still exposed to SPOF (single point of failure) if the underlying hardware fails. In the case of clustering, you duplicate resources that get used only in the case of failure, which is wasteful.

You can achieve the robustness of clustering while achieving the high utilization rates of simple failover. It goes by the name of *load balancing*. Simply put, load balancing involves running two instances of a virtual machine on separate pieces of hardware and dividing the regular workload between them.

Load balancing protects against SPOF. By running two instances of the virtual machine, if one machine crashes, the other continues to operate. If the hardware underneath one of the virtual machines fails, the other keeps working. In this way, the application never suffers an outage.

Load balancing also makes better use of machine resources. Rather than the second VM sitting idly by, being updated by the primary machine but performing no useful work, load balancing makes the second VM carry half of the load, thereby ensuring that its resources aren't going unused.

The use of duplicate resources can extend beyond the virtual machines. Companies concerned with achieving high levels of availability often implement duplicate networks with each physical server cross-connected to the rest of the network, which ensures that the virtual machines will continue to be able to communicate even if part of the network goes down.

Moving to virtualized storage is a prerequisite for load balancing because each virtual machine must be able to access the same data, which is necessary because application transactions can go to either virtual machine. In fact, depending on the application and how the load balancing is configured, transactions might go through both virtual machines during the execution of an extended transaction. Therefore, both machines must be able to access the data, and therefore, virtualized storage is required.

You can also configure load-balanced virtual machines to act as clustered machines and share state between them. That way, if a virtual machine crashes, the other can pick up the work and continue it.

Products for failover/high availability/ clustering/load balancing: The usual suspects

When you're ready to start shopping for failover, high availability, clustering, and load-balancing products, start with this list. A lot of these names are going to look familiar from my discussion of server consolidation products.

- ✔ **VMware ESX Server:** Right out of the box, you can configure this commercial hardware emulation virtualization product to automatically restart a crashed virtual machine.

- ✔ **VMware Virtual Infrastructure 3 (referred to as VI3):** Provides sophisticated management services for collections of ESX Servers; load-balancing capabilities as well as HA and clustering functionality are available as features (called VMotion and HA) within VI3.

- ✔ **Virtual Iron:** This company's commercial product, based on the Xen hypervisor, provides the ability to automatically restart a virtual machine on a second server should the original server become unavailable. (Okay, you probably expected that, but the product also provides for load balancing and clustering.) Virtual Iron offers a free single-server version of their product that provides basic failover.

- ✔ **SWsoft Virtuozzo:** This commercial container virtualization product can be configured to automatically restart a crashed emulated OS.

- ✔ **Sun Solaris containers:** Similar to SWsoft's Virtuozzo, Sun Solaris containers can be configured to automatically restart an emulated OS.

- ✔ **Xen:** The open source paravirtualization Xen product can be configured to bring up a new instance of a guest OS that crashes. It's available in a number of Linux distributions, such as Red Hat Enterprise Linux and Novell's SUSE Linux Enterprise Server.

- ✔ **XenSource XenServer and XenEnterprise:** These commercial products from XenSource, the commercial sponsor of Xen, are capable of simple failover when configured appropriately. XenSource distributes XenExpress at no cost. XenExpress shares a code base with XenSource's other products.

Future directions in high availability

One thing that none of the high-availability solutions provide is the ability to recover from the loss of application state; in other words, any data located in machine memory is lost when a virtual machine goes down.

Because the hypervisor needs to keep track of every virtual machine's memory, it would seem possible for the memory state of each machine to be automatically transferred to somewhere off the physical server the hypervisor resides on, ready to be re-created in a new virtual machine should the original go down.

There are some developments in that direction. Today the effort is mostly focused on Xen, because its open source characteristics make it possible to add additional software to track and communicate virtual machine memory state. I expect that there will be much more of this in the future, as virtualization is extended to enable the highest possible availability. To put it another way: It's a future development, but expect it in the *near* future.

Server pooling

If you've read through all the other descriptions of how virtualization can be applied, you're probably thinking "Wow, virtualization sure can be applied in a lot of useful ways, but there seems to be a lot of installing and configuring in those descriptions. Wouldn't it be great if the virtualization software was arranged for the installation and configuration so that I automatically got failover and load balancing?"

And in fact, that functionality exists. It's called *server pooling,* and it's a great application of virtualization.

With server pooling, your virtualization software manages a group (or pool) of virtualized servers. Instead of installing a virtual machine on a particular server, you merely point the virtualization software at the virtual machine image, and the software figures out which physical server is best suited to run the machine.

The server-pooling software also keeps track of every virtual machine and server to determine how resources are being allocated. If a virtual machine needs to be relocated to better use the available resources, the virtualization software automatically migrates it to a better-suited server.

You manage the pool through a management console, and if you notice that the overall pool of servers is getting near to your defined maximum utilization rate, you can transparently add another server into the pool. The virtualization software then rebalances the loads to make the most effective use of all the server resources.

Because you have no way of knowing which physical server will be running a virtual machine, your storage must be virtualized so that a VM on any server can get access to its data.

In my view, this is the future of virtualization. (For more of my predictions about the future of virtualization, check out Chapter 4.) In the near future, you'll look back on manually installing operating systems on individual servers, or even on managing groups of virtual machines on individual servers, as a crude, inefficient practice.

But in the here and now, server pooling is a relatively new concept. Most IT organizations haven't moved toward server pooling — yet. But it's on the horizon.

Two virtualization products for virtualization server pooling are (you guessed it):

- ✔ **VMware ESX Server:** VMware's Virtual Infrastructure 3 (VI3) uses a product called VMware DRS (*D*istributed *R*esource *S*cheduler) to offer server-pooling capabilities.

- ✔ **Virtual Iron:** Can you say Iron Man? This company's commercial product provides server-pooling functionality — in addition to all its other offerings.

Server pooling and DRS, in addition to intelligently moving and migrating machines to other machines that have more resources (load balancing), help with moving machines when a hardware failure hits. So, rather than using clustering for failover, DRS can help move a machine when its base hardware has an issue.

Disaster recovery

Disaster recovery (DR) refers to products and processes that help IT organizations respond to catastrophic situations, ones far worse than a single virtual machine crashing or a piece of hardware failing. Disaster recovery comes into play when an entire data center is temporarily or permanently lost. In complete data center loss, IT organizations need to scramble to keep the computing infrastructure of the entire company operating. Think of Hurricane Katrina: When it struck, many IT shops lost all processing capability because their entire data centers were inundated. If that weren't enough, Internet connectivity was lost as well due to telecommunications centers being flooded. Spare capacity inside your data center when a catastrophe strikes won't help. To protect yourself from truly awful weather, earthquake, or man-made disasters, you need disaster-recovery capability.

Discussing the overall requirements for DR is too large a subject to be addressed in this book, but suffice it to say that you need spare data center capacity, the ability to bring operating systems and applications back up, and a way to manage the migrated infrastructure. In addition, you need a well-considered DR process so that if a disaster occurs, the IT staff can execute a documented — and rehearsed — plan.

Virtualization can help with the application recovery and ongoing management tasks. Any of the failover, HA, load-balancing, or server-pooling virtualization capabilities may be applied in a DR scenario. Their application just depends on how much you want to physically manage during the DR process.

Because virtual machine images can be captured in files and then started by the hypervisor, virtualization is an ideal technology for DR scenarios. As you can imagine, in a time of a disaster, needing to locate physical servers, configure them, install applications, configure them, and then feed in backup tapes to get the system up to date is a nightmare. However, keeping spare computing capacity in a remote data center that completely mirrors your primary computing infrastructure is extremely expensive.

With virtualization, a much smaller set of machines can be kept available in a remote data center, with virtualization software preinstalled and ready to accept virtual machine images. In the case of a disaster, such images can be transferred from the production data center to the backup data center. These images can then be started by the preinstalled virtualization software, and they can be up and running in just a few minutes.

If you're uncomfortable with the risk that some transactions might be lost in the case of a disaster that strikes suddenly, leaving no time to migrate virtual machine images, you can run load-balancing virtualization configurations, enabling the two data centers to remain consistent. Of course, to do so, you need to implement storage virtualization; in fact, you have to implement the most sophisticated (and expensive) form of it because storage virtualization is generally designed to operate within the confines of a single data center.

Both Virtual Iron and VMware VI3 provide DR capability.

Because virtualization abstracts hardware, it is possible to move a virtual machine from one hypervisor to another, whether the hypervisors are on machines in the same rack or on machines in data centers halfway around the world from one another. Because the virtual machines can be moved to any available hypervisor, it is possible to more easily implement a disaster recovery plan, with no need to replicate an entire data center.

Just to make all the foregoing more comprehensible, here is a table (Table 3-2) that includes a summary of all the different applications of virtualization, a listing of all the products providing the application functionality, and some comments as well.

Table 3-2	Virtualization Applications	
Application	*Product*	*Comment*
Development and Testing	VMware Server	Free; good for low-density use.
	VMware ESX Server	Commercial; very scalable; might be expensive for development and test environments.
	Xen	Free; open source; available for free download as well as in numerous Linux distributions, including Red Hat Enterprise Linux, Novell SUSE Linux Enterprise Server, Fedora, and OpenSUSE.
	XenSource	Commercial products; free XenExpress for limited workloads; XenEnterprise for high-density workloads.
Server Consolidation	SWSoft	Open source OpenVZ and commercial Virtuozzo products provide scalable operating system virtualization; good for homogeneous workloads.
	Sun	Solaris operating system provides container OS virtualization; available in open source OpenSolaris as well as commercial Solaris products; very scalable for homogeneous workloads.
	VMware ESX Server	Commercial; most widely deployed virtualization product; very scalable hardware emulation virtualization product.
	Xen	Open source paravirtualization product is offered in many Linux distributions; depending on underlying hardware, may or may not support Windows or unmodified Linux guests; good scalability.

(continued)

Table 3-2 *(continued)*

Application	Product	Comment
	XenSource	Commercial paravirtualization product provides good scalability and focus on supporting Windows guests.
	VirtualIron	Commercial virtualization product using Xen technology; very scalable.
Failover	SWsoft	Commercial Virtuozzo product provides failover functionality.
	Sun	Solaris operating system virtualization can be configured to provide failover.
	VMware	ESX Server can be configured to automatically restart crashed virtual machine.
	Xen	Open source paravirtualization product contained in many Linux distributions can be configured to automatically restart crashed guest operating systems.
	XenSource	Commercial paravirtualization products can be configured to automatically restart crashed guest operating systems.
	VirtualIron	Commercial virtualization product can be configured to automatically restart crashed guest operating systems.
High Availability (HA)	VMware ESX Server	Virtual Infrastructure 3 (VI3) provides sophisticated management services for collections of virtual machines.
	VirtualIron	Commercial product incorporating Xen hypervisor provides high availability functionality.
Load Balancing	VMware ESX Serve	VI3 provides load-balancing capability.
	VirtualIron	Product provides load-balancing capability.

Application	Product	Comment
Server Pooling	VMware ESX Server	VI3 feature called DRS provides server pooling.
	VirtualIron	Product provides server-pooling capability.
Disaster Recovery	VMware ESX Server	VI3 provides ability to failover virtual machines to alternate server; requires sophisticated storage virtualization implementation.
	Virtual Iron	Requires sophisticated storage virtualization implementation.

So there you have it. You now have a good understanding of the lay of the land with respect to virtualization technologies and applications. As you have seen, there are a plethora of options for how you move forward with your virtualization project. By carefully looking at your virtualization plans — and the potential destination of your virtualization journey — you can more surely select the right virtualization technology and product for your needs.

Chapter 4

Peeking at the Future of Virtualization

*T*he virtualization trend is sweeping through IT like a brushfire through a bone-dry forest. The potential for getting higher utilization from hardware, better responsiveness to changing business conditions, and lower cost operations has IT shops enthusiastically implementing the current generation of virtualization solutions.

I spend a good deal of time in Chapters 1 and 2 going over the business benefits of virtualization and how it can be applied in your organization, and I also linger a bit in Chapter 3 over the different types of virtualization out there in the marketplace. If you've taken the time to look over those chapters, it's probably begun to dawn on you that virtualization isn't just one more entry in the long line of "revolutionary" products that have hit the technology marketplace. You're absolutely right. Virtualization is a new infrastructure platform. It will affect many parts of the technology ecosystem as the paradigm shifts from the old one-to-one correspondence between software and hardware (bad!) to the new approach of software operating on whatever hardware happens to be most convenient to use (good!).

As virtualization diffuses deeper and deeper into the technology ecosystem, I expect that eventually there won't be a separate technology called *virtualization:* Everything will just come virtualization ready. In this chapter, I put on my fortune teller's turban and gaze (not so) far into that future to look at how this diffusion might act itself out. I also take a look at some of the implications such diffusion might have on the future of virtualization.

Virtualization Gets Integrated into Operating Systems

Really, you don't have to be much of a fortune teller to predict that virtualization will become a regular feature of operating systems, just like hundreds of other features that come pre-integrated into the core operating system.

In fact, you don't have to be a fortune teller at all. Both Red Hat and Novell include Xen virtualization as part of their core operating systems. And Microsoft is scheduled to deliver virtualization as part of its upcoming Microsoft Server 2008 release.

The inclusion of virtualization in operating systems reflects the OS providers' recognition that virtualization is so critical a technology that it needs to be a fundamental part of the operating system. Of course, you might take a more cynical view: The OS vendors recognize that the virtualization market is too important to cede to competitors like VMware. More importantly, OS vendors don't want to lose their primary role in the data center. If end users focus their attention on how well their applications integrate with software other than the underlying OS, that means OS vendors no longer are the key supplier to those end users. This is bad from their perspective.

So, you can expect to see increasing virtualization integration from OS providers in their flagship products. In the future, look for this integration to be extended even further into areas like virtualization management, storage, and server pooling.

Of course, such integration will present a challenge to independent vendors of virtualization products, particularly the leading vendor, VMware. Currently, it has significantly better functionality compared with the virtualization functionality present in operating systems, but that advantage will undoubtedly be reduced as OS vendors improve their products.

The cliché in the virtualization world is that basic virtualization functionality will become a commodity — just another assembly-line product — and that future differentiation in virtualization products will be at the management level; in other words, what will distinguish virtualization products will be how easy they are to run on a day-to-day basis. VMware offers significant capabilities in this area and is continually improving this dimension of its products. It remains to be seen, however, how successfully it can compete against virtualization capabilities that are present as a default (and free) feature in the underlying OS.

Don't count VMware out by any means, though. Although many OS features started out as separate products (for example, TCP/IP stacks were once a separate product but now are included by default in every OS), other products (such as content management) still stand as separate product categories, even though logic might dictate that the functionality could be included in an operating system. And, of course, just because something is included in the operating system at no cost doesn't mean that the option is the right one for you. If you read through Chapter 3, you saw that the right virtualization technology for you can vary depending on your use profile — so *free* and *included* might still be trumped by an add-on product that meets your needs better.

Just because something is free doesn't mean it's the right solution for your problem. Take time to evaluate your requirements before you commit to a technology or product.

Einstein once defined the role of time as "keeping everything from happening at once." Keep in mind that I'm discussing the *future* of virtualization here; you'll need to make plans to accomplish virtualization tasks today while keeping an eye on future developments. The important thing is to get started, not wait for some future point in time when everything will be virtualization perfect.

What you can expect to see in the future is that operating systems will come preconfigured with a virtualization hypervisor that begins running at boot time, ready to support virtual guests. (Chapter 3 discusses hypervisors.) In fact, virtualization won't even be an install-time checklist item as it is today — it will just be a normal part of operating system services. You won't have to worry about configuration. It'll just be there, ready to support virtualized payloads. Speaking of preconfiguration, that's the next item!

Virtualized Software: Delivered to Your Door Preinstalled

You may have noticed a seeming paradox in the world of virtualization. Server virtualization does a great job of several tasks, such as abstracting an operating system/application bundle from underlying hardware; improving IT operations by enabling failover, load balancing, and server pooling; and even converting existing servers into virtualized servers via physical-to-virtual (or P2V) software. But virtualization doesn't really do much to help with the initial installation of software.

Right now, you have to install software yourself, which has many drawbacks, as I discuss in the following section. However, I also discuss the future of the virtual appliance, which is brightening on the horizon.

The software installation headache

To get a machine — any machine, whether it's physical or virtual — up and running, a system administrator has to perform the following tasks:

1. **Install the operating system.** Depending on whether this is done from scratch with disks or done via a preconfigured network install, this task can take anywhere from 30 minutes to several hours.

2. **Configure the operating system.** This task makes the OS ready to run applications. Individual work items include configuring file systems, Web servers, user accounts, and system services. This task can be quite time consuming and is prone to error because many of the individual work items require manipulation of text files, in which a minor error like a misplaced semicolon can cause a problem that can take tons of time to track down. Furthermore, software patches need to be applied, after which the entire operating system needs to be examined for security vulnerabilities, which also need to be addressed.

3. **Install the application software.** Like the OS install, this task can take anywhere from minutes to days, depending on how automated the installation process is.

4. **Configure the application software.** This can be the most challenging system administration task of all. Every piece of software has its own configuration needs and can require poring over documentation and frantic Internet searches to find necessary information. Moreover, the problem compounds because it's necessary to get the entire software aggregation working properly, so the individual applications have to be configured to work together well. This task definitely can be a nightmare.

As you might expect from the foregoing list, installing a new system is a real headache.

Also, consider the installation process from the application vendor's point of view. If you run into problems while installing a vendor's product and you have a support agreement, you're likely to call the vendor for help. And, you're likely to call whether the problem resides with their software or with something unrelated to their software — with the Apache Web server, for example.

Getting all these calls is expensive for software vendors, particularly when the call relates to another part of the software stack. If they're trying to be good citizens, they need to have staff members who have expertise with all the products in the stack, which raises the vendors' costs.

Many software vendors find that the vast majority of their support calls are related to initial installation and configuration. If they could find a way to reduce the difficulty of initial installation and configuration, they could reduce the total amount they have to spend on support as well as focus their support resources on solving more critical issues.

One initiative that many vendors have pursued to reduce installation complexity is to deliver the software preinstalled on a piece of hardware. These bundles of software and hardware are called *appliances,* and they can be a powerful way of delivering functionality to users. If you've ever installed a home wireless router, you've experienced how easy appliances can make bringing up a new software application; most consumer wireless routers are nothing more than a preconfigured Linux system installed in an inexpensive piece of hardware.

Hardware appliances — those special-purpose pieces of hardware that are delivered with both an operating system and application preinstalled and preconfigured, ready to operate — are much easier to install when compared to the four-step process outlined earlier. Typically, you install the hardware in a server rack, power it up, and give it network connectivity. You don't need to do any further work to get the software installed and configured. You take a Web browser interface (typically sporting an easy-to-use wizard) for a spin to configure the necessary network and user account information. That's it. The appliance is installed and ready to use.

The past few years have witnessed a blizzard of appliances being released into the marketplace. You can find security appliances, e-mail appliances, antispam appliances, and WAN (Wide Area Network) optimization appliances — and that's just a short list of the universe of available appliances. In fact, the stupefying array of these appliances points to a drawback: Many companies feel they are drowning in appliances — too many pieces of hardware, too many different hardware vendors, and the inevitable appliance sprawl, analogous to the server sprawl that is driving organizations to virtualization in the first place. Also, many IT organizations are uncomfortable adding unfamiliar hardware to their infrastructures — you might say they don't trust vendor promises of self-managing appliances and are wary of taking on any more (and different) hardware.

What's needed, obviously, is a *software* delivery mechanism that provides the convenience of hardware appliances without causing the complexity of appliance sprawl. Enter virtual appliances!

The virtual appliance: Oh, what a relief it is!

A *virtual appliance* is a preconfigured software bundle containing the operating system, an application, and all necessary software components to make the application ready to run. The software vendor builds a virtual machine containing the configured components and then saves the software image of the virtual machine. It then distributes that image to anyone who wants to implement the vendor's product. The user receives the image, points the virtualization management software at it, brings up the virtual machine, and presto! The application is up and running.

Unfortunately, virtual appliances aren't quite as simple as that last sentence. You'll still need to perform some minimal configuration in terms of assigning an IP address and making the rest of your machines aware of the new system. Overall, though, this kind of configuration is like a walk in the park compared to the traditional drudgery of installing new software.

Software vendors love this approach, because it means

- **Fewer support calls:** Even with the best of intentions, users make mistakes during installation and configuration, resulting in support calls to the vendor. Cutting installation and configuration out of the picture means fewer user mistakes and fewer support calls, which translates into lower support costs.

- **Easier problem debugging:** If a support call comes in, the vendor can dispense with much of the usual back-and-forth required to confirm that the product is installed properly (though, of course, they'll still need to confirm the classic reason a system isn't working properly — it isn't plugged in). This will enable easier and quicker problem resolution, and thereby lower support costs.

- **Happier customers:** Encountering problems during application installation is frustrating, particularly when the installation is performed under a deadline. Making application installation simpler and faster makes for more satisfied customers, which results in quicker application adoption and additional sales.

End users will love virtual appliances as well, for the following reasons:

- **Virtual appliances align with the move to virtualization:** If you have a virtualized infrastructure, it's natural to run new applications in virtual machines.

- **Virtual appliances reduce the manual effort involved in bringing up new applications to a minimum:** The vendor, rather than IT staff, does all the configuration, shifting the work from user to vendor. Users are bound to like that equation.

- **Virtual appliances reduce the chance for error:** There are so many steps required to provision a new application that one or more things are bound to go wrong with the process, particularly when the work is, inevitably, being done in a hectic, interruption-filled, work environment. Avoiding the need for this work means far fewer problems.

- **Virtual appliances get applications up and running much faster:** The speed of provisioning a virtual appliance versus installing and configuring applications by hand means that applications are available for use much more quickly. Because the whole point of the exercise is to make applications available for real work, using virtual appliances speeds availability.

You may have noticed I used the future tense to describe end user reaction. Why did I do so? Mostly because this form of software distribution is still in its infancy. It isn't widely used today, although I predict it will soon become a major, if not dominant, form of software distribution. Anything that both vendors and users like is bound to get lots of momentum.

Virtual appliances are a win-win for users and vendors. I've learned not to overlook the role of inertia in human affairs, so don't be surprised if this movement takes longer to come to fruition than would seem to make sense. It *will* happen, though. To quote the tech giant Bill Gates: "People overestimate the amount of change possible in the short term, but underestimate it in the long term." This will certainly be true of virtual appliances.

If you want to see virtual appliances in action, you're in luck. VMware offers a large number of virtual appliances that can run on its VMware Server product. Actually, it would be more accurate to say that VMware provides a repository of user-created virtual appliances, which are available on its Web site. The company held a big contest last year for people to enter their own VMware Server virtual appliances. The range and capability of submissions was staggering, and all the submitted virtual appliances are available for you to use at no cost (and remember, VMware Server itself is available for free, too). You can find out more about all the VMware Server appliances at `www.vmware.com/vmtn/appliances/index.html`. Also, Chapter 12 covers installation and use of VMware Server and includes an example of installing a VMware Server virtual appliance, showing how simple and quick it is. I encourage you to take a look and experiment on your own to see how easy the future world of virtual appliances will be.

This trend isn't limited to VMware, by the way. Microsoft is making many of its operating systems and applications — as well as applications from partner companies — available as virtual appliances in a "try before you buy" program known as VHD Test Drive.

Virtual appliances allow you to skip all that boring software loading and configuration, but they require you to know how to load virtual machine images into your virtualization software. If the idea of virtual appliances intrigues you, be sure to research how you load virtual machines in the virtualization software of your choice before experimenting.

As I point out in an earlier prediction, virtualization will soon be a normal part of the operating system. Just as a typical server will soon come to you as "virtualization capable," you'll soon see software products delivered in a format that assumes you'll run them as virtual appliances. It won't be too terribly long before you look back on the manual install process the way you look back on having to hand-crank cars to get them started.

Virtualization Diffusing into the Internet

Have you ever gone out to breakfast in a restaurant and ordered pancakes? It's a wonderful moment when you pour the syrup onto the warm flapjacks and anticipate tasting the delicious flavor from the first bite. But have you ever taken a sip of coffee, looked down, and gasped in shock when you found that all that tasty syrup disappeared? Where did all that beautiful delicious syrup vanish to?

Actually, the syrup didn't really disappear. It just soaked into the pancakes, its delectable flavor diffused throughout them, ready to be savored in each scrumptious mouthful.

Well, that's the future of virtualization. It's going to go from something added onto computing infrastructures to a capability universally diffused throughout the Internet. Virtualization's presence will surround computing the way air surrounds us — unseen and ubiquitous, and a fundamental part of life. And when you understand the implications of a diffused virtualization, well, as the immortal saying goes, "You ain't seen nothing yet."

Software as a Service (SaaS)

One particularly neat use of virtualization, especially the operating system flavor of virtualization often referred to as containers, involves harnessing virtualization's many talents to create more efficient Web-hosting applications. Software as a Service (widely referred to as SaaS) is the next frontier of Web-based services that will take advantage of virtualization.

SaaS is the delivery of computing services over the Internet. Google's Web searching is a form of SaaS. Google's search makes it available via a Web page; you fill in the box with your desired search term, and Google's enormous server farm remotely executes your search and returns the results in a set of Web pages.

That same sort of remote execution of application processing is being widely applied to a broad range of business services. Perhaps the most famous SaaS offering is Salesforce.com, which offers Customer Relationship Management (CRM) services to businesses.

The advantage from the customer's point of view is that SaaS delivers the benefits of using the software without needing to physically install it. SaaS products are usually offered on a subscription basis, which reduces the upfront costs associated with software package licensing. Furthermore, because the SaaS vendor takes care of keeping the application updated and patched, SaaS reduces the maintenance headache associated with on-premises software package installation.

The concept of SaaS has emerged gradually, and it wasn't the first kid on the block. About ten years ago, the first stab at providing remote applications services came on the market. At that time, the providers were known as Application Service Providers (ASPs). The ASP concept quickly fell into disfavor because the economics of the industry were all wrong. ASPs just provided remote system administration of packaged software; in other words, it was as if you picked up a server running an application from your data center and moved it into the ASP's data center. ASPs followed the "one application, one server" rule, so their cost typically wasn't much better than what a company could achieve on its own.

SaaS has taken a different approach to the problem. Instead of running multiple instances of the application, one for each customer, with each application instance running on a dedicated server, SaaS applications have been designed as "multitenant" applications, which reduces their costs because a single application instance hosts multiple customers. This raises the obvious question about how isolated a customer's data is because mixing data in the same application seems to pose the threat that data could leak from one customer to another. Although SaaS providers have a good track record in this regard, many companies refuse to use a service that has the potential for data security issues.

Virtualization provides a way to address the shortcomings of SaaS while avoiding the cost issues of ASP. SaaS providers will soon begin to offer customers both multitenant and dedicated SaaS versions. If a company strongly desires its own dedicated instance, the SaaS provider can create a virtual machine running the customer's own instance of the application. In this way, SaaS companies can offer increased security without taking on significantly larger costs. There will undoubtedly be price differences between the two types of offerings, but virtualization enables service providers to make different options available cost effectively.

Ever more virtualization = ever less hardware

Well, SaaS is just fine and dandy for remote computing services being offered by a commercial provider. In fact, I'd call SaaS a great model for offering (in a more convenient form) what previously would have been packaged software applications.

But what about home-grown applications? These are systems developed in-house to meet company-specific needs. Of course it's possible to run these applications in a virtual machine within the company's own data center. But what if the company doesn't have room in its data center? Or what if it doesn't want to manage hardware, either because it's a hassle or because the company doesn't consider managing hardware to be something it wants to focus on?

For a solution, how about a remote data center, managed by professionals, ready to let you install your application immediately, all with pay-as-you-go pricing? With a service like this, you can bring up a machine, install your application, and be ready to go in minutes — all without the hassle of waiting for hardware to be purchased or administered.

Such a service exists today, offered by your online superstore, Amazon. Amazon Web Services (AWS) is a little-known service from the company that brought you online book ordering. Amazon's shorthand reference for their new offerings: Infrastructure as a Service (clever, no?).

Amazon offers both remote machines (via a service called Elastic Compute Cloud, or EC2) and remote storage (called Simple Storage Service or S3). Both services provide remote capability (that is, virtual capability, because Amazon provides computing *services,* not a specific machine, and storage *services,* not a specific hard drive partition) on an inexpensive metered basis. You can rent processing services on an EC2 virtual machine for only 10 cents per hour. Storage on S3 runs only 15 cents per GB per month.

Amazon provides these services in an extremely clever way. All signup and control of the services is accomplished via a Web services interface. Without going into detail about how it works, suffice it to say that you can remotely install, run, manage, and manipulate data without ever having to interact with an Amazon employee. In other words, Amazon provides a completely virtual environment that you can run in a completely automated fashion. You can install your home-grown apps on an Amazon-hosted virtual machine without ever needing to worry about hardware. Amazon provides the processing capability and manages the hardware infrastructure — and, face it, Amazon is probably better at it than you are.

Interestingly, Amazon implements EC2 by running virtualization software on top of its physical servers. Amazon uses Xen, discussed throughout this book, as the foundation's technology for its offering. As just noted, Amazon then surrounds the basic Xen product with a set of management wrappers that enable remote management by customers.

AWS points the way to one certain future direction for computing. Many people use electric power as the metaphor for what this future direction looks like. No one really worries about where "their" electric generator is; they just expect the service provider to keep the electric grid running reliably so that power is available as needed. In a similar fashion, computing capacity will one day come to be provided this way; after all, what do you care if the computing capacity you need resides a few miles away in your data center, or a hundred miles away in Amazon's data center?

Enterprising entrepreneurs are already developing businesses that take advantage of Amazon's offering. To offer a SaaS-type service, you used to need to build out your own data center to hold all the machines necessary to provide service, which is an expensive proposition and a real challenge for young companies to finance. A number of new companies have sprung up to offer remote computing services based on using Amazon's AWS as the computing infrastructure. This situation enables these new companies to start offering their services without any need to invest in an infrastructure. They can also offer their services at a lower price point.

It's only a matter of time before AWS becomes a ubiquitous method of computing. I wouldn't be surprised to see Amazon begin to offer hosting of its customers' Xen images; in other words, a user might convert his own physical servers to Xen virtual machines and then transfer those Xen images to EC2, thereby getting out of the hardware-management business altogether. In fact, a small virtualization company called rPath offers a product that performs that very task — taking a physical machine and moving its Xenified image into EC2. So, if you want to get out of managing hardware altogether, it's possible today. To find out more, go to www.rpath.com/corp/amazon. html.

AWS is, as of this writing, an excellent — but not perfect — offering. In particular, there is no way to assign a permanent IP address to the virtual machines EC2 creates. IP addresses are analogous to street addresses, in that they offer a stable place of contact — if the IP address changes, it's difficult for other machines on the Internet to know how to connect to the machine with the changing address. Amazon is addressing this drawback, and I expect that the issue will be resolved in the near future. Should you decide to look into using EC2, be sure to find out whether you require a permanent IP address for your application.

The Changing Skill Set of IT Personnel

Each of the trends I discuss in the preceding sections of this chapter indicates that virtualization is changing traditional ways of doing IT. Time to focus more directly, then, on how the folks in IT will respond to the change.

Today's virtualization is often nothing more than doing the same thing (except more of it) on a single machine. But tomorrow's virtualization will mean doing a different thing, not just the same thing more efficiently.

Two key developments that go hand in hand are operating systems being virtualization ready right out of the box and software applications being delivered as virtual appliances. When these two developments become widely practiced, the everyday tasks of operations personnel will change significantly — there will be less routine work, but proportionally more complex work.

Every new wave of computing infrastructure has shaken up the established way of doing things in IT organizations and changed the nature of people's jobs within those organizations — just think of the PC. Before the advent of the PC, the help desk didn't exist; after the PC, every organization needed one. Virtualization will have the same kind of effect on IT workers. Get ready for it!

With the coming of virtualization-ready operating systems and virtual appliances, the time-honored tasks of software installation and configuration will dwindle. Rather than repetitively shoving CDs into machines and then spending precious time setting configuration parameters, system administrators will take preinstalled and preconfigured virtual machines and let the server's virtualization software load and run them.

So virtualization means that a lot of boring manual work will fade away. But does virtualization just mean less work for IT operations?

Far from it. Just as the smart money is on virtualization management becoming the battleground between competitive virtualization products, so too will IT operations begin to shift from low-level installation work to higher-level management and optimization tasks.

The press of daily grunt work has meant that many desirable IT tasks have largely gone undone. Too few IT organizations can monitor performance of the infrastructure and proactively take action to prevent problems. In the virtualized future, these previously unaddressed tasks will become the primary focus of IT operations.

Are you curious about just what types of tasks IT operations will take on in the virtualized future? Here are a few to ponder:

- ✔ **Ongoing monitoring** of load factors on servers to ensure that all virtual machines have adequate resources

- ✔ **Capacity planning** for new virtual machines to ensure adequate resources are available to run them

- ✔ **Management of virtual machines** across a pool of servers to take advantage of load balancing and to respond to changes in system demand

- ✔ **Creating an integrated infrastructure** to ensure server, network, and storage all operate efficiently to support a thoroughly virtualized environment

Although these tasks might seem to present an attractive future — after all, who doesn't want to get rid of mind-numbing repetitive tasks? — they will cause challenges for IT operations groups and for individual operations employees.

Managing the IT infrastructure from a higher-level perspective will require new skills in areas such as capacity planning and monitoring. For many system administrators, this situation will require a skill upgrade and a shift in perspective from tactical to strategic. It's not too early to begin assessing your current duties and skills to see where you're likely to need to develop new capabilities. Consider how you can begin to learn these new skills and seek out developmental opportunities. But whatever you do, recognize that the traditional way of running IT infrastructures will undergo a rapid transformation.

Some IT personnel may resist the shifting nature of their responsibilities. You can minimize this resistance by pointing out that changing skill sets is the nature of IT because it evolves so rapidly. Emphasize the opportunity to learn new skills as a way of keeping current on the mainstream trends in IT.

Software Pricing: How Will It Respond to Virtualization?

Breaking the mold of the old "one application, one server" paradigm and moving to an environment in which a single piece of hardware can support ten or more virtualized machines is revolutionary. Cutting out all that hardware definitely makes it less expensive to implement more computing capacity. Based on the law of supply and demand, one would expect that, with the price of infrastructure coming down, demand for virtualized server instances would increase. One might also expect that software vendors would eye this as an incredible opportunity and be ready to cut prices in order to capture much of the larger market made possible by the lower cost of computing.

The evidence to date, however, is that software vendors are reluctant to consider any pricing changes due to virtualization. Perhaps they hope that more server instances will equal more demand and thereby support even higher prices. More likely, in my view, is that virtualization users will see the current high prices of software as a barrier to virtualized system implementation, which will hinder the growth of the universe of systems made possible by virtualization. It's often the case that vendors fail to understand the opportunity made possible by vastly larger and lower cost markets; just look at the music business's response to digital music to understand how an industry can fail to change pricing in an appropriate response to a dramatically changed market. The danger is that software vendors will fail to see that lower prices would allow them to achieve much higher volumes, consequently achieving much larger revenues. It's simple economics, really — if reducing prices by 80 percent allows you to sell ten times as much product, you come out way ahead.

It seems clear, however, that software pricing will need to respond to the vastly larger software infrastructures that will result from virtualization. Customers will demand that their software providers offer pricing more appropriate to virtualization. Failure to do so will motivate customers to move to less expensive options, particularly open source software.

When beginning your virtualization journey, take a close look at your software licenses and the fees you're paying. You may be surprised to find that you're paying for software that is no longer around or that you're paying for more software than you're actually using. Transferring inefficient and bloated license fees to virtualization is a recipe for continuing the same old wasteful ways. So look over your current licenses and fees before moving to virtualization.

In the near term, you can expect to see confusion from vendors regarding the pricing of their products. Should they continue to charge you a set fee for using their software on a single piece of hardware, as they've always done? Or should they charge you a separate fee for each virtual machine in which you install their software? One vendor (Oracle) is currently planning to charge customers a fee per virtual machine installation based on the overall hardware capability of the underlying server, despite the fact that the virtual machine instances might use only a fraction of the server's resources. For example, on an eight-way server, you would pay for an eight-way Oracle license even if you were running Oracle in a virtual machine that uses only two of the machine's processors.

Taking a different tack, Microsoft has responded to virtualization by making it possible to support a number of Windows-based virtual machines at no cost if hosted by Windows Server. This is clearly a pricing model more suited to the new world of larger markets made possible by virtualization.

In the midterm, as the use of virtualization spreads, expect to see customers demanding better pricing terms for software products. This will, in part, be driven by differences in the implementation patterns of virtualization as users become more comfortable with the technology. Today's implementation, which is typically a *physical-to-virtual* transfer (where existing physical machines are migrated to virtualized instances), will give way to a new pattern of implementation. That new pattern will reflect the lower cost and ease of implementing virtualized systems. Organizations will implement far more systems when doing so becomes easier and cheaper.

In the long term, pricing will need to change to reflect the shift to delivering software as virtual appliances. Expect to see vastly different pricing mechanisms come into play in that world because customers will no longer be purchasing products; instead, they'll be purchasing the functionality of software. That is to say, they'll be purchasing software functionality as a service provided by a virtual appliance. And that will entail very different pricing expectations on the part of customers.

Be sure to examine your software pricing assumptions when you begin your move to virtualization. Don't assume your vendors will provide better pricing for a virtualized world. And definitely don't assume your vendors will approach virtualized pricing consistently.

Part I
Getting Started with a Virtualization Project

The 5th Wave By Rich Tennant

"Why, of course. I'd be very interested in seeing this new milestone in our server virtualization project."

In this part . . .

*V*irtualization is a hot topic. But what if you don't know enough to even fake it around the water cooler? Not to worry. This part gives even the virtualization-challenged a thorough introduction to the subject of virtualization.

It begins with an overview of virtualization — what it is and what all the different types of virtualization are. You didn't know there are different types? Well, this part is perfect for you.

For good measure, this part also includes an in-depth look at the technologies and applications of virtualization so that you can form an opinion of how it might be usefully applied to your own environment.

I conclude this part with a look at the future of virtualization. The area is evolving rapidly, and looking forward to future developments is exciting and, perhaps, sobering. Certainly I expect that virtualization will transform the way hardware and software is sold, so a peek into the future is well worth your time.

Chapter 5

Deciding Whether Server Virtualization Is Right for You

. . . .

In This Chapter

▶ Deciding whether you should use server virtualization

▶ Finding out when not to use virtualization

. . . .

*V*irtualization (in case you're not in the know) is a software technology that helps you achieve better financial and operational results from your computing infrastructure. As such, it has benefits perhaps too numerous to mention, but here are the really good ones:

✔ **Increased utilization of hardware:** Many data centers have machines installed running at no more than 10 or 15 percent capacity. Although it's good to provide extra capacity (often called *headroom*) for spikes in processing requirements, too much headroom translates into wasted capacity. Virtualization can consolidate many operating systems (OSes) onto a single physical piece of hardware, increasing utilization dramatically.

✔ **Decreased power costs:** Every server uses electricity to power its processor, memory, hard drives, and fans — whether it's working at 10 percent of capacity or 90 percent of capacity. The racks full of machines in data centers suck up an enormous amount of power, so reducing the total number of physical servers through the application of virtualization technology can reduce the amount of power consumed in the data center. Also, servers throw off heat while they run; this heat must be removed from the data center so that the machines continue to operate properly. Using virtualization to reduce the overall number of physical servers also cuts down on the amount of heat generated, thereby reducing the power needed for air conditioning.

✔ **Reduced system administration costs:** Managing servers takes skilled system administrators, but by reducing the overall number of machines, virtualization can reduce the total system administration load and thereby reduce the overall cost of system administration.

Wow, impressive, eh?

Wait just a moment, though. Deciding to do a virtualization project might seem like a slam-dunk, but it's important to determine whether virtualization is right for your organization. Also, although you might intuitively know that virtualization is a good idea, undoubtedly others in your organization need to be convinced, so evaluating whether virtualization is a good fit for your organization can also help you convince others of your conclusions.

This chapter covers the pros and cons of virtualization and helps you understand whether it's a good option for your organization. Chapter 6 outlines how to do a financial analysis of the benefits and costs of your virtualization project to understand the bottom-line impact of virtualization for you.

How to Decide Whether You Should Use Server Virtualization

Well, you're reading a book on virtualization, so clearly you're interested in the topic and even, perhaps, in implementing virtualization in your infrastructure. So, how can you decide whether virtualization makes sense for you and what its benefits are?

Figuring out whether virtualization is right for your organization

It might seem obvious, but every organization's circumstances are different. Even though virtualization is a great technology, it might not be right for your organization.

Before charging headlong into a virtualization project, it makes sense to do some upfront research to determine whether it will benefit your organization. This work is also good to do because it helps you create a clearer picture of the benefits that you can share throughout the organization as you go through the inevitable sales process that's necessary to get management buy-in and commitment for a new technology. Finally, the planning you do as part of your due diligence in this process helps you form a project plan that you'll use as the basis for your implementation.

Only if you can convince yourself and others that virtualization will show benefits for your organization should you move forward. This chapter helps you understand what to look for to determine whether virtualization makes sense for your organization as well as what things might be red flags alerting you that virtualization isn't appropriate for you.

So, what things should you examine to determine whether virtualization is for you? The following sections give you a place to start.

Looking for clear financial benefits

Nothing is more comforting to a bean counter than a financial projection that indicates using a technology will deliver bottom-line benefits. As you go through your assessment process, part of your job is to create a financial cost-benefit analysis.

Although comparing the cost of a virtualization product against projected savings in hardware expenditures is relatively straightforward, calculating the benefits of virtualization can encompass much more than how much you save on server purchases. For this reason, it's important to think through how you'll use virtualization, and how you might extend your use of virtualization with shared storage to achieve some of the benefits of failover and high availability (as discussed in Chapter 3).

With a more comprehensive view of how you'll use virtualization, you can generate a more sophisticated financial analysis demonstrating the true costs and benefits of your move to virtualization.

This analysis should illustrate a clear financial win in going to virtualization. If you can't find demonstrable financial benefits, perhaps you should rethink your desire to pursue virtualization.

Chapter 6 focuses on how to make a financial analysis of your virtualization project, including determining all the costs and benefits, as well as creating a spreadsheet documenting your findings.

Checking to see whether important prerequisite conditions are in place

Demonstrating that the numbers line up for virtualization within your organization isn't enough. Other nonfinancial aspects of virtualization must also be in place for your organization to take advantage of it. In some respects, these nonfinancial aspects are more important than whether you can demonstrate a financial payoff — if the right conditions are absent, the project will almost certainly fail.

As you examine these nonfinancial conditions, think very carefully about how well you meet their requirements. If the organization doesn't currently meet them, give thought to what you can do to improve the situation.

Verifying that your software providers can support their products when virtualized

A critical question is whether your software suppliers can support your applications when they run in a virtualized environment. Unfortunately, some software vendors refuse to support their products if they aren't running in a certified configuration, and they might not have certified their products running in a virtualized environment.

This issue gets even trickier when you consider that some software vendors will support their products when they're running on one virtualization product but not another. For example, Microsoft (naturally enough) supports its products when running on Microsoft Virtual Server, but it also supports its products when running on Xen — if the Xen instance is part of a Novell SUSE Linux system. On the other hand, Microsoft won't support its products running on Xen on Red Hat — at least at the time of this writing. (Because the world of virtualization is evolving so rapidly and companies keep forming what once would have been unlikely alliances, anything can happen.)

Therefore, it's critical that you don't assume that software support will or won't be available. You need to research the subject and perhaps talk to individual vendors to truly understand what the real situation is.

As virtualization becomes more popular, the issue of software support is rapidly changing, but it's vital for you to evaluate your list of important applications for their suppliers' willingness to support them running in the virtualization environment you're planning to implement.

A more subtle issue is the level of enthusiasm a software vendor brings to solving problems that its application experiences when running in a virtualized environment. Software vendors are notorious for finger pointing at one another when multiple vendors' products are operating. Having an important software vendor that immediately blames the underlying virtualization product when a problem arises is a significant obstacle for successful virtualization.

The problem of having no virtualization support or reluctant support can be mitigated by keeping a nonvirtualized piece of hardware available on which you can reproduce problems, but that's clearly not a desirable situation. Far better is for the vendor to embrace virtualization and fully support its products in a virtualized environment.

Obviously, it's important that you evaluate the software support levels your vendors offer for their products running in a virtualized environment.

Understanding whether your organization is willing to invest in virtualization

How willing is your organization to invest in training and pilot implementations? A learning curve is associated with every new technology, and virtualization is no exception.

Depending on the virtualization product you select, employees will probably require training on how to install, configure, and manage the product. This training, whether online or live, will come with a price tag and will require the organization to invest in it. Moving to a new technology without ensuring that employees have the necessary skills falls under the expression "Penny wise, pound foolish."

If your organization typically is supportive of investing in important secondary aspects of projects, such as training and test implementations, your virtualization project has a good probability of success.

Determining whether your co-workers are willing to learn new skills

Every new technology is a learning opportunity — one that some employees might grasp and some employees might avoid. Implementing and tuning virtualization products can be challenging. If many of your fellow employees resemble the characters in a *Dilbert* cartoon, you might need to reevaluate your virtualization plans.

All is not lost, however. In every organization, no matter how filled with stick-in-the-muds, there are a few eager beavers who love to explore new technologies and treat challenges as a gift. If you make sure your early virtualization efforts are staffed with these types of employees, you're on the way to success because the rank-and-file will eventually fall in line and reluctantly learn new skills. Just be sure you staff your first virtualization project with eager beavers!

Evaluating whether your future organizational plans dictate change and growth

One of the primary virtues of virtualization is how easy it makes bringing up new machines, migrating them to new hardware, and balancing computing workload across a number of machines. If your organization's infrastructure is fairly static and unlikely to change much in the future, virtualization is much less useful.

Therefore, an important part of your virtualization decision is based on whether the flexibility that virtualization technology potentially offers is important to where your organization is going. Think about whether the following characteristics are important to your company:

✔ **Ability to grow:** Do you foresee rapid growth for your company in terms of revenues? How about number of customers? Will the overall number of transactions increase significantly? If your company is on a steep growth curve, the ability to quickly deploy new systems is an important characteristic. Virtualization can help you a lot. Conversely, if your company isn't likely to grow or is part of a relatively static industry, virtualization will be less important to you.

✔ **Agility to respond:** Are there rapid changes in your business conditions? Perhaps your company experiences heavy seasonal variation in demand — for example, many retailers do a significant part of their overall business in November and December, with little business in the spring. Of course, if your company sells travel packages, summer is the busy season. For companies with high order variability, having the agility to respond by rapidly adding systems or removing them during low-demand periods makes virtualization a very good technology candidate for implementation.

✔ **Requirement for flexible infrastructure:** You live in a time of rapid economic change. Companies enter new businesses, markets, and regions seemingly overnight. The rise of private equity has made buyouts, acquisitions, and mergers very common experiences for most companies. Translated into technology, this means the ability to quickly consolidate data centers, move applications to new machines, and the like are vital for IT organizations. Virtualization can help create a more flexible infrastructure that enables IT organizations to quickly change computing infrastructures.

When Not to Use Virtualization

Just as important as knowing when to use a tool is knowing when not to use it. Although virtualization is a great tool for many IT organizations, it isn't perfect for every situation.

How can you know when virtualization isn't worth pursuing? Mirroring my "How to Decide Whether You Should Use Server Virtualization" discussion that makes up the bulk of this chapter, the following sections make up a handy "When Not to Use Virtualization" list.

When your computing environment is static

If you foresee little change in the type and scale of computing your company is going to need in the future, why upset the apple cart? Your infrastructure is probably running just fine and there's little need to change it. In this situation, virtualization might not be something you need to pursue.

Be aware, however, that even in relatively static environments, virtualization can become important to you. Many organizations that have one or more applications certified to run only on ancient operating systems (for example, an application is certified to run only on Windows NT 4.0) run into problems when their hardware vendor no longer supports the system the application runs on. In the past, this type of situation caused enormous headaches for companies. With virtualization, you can often migrate the old OS and application onto new hardware and thereby extend the useful life of the application.

When your software providers refuse support within a virtualized infrastructure

Some software providers simply refuse to support their applications running in a virtualized environment. Although it's possible to work around this situation by keeping a spare piece of hardware around that matches the vendor-supported configuration, it's obviously not a desirable situation. Moreover, this setup causes extra work and downtime while attempting to reproduce problems in the "official" configuration — work and time that you might not be able to afford, not to mention the cost of keeping spare hardware sitting around to be available if needed to reproduce a bug.

Even if you're willing to keep a parallel nonvirtualized server/application combination running to use for bug reproduction and support calls, be aware that some application problems might arise only when you run the application in a virtualized environment. In other words, you won't be able to reproduce the problem in your "standard" configuration. This situation can clearly cause problems for you if your vendor refuses to offer support for its applications in a virtualized environment. If you run into this situation, you might consider keeping this particular application running on its original hardware while migrating the rest of your applications into the virtualized environment.

When your applications don't lend themselves to virtualization

Another reason you might consider keeping nonvirtualized applications running is if the applications themselves run better in a nonvirtualized environment. If specific characteristics about the applications preclude sharing hardware, you'll be better served keeping those applications running on dedicated hardware. Here are a few application profiles that don't lend themselves to virtualization:

✔ **Applications with high processing or I/O loads (such as databases):** Databases are typically a critical resource in a company's computing infrastructure. Performance is paramount, and much time and attention goes into tuning databases to account for their data characteristics, typical data values, and so on. A key aspect of this tuning process is ensuring that the database software is configured properly for the hardware it's running on. If these systems are virtualized, the hardware capabilities the tuning took advantage of are no longer present. Instead, the database software now shares the underlying hardware with other applications. This might negatively affect database performance, so it might make sense to keep any performance-sensitive, carefully configured systems running on the original hardware.

✔ **Applications that require specific hardware:** Some applications require add-in cards or USB *dongles* (small hardware devices that are connected to USB ports on the machine). Some virtualization products don't provide the ability for virtual machines to access nonstandard hardware devices, which would make the application unable to perform properly. Even if the virtualization product enables virtual machines to "see" the hardware, it might not provide enough throughput or a quick enough response time for the application to work properly. Consequently, it's often a good idea to leave hardware-dependent applications running on their original systems.

✔ **Applications that are graphics intensive:** One area that virtualization isn't very good at yet is rendering high-quality graphics, particularly 3-D graphics. If your application is graphics intensive, it probably isn't a good candidate for virtualization.

✔ **Applications suffering from performance issues:** If an application is already suffering performance issues due to inadequate CPU or memory capacity, virtualization probably isn't a good option. On the other hand, if you're moving to much more powerful hardware that will underlie the hypervisor, it might be that the application will finally have enough hardware capacity to perform well. If you have application performance issues, be sure to look at the situation carefully before deciding to move to virtualization.

✔ **Applications running on multimachine or grid architectures:** Virtualization does a great job of taking applications designed to run on standard hardware and enabling them to run in a shared environment. Some applications, however, don't run in a standard hardware configuration; instead, they might run only in specialized software infrastructures that aggregate multiple machines and present a "single" processing environment. Grid computing systems, used for applications such as video rendering and bioinformatics processing, are an example of multimachine configurations. Because these application architectures require unusual hardware configurations, they aren't good candidates for virtualization. Your time and energy would be better spent seeking standard application environments that can be easily migrated to virtualization.

The electric company: Your virtualization partner

With the cost of electricity climbing every day, power is an important reason organizations pursue virtualization. For every machine you don't run, you save power — and more important, money.

But what about the company that provides your power? What's its perspective on virtualization? Isn't its financial interest bound up with selling as much power as possible? Wouldn't it detest virtualization's ability to reduce the amount of power an average data center consumes?

Surprisingly, for some power companies, the answer is no. In fact, the power company that serves Silicon Valley, Pacific Gas & Electric, is enough of an enthusiast of virtualization to have put a virtualization rebate program in place — you can get money back if you implement virtualization!

Although it might seem counterintuitive that a power company would pay you to not consume electricity, the PG&E program reflects its desire to reduce overall power consumption growth in its service territory, because building new power plants is expensive. PG&E can operate more efficiently if it reduces peak power demand from heavy users such as data centers.

Therefore, in the interest of meeting its customers' power needs, as well as to avoid building new generating plants, PG&E created the virtualization rebate program. The rebate program applies to any virtualization project undertaken within PG&E's service territory. The program rebates up to half of a customer's power savings for the first year of using virtualization and is capped at $4 million.

Keep in mind that the rebate amount is in addition to the financial benefits companies usually achieve by moving to virtualization: a savings of $300 to $600 in energy costs per physical server removed, plus additional savings from reduced cooling needs due to fewer servers being present in the data center.

A broad range of costs are eligible to be included in a virtualization project rebate: new hardware, new software, and internal and external personnel costs. Unfortunately, reduced HVAC costs can't be applied to the overall power savings.

As an example, suppose you replace 50 machines with 5 of the latest-generation, power-sipping, virtualization-specialized machines now available from manufacturers such as Sun and IBM. You save $30,000 in power costs by no longer running those machines. You can apply for a rebate of up to $15,000 to offset the cost of the new machines, any software you need to purchase to run virtualization, and the cost of your employees or any outside consultants you employ to assist you with your virtualization project.

This program can significantly increase the attractiveness of implementing virtualization, which should be factored into your decision process and into the financial calculations that make up your cost-benefit analysis.

What if you're not lucky enough to be located in PG&E's service territory? The company is working with other power companies located in California to extend the rebate program throughout the state. It doesn't take much imagination to see the rebate program being taken up by other power companies in the rest of the U.S. because many of them now face, or will soon face, the challenge of capacity constraint. Look for a rebate program like PG&E's to be available in your neck of the woods soon. If you'd like to understand the PG&E program in more detail, check out PG&E's pertinent Web site at www.pge.com/rebates.

When your organization is unwilling to invest to improve operations

If your organization is unwilling to invest in order to run its IT operations better, it's unlikely to respond favorably to implementing virtualization, despite its potential for reducing IT spending. Apathy is a powerful force, and many organizations are more comfortable continuing to do things "the way they've always been done," rather than doing something different. Organizations with this attitude aren't good candidates for virtualization (or for any other new technology, no matter how powerful or cost effective).

In particular, if your organization is unwilling to invest in hardware, virtualization probably isn't a good idea. Most organizations that move to virtualization do so on newly purchased servers that are significantly more powerful than the previously used servers.

Generally speaking, old servers just don't have the horsepower to serve as virtualization platforms, and attempting to repurpose old servers is a recipe for a virtualization mess.

Chapter 6

Performing a Server Virtualization Cost-Benefit Analysis

*I*n many organizations, deciding whether to go forward with a project is tied up with a project's financial benefits. Certainly a primary reason virtualization is so hot these days is that it promises significant payback. In any case, having a documented financial analysis is sure to help you communicate the benefits of the project as well as "sell" it to decision makers.

This chapter outlines six steps to creating a financial analysis of your virtualization project and even includes examples of the spreadsheets that you can use to document your project. Armed with these items, gaining commitment for your project should be much easier.

Getting Your Cost-Benefit Ducks in a Row

I won't keep you in suspense any longer. Here are my five steps to performing a server virtualization cost-benefit analysis in all their succinct glory:

1. Define your proposed virtualization solution.

2. Establish your current cost structure.

3. Identify your virtualization project costs.

4. Define the benefits of your proposed virtualization solution.

5. Create your virtualization project overview spreadsheet.

The upcoming sections examine each of these steps in greater detail.

Defining a solution

Clearly, your first task is to look at your current infrastructure and consider how you might apply virtualization to it. Should you consolidate a number of physical servers onto a smaller number of machines, each of which hosts a number of virtual machines? Do you need to construct a redundant infrastructure to allow guests to be migrated between machines to ensure high availability? Or do you need to virtualize your storage as well as consolidate servers?

Based on your assessment of the situation (see Chapters 3 and 7 for more on assessment criteria), you can identify what portion of your existing infrastructure is suitable for virtualization. You can then identify the right virtualization solution to use. (The section on products in Chapter 3 can help here.)

After you've identified the existing infrastructure that will be affected as well as the proposed virtualization solution, you have the basis for performing a comparison between your previrtualization setup and your post. When that comparison is done, you can calculate the financial impact of going to virtualization as well as the operational benefits you'll derive from the move.

Looking at current costs

Understanding how much your infrastructure costs you to run today is vital to figuring out your current baseline. It might surprise you to discover that most IT organizations don't track their costs with much granularity; that is, IT organizations track their budgets in fairly broad categories without assigning costs in significant detail. As a result, you probably can't request a report that shows the current costs of the part of your infrastructure that you want to virtualize. However, you can, with a bit of work, create a fairly accurate estimate of the current cost of your infrastructure, which serves as the baseline with which to compare the potential benefits of going to virtualization.

Hard costs and soft costs

The first thing to recognize about costs is that there are two broad categories: hard costs and soft costs. It's much easier to document hard costs, but soft costs often represent the preponderance of the total cost structure.

Because documenting hard costs is easier, you'll probably have more confidence in their accuracy with respect to your cost structure. Therefore, I recommend that you keep the two types of costs separate in your analysis. Many times, even the hard costs are enough to justify a virtualization project, so the soft costs serve as backup in the decision, which makes their lower accuracy less of an issue.

So, time for some definitions. *Hard costs* are any costs that require paying actual money to an entity. Hard costs are usually associated with a specific product and service. For example, if you use an outside company to run security scans on your servers, the fees you pay to that company are a hard cost.

Hard costs don't have to be associated with an outside company, however. If you have a chargeback system in place in your organization, part of your budget might be assigned to another entity within the company. In this case, you would transfer budget dollars to that entity to pay for the service it provides.

The point is that actual money flows out of your organization to someone else. These flows — and their size — can be identified. Typically, an invoice is associated with hard costs from an external company; although chargeback systems might not include invoicing and check cutting, some system must be in place to cause the budget transfer, and you can discover the types and sizes of budget flow.

Soft costs, on the other hand, are typically associated with internal personnel or internal services for which no explicit chargeback system is in place. Soft costs are what the organization spends on an ongoing basis doing its daily work.

Soft costs are notoriously difficult to establish with any degree of accuracy. Very few organizations systematically keep track of the specific tasks its members perform, not to mention the amount of time its members devote to each task.

This lack of granularity is also present in many internal company services. In a data center, for example, air conditioning is a significant expense, yet it's typically assessed as a lump sum applied to the general IT budget.

The lack of cost tracking for individuals and services means it can be extremely difficult to understand how much budget an organization uses for any particular part of its work. In the case of virtualization, this means it's not easy to find out the cost of running an individual machine, which serves as the basis for developing the baseline cost structure.

However, to truly develop an accurate picture of an organization's cost structure, you must examine soft costs. This is because soft costs — particularly employee costs — can represent a large percentage of the total cost base for the organization. In most IT organizations, personnel represent the preponderance of total expenditures; therefore, assessing soft costs as part of the overall baseline cost structure is extremely important.

In your financial analysis, separate hard and soft costs. Because soft costs are more difficult to specifically identify, many people are skeptical about them. By separating the two types of costs, you increase the clarity of your financial analysis.

Hard costs in the data center

In the previous section, I let you know that hard costs require a direct outflow from an organization's budget. When developing a baseline budget, you must track these three hard costs:

✔ **Power:** You know what power is — it's the stuff that comes out of the wall socket. Except for the rare company that creates some or all of its own power through cogeneration, power is most assuredly a hard cost.

  Your company likely has its overall cost of power itemized at the data center level of granularity. Consequently, finding out the total amount spent on power should be relatively straightforward.

  However, calculating the cost of power for the machines in your virtualization project might be a bit trickier. Some tips on how to calculate power cost at that level of detail are contained in the "Identifying the financial benefits of virtualization" section, later in this chapter.

✔ **Server maintenance:** The existing machines in a data center most likely are under a service plan. A service plan covers maintenance on machines, ensuring that, should some component within the machine fail, a vendor will take responsibility to get the machine back up and running.

  Service plans come in many different forms; users can usually choose one of several levels of response time guarantee. For example, a report problem will be worked on in two hours, four hours, and so on. (These service levels are often named after precious metals: Bronze is okay responsiveness, Silver is faster, Gold faster yet, and Platinum . . . well, it doesn't get any more responsive than that.) As you might imagine, quicker response times cost more money.

  Organizations often vary the level of service plan according to the importance of the machine. After all, it's not very cost effective to purchase extreme responsiveness for a machine used to generate low-priority reports. If, on the other hand, those reports are used to schedule the company's workforce, keeping the report generator machine up and running might be vital.

  Server maintenance costs should be fairly easy to establish because the costs are directly associated with individual machines. Of course, the company might have a blanket policy that covers a large number of machines, but it should be fairly easy to identify how much maintenance costs per machine, and you can use the cost as an input to the assessment of baseline costs.

✔ **Outside services:** It might be that your company engages an outside organization to perform services within your data center. In this world of outsourcing, it's often more cost effective or just plain simpler to use an outside vendor to perform work rather than rely on internal personnel.

If your company uses outside vendors for anything associated with keeping its infrastructure up and running (for example, someone to run backups on your machines), you have outside services hard costs that you must assign to the baseline cost structure you're creating. You might need to divide the cost of the service if it covers a larger number of machines than you're considering for virtualization, but simple mathematics enable you to come up with the cost of the outside services devoted to those machines.

Soft costs in the data center

Here's where things get tricky. Trying to assign soft costs to specific servers can be like trying to nail Jell-O to the wall. Nevertheless, with some diligence, you can establish how much your organization spends on soft cost items for the machines in question. Soft costs are

✔ **Machine administration:** Machine administration refers to the work done by internal personnel keeping the technology infrastructure humming. Although this term can include system administrators, network administrators, and database administrators (noticing an administration pattern?), you should look solely at the personnel directly involved with the machines in question and leave out those whose work will be unaffected whether the machines are physical or virtual. For example, a network administrator who spends time ensuring that machines can connect to the network efficiently does so whether the machine is physical or virtual, so it probably makes sense to leave him or her out of the baseline cost creation. However, someone who spends time administering the hardware in a data center (that is, moving applications from one server to another so that the original server can have parts replaced) performs duties directly related to the systems in question, and costs associated with him or her should be included in the cost structure.

Most organizations have very little awareness of how much time internal employees actually spend on specific tasks and even less awareness of how much time is spent on those tasks for each machine in the data center. So identifying the amount spent on machine administration requires some dexterity of judgment. You need to consult with the actual personnel to develop an estimate of how much time people spend on machine administration per machine.

If, despite all your best efforts, you can't find a way to determine actual numbers for your organization's costs, you can always turn to the information hunter's best friend: Google. By doing some Internet searching, you should be able to find a number of studies and estimates on the cost of administering a machine. Choose a study that tracks costs in an environment similar to yours and use its costs in your estimates. I suggest you make a note of the source of your cost in the spreadsheet you create. That way, if someone questions your numbers, you can cite an authority as your source, which should raise everyone's confidence in your financial projections.

Bottom line: It might not be easy to track machine administration costs with any real accuracy, but with a little effort, you should be able to create a rough estimate of the cost per machine for administration. Even a rough estimate is better than throwing up your hands and giving up.

✔ **Backup:** Backup refers to the process of creating a secure copy of the data on individual machines. You can do so by copying the data to a tape that the administrator inserts, by replicating the data across the network to another server, or even by sending the data outside the organization (a so-called "outside the firewall" backup) to a remote backup service.

No matter what method is used to back up existing data, someone probably spends some time making sure it happens. Although a number of vendors offer software designed to automate the backup process, many organizations still rely on manual work by employees to either do the work directly or serve as nonautomated tape changers.

As with machine administration, you'll probably find it difficult to get an accurate picture of the amount of time employees spend on this activity, but if you do some poking around, you should be able to discover how much work it takes to perform reliable backups. This number then serves as an input into the current-state financial picture.

Identifying virtualization costs

After you establish the current running costs of your as-is infrastructure, you need to understand the potential benefits — and costs — of moving to virtualization. This part of the assessment process can be trickier than establishing your current cost structure because it requires estimation rather than documentation. Nevertheless, to understand the complete implications of moving to virtualization, you need to know the financial impact of the virtualization scenario you select.

Selecting a virtualization deployment scenario

The first step in estimating your after-implementation virtualization costs is to define the configuration you'll most likely install. Because you can choose from many virtualization products and many potential configurations (for example, individual virtualized servers or a virtualized pool of servers, possibly including virtualized storage, as well), making the choice can be a difficult process.

Despite the difficulty, deciding on what to implement is critical. Without a defined configuration, you can't accurately estimate the cost of moving to virtualization. In addition, most organizations frown on project plans that are ambiguous about what will actually be implemented.

I spend quite a bit of time in Chapter 7 discussing how to choose your virtualization scenario, so that information can be a big help here. If you use that coverage as the basis for your technical discussions, I'm pretty sure you can reach a consensus on the configuration you'll want to move forward with. When you have a concrete picture of the final virtualization configuration, you can begin documenting your likely costs.

There's no such thing as a free lunch, and virtualization, despite its obvious benefits, isn't free, either. You'll incur a range of costs as you move to virtualization, and it's important to recognize them and estimate them in your overall cost-benefit analysis. Only by identifying the likely costs can you be confident that your overall virtualization picture is accurately drawn.

You also need to acknowledge and estimate these costs to ensure you aren't perceived as an overzealous advocate of the technology. By realistically documenting the costs of moving to virtualization, others are more likely to view you as an impartial assessor of virtualization.

Being identified as a zealot pushing a virtualization agenda is a good way to slow the progress of your virtualization project. Arriving at a planning meeting with a slide show outlining the proposed virtualization architecture and with a stapled set of papers outlining the financial impact of the project will speed your project's approval and identify you with its success. It's not much work to create an impressive set of supporting documentation, but it can make all the difference in the world.

Identifying new hardware needs

Although virtualization is a very flexible technology and is capable of running on a very wide range of hardware — including repurposed hardware you already have running in your data center — you might very well want to use the latest generation of virtualization-oriented hardware to host your virtualized servers. The ongoing march of hardware performance improvement means that this new generation of hardware delivers incredible performance at a price that would have been unthinkable just a few years ago. Bringing in new hardware as part of your virtualization project might make good sense. If you decide to do so, naturally you need to add those costs to your analysis.

If you want to take advantage of some of the more advanced characteristics of Xen, like the flexibility to avoid guest operating system modification (see Chapter 3 for a more detailed description of paravirtualization and the operating system modifications it might require), you'll need new hardware with the virtualization-enabled chips from Intel or AMD.

If you're moving forward with a product from VMware, however, its products only run on certain hardware, which is listed on their hardware compatibility list. So a hardware upgrade probably will be a prerequisite for your project.

Consider creating two versions of the cost analysis: one with new hardware and one without. Because the new generation of hardware is also extremely efficient in terms of the amount of power required, you might find that the increased cost of the hardware is partly or totally offset by the power savings you'll realize.

You need to estimate how many servers you'll require. The primary driver of how many machines you'll require is the distribution of virtual machines; that is, how many guest systems each server will support. If you're planning to migrate 20 current servers and don't want to run more than seven guests on each physical server, you need three physical servers.

Again, hardware is a hard cost (perhaps the hardest of hard costs!), so the cost of the physical servers goes into the hard costs section of the detail spreadsheet containing your project's financial projections.

The cost of the physical servers can vary widely, depending on how you've decided to implement your virtualization infrastructure. Again, you might choose to repurpose existing hardware, in which case the primary physical hardware expense will be maintenance. You might, however, conclude that you want to move to new hardware that's better suited to support virtualization. (For a discussion of your hardware options, see Chapter 8.) In summary, many newer machines are designed to support more memory and more processors, making them better suited for virtualization.

If you decide to move to new hardware, your cash flows will be a large outflow in Year One, when the purchase is made, with smaller ongoing amounts for maintenance fees.

Considering other physical equipment

Depending on the envisioned configuration you've designed, you might also decide to include other physical equipment such as Network-Attached Storage or a Storage Area Network. (See Chapter 11 for a discussion of your storage virtualization options.)

Any additional physical equipment is, naturally, a hard cost and should be documented in that section of the detail spreadsheet.

Software licenses might also be required to implement other physical equipment, so you might need to estimate and document an additional hard cost in the new software section of the worksheet. Speaking of which . . .

Purchasing new software

Based on your review of your use cases (see Chapter 7 for more on that), you have a pretty good idea of how many of your current servers you'll migrate to virtual machines. Depending on the load they place on the underlying physical hardware, you'll be able to estimate how many virtual machines you can support per physical machine. In turn, that estimate should tell you how many virtualization software licenses you require for your project.

Of course, if you're using one of the free or open source products, you don't have any license costs, although you might choose to purchase software maintenance, thereby incurring ongoing costs despite the absence of license fees.

Software licenses are a hard cost, so document them in the hard costs section of your detail worksheet. Presenting an annualized view (such as yearly costs over a five-year period) is important because software licenses typically carry a significant cost in Year One and then a lower ongoing cost for software maintenance.

Training employees

A learning curve is associated with beginning to use *any* new software product. Many organizations educate their employees through training classes to get them up to speed more quickly. If you're likely going to take advantage of training for this purpose, the cost of the training should also go into the costs section of the spreadsheet.

Identifying the financial benefits of virtualization

After you define the configuration of your virtualization solution and identify the costs associated with it, you can estimate the financial benefits you'll receive by moving to virtualization.

Because virtualization enables multiple systems to run on a single piece of hardware, most organizations find that they can reduce their current cost structure by using virtualization.

Because you're developing an overarching view of what this virtualization project will mean to your organization, identifying the savings you'll achieve is important. Be sure to explicitly document the achievable savings.

You can receive two types of financial benefits by moving to virtualization:

- Cost savings through not having to spend money you're currently spending on your existing infrastructure
- Cost savings through more effective and efficient operations

As you might expect, the two types of savings fall into hard and soft categories.

Reduced hard costs

As you migrate operating systems and applications from physical to virtual servers, you have the opportunity to run fewer physical machines. For every machine you retire, you save on hardware maintenance and power costs.

If you've done your work on assessing your current infrastructure, you have a very good estimate of the costs directly associated with every machine. However, estimating power savings can be difficult. Keep the following topics in mind:

- ✔ **Reduced hardware maintenance:** Every server that has an operating system and applications that will be migrated to a virtualized infrastructure is a candidate to be yanked out of the data center. Because even modest virtualization servers can support four or more simultaneous virtualized servers, you might be able to retire a number of machines from your infrastructure.

    Part of calculating your current costs is identifying the ongoing maintenance costs for every machine; for every machine that can be retired, you can identify the maintenance fees that will no longer be necessary and add them to the cost savings.

- ✔ **Reduced software licenses:** By moving to a virtualized environment, you might be able to realize savings on your software licenses and maintenance. If your research establishes that you can do so, you should enter these savings into your spreadsheet.

    However, most software vendors are still grappling with the implications of virtualization, so you probably won't obtain any savings on software. Indeed, if you migrate systems to more powerful systems, even if you don't use the processing power for the migrated system, you might end up paying more for your software! This is because some software manufacturers charge by how many processors the underlying hardware has; if you're running your virtualized server on a four-way machine but using only one processor's power, with these software vendors you might be charged a license fee for a four-processor box.

    So don't be surprised if your software license and software maintenance costs don't show any savings due to virtualization.

- ✔ **Reduced power costs:** When it comes to identifying the potential power savings, the process is straightforward. Each machine should have some documentation about how much power it draws. If you don't have the documentation any longer, the manufacturer's Web site should have it. The documentation will provide several power measurements associated with various loads. Use the power draw level associated with the most typical load factor for the machines in your data center.

If you're uncomfortable working from these estimates, you can establish power draw more accurately. You can get a test tool (called, naturally enough, a power meter — you can find them easily via an Internet search; my favorite is one called the "Kill-A-Watt") that measures how much power a physical device is using. This tool enables you to be very specific about the power each machine uses. However, repeatedly measuring power draws on servers is a lot of work, so you're probably better off avoiding this and using the method described in the previous paragraph. If you're not comfortable with that level of accuracy, you can always measure one machine and use that machine's power draw as a general number to be used for all machines.

If you go the physical measurement route, be aware that the actual load can vary significantly, depending on what the machine is doing at the time of measurement. If it's loafing along, waiting for an application load, its power consumption will be quite low; on the other hand, if it's processing a giant Web request, its consumption will be much higher. Try and figure out the average load and measure power consumption at that point in order to establish an accurate estimate of power draw.

You're not only saving power by getting rid of machines. You're probably going to be bringing some new, more efficient machines into the data center to serve as virtualization platforms. You will also achieve some power savings by replacing some existing machines with more efficient ones.

Put another way, your total power savings include both the amount of power you save because you remove machines and the amount of power you save because you replace some machines with more efficient servers. If you use a five-to-one virtual machine ratio — you take five old servers and turn them into virtual machines running on one new physical server — your power savings are the amount of power to run four old servers plus the difference between the power draw of an old server and the power draw of the new server.

If the manufacturer doesn't provide documentation on actual power costs and you don't feel like going through the work of physically measuring actual power consumption in your data center, all is not lost. Just as you could draw upon Internet research to determine system administration costs (see the discussion in the "Soft costs in the data center" section, earlier in the chapter), you can also find many estimates of server power consumption on the Internet. As before, I recommend you cite the source of your information to ensure credibility.

Perhaps an example is in order. Suppose you have 15 machines currently operating in your data center. You decide to migrate all the operating systems and applications to new virtualization servers, which are of the low power-draw variety. You conclude you can run five virtualized servers per physical machine. This means you need three of the new servers to replace all 15 of the old servers.

You'll completely retire 12 machines, so you can add the power consumption of each machine to your power savings. In addition, you'll be replacing three of the old machines with new, lower-power-draw machines. The power you save for these three machines will be three times the difference between the power requirements of the old versus new machines, and you can add that difference to your total power savings.

At the end of this step, you get a good idea of how much power you might save by moving to virtualization, both by retiring machines and by replacing old machines with new.

Reduced soft costs

After you identify all the costs you're likely to save that are closely tied to physical hardware, you can identify the internal, employee-based costs that you can save by moving to virtualization. Need a checklist of such costs of what to look for? It's not a particularly long list, but here you go:

- ✔ **System administration work is reduced.** Keeping a physical server up and running takes a lot of work. It needs to be monitored, have its hardware upgraded occasionally, and have tape backups run. If that server is virtualized, the effort needed to keep it up and running typically is reduced, perhaps by 30 to 50 percent. This is due to the fact that you no longer have to worry about hardware issues (you have only the host machine's hardware to worry about) and the fact that your hardware system administration tasks no longer have to be done during expensive off-hours timeframes. If the underlying hardware requires work, you can simply migrate the virtualized server to another piece of hardware at your convenience and work on the now-empty hardware at your leisure.

- ✔ **Soft costs might require rough estimates.** Estimating the reduced work necessary due to virtualization can be difficult. It might be easier to make rough estimates and then include the soft costs section separately on your benefits spreadsheet. This enables you to include the estimates in your overall assessment, but you also have them clearly broken out. So, if any controversy arises regarding the soft benefits of virtualization, they can easily be set aside so that you can focus on the other considerable virtualization benefits.

Creating your virtualization cost-benefit spreadsheet

After you establish all your as-is and will-be costs and identify savings, you can capture them in a spreadsheet. You might feel this is overkill, but after you prepare one, you'll be surprised at how quickly it becomes the common currency of discussion about your virtualization project.

My sample spreadsheet set

As a guide to help you through this process, I've put together a sample spreadsheet set. For purposes of clarity, I simplified these spreadsheets somewhat, but they nonetheless provide a model for how to document your cost findings. In the example I put together, I'm assuming an existing infrastructure of 20 machines that will be migrated onto three next-generation (specialized for virtualization) servers. I use VMware ESX Server as the virtualization solution, and I take advantage of the existing storage virtualization infrastructure. (Assuming a SAN — Storage Area Network — is already in place allows me to simplify the example, but if new SAN equipment and software had been necessary, I would have added it to the hard costs section of the "Virtualized Cost Structure" spreadsheet.) There are three spreadsheets:

✔ **Current Cost Structure:** This documents the costs of your current nonvirtualized infrastructure, using a five-year time horizon. (See Figure 6-1.)

✔ **Virtualized Cost Structure:** This documents the costs of running your infrastructure after virtualization is enabled and includes all the costs of implementing your virtualization solution. Again, it uses a five-year time horizon. (See Figure 6-2.)

✔ **Project Cost Summary:** This spreadsheet identifies the financial outcome of moving to virtualization. (See Figure 6-3.)

Figure 6-1: Your previrtualization cost structure worksheet.

Category	Cost Year 1	Year 2	Year 3	Year 4	Year 5	Notes
Current Yearly Costs						
Hard Costs						
Power	12,000	12,000	12,000	12,000	12,000	20 Dell PowerEdge servers X $600/yr/machine
Server Maintenance	6,000	6,000	6,000	6,000	6,000	20 Servers X $300/server/year
Outside Services	0	0	0	0	0	All operations handled by staff
Total Yearly Hard Costs	18,000	18,000	18,000	18,000	18,000	
Total Five Year Hard Costs	90,000					
Soft Costs						
Machine Administration	60,000	60,000	60,000	60,000	60,000	Estimate: 1 week/machine/year X 20 machines (Loaded admin cost $150K/yr)
Backup	93,750	93,750	93,750	93,750	93,750	Estimate: 15 mins/workday X 20 machines
Total Yearly Soft Costs	153,750	153,750	153,750	153,750	153,750	
Total Five Year Soft Costs	768,750					
Total Current Yearly Costs	171,750	171,750	171,750	171,750	171,750	
NPV Total Costs	651,068					

Current Cost Structure / Virtualized Cost Structure / Project Cost Summary /

For each spreadsheet, you should also include a net present value (NPV) calculation. NPV is a calculation that collects the project's cash flows over its life span and — using a discount factor to account for time differences of the various cash flows — comes up with a single number to reflect the current value of all future cash flows. NPV captures the entire lifetime of a project in a single figure and is extremely helpful in analyzing the financial implications of projects. It's also very impressive to finance types and can help convince them to support your project. The example spreadsheets contain an NPV for the as-is, the will-be, and the cost summary spreadsheets.

Figure 6-2:
Your postvirtualization cost structure worksheet.

Virtualized Infrastructure Yearly Costs

Category	Cost					Notes
	Year 1	Year 2	Year 3	Year 4	Year 5	
Hard Costs						
Machine Purchase	63,000					3 Sun SunFire X4600 X $21k/server
Software Purchase	12,000					3 Vmware ESX Server
Software Maintenance		2,400	2,400	2,400	2,400	3 VMware ESX Server @ 20% maintenance
Power	900	900	900	900	900	3 Sun SunFire 4500 X $300/yr
Server Maintenance	6,300	6,300	6,300	6,300	6,300	3 Sun SunFire 4500 X $2100/yr
Training	3,000	1,500	1,500	1,500	1,500	2 employees trained year 1, 1 employee thereafter
Outside Services	0	0	0	0	0	All operations handled by staff
Total Yearly Hard Costs	85,200	11,100	11,100	11,100	11,100	
Total Five Year Hard Costs	129,600					
Soft Costs						
Machine Administration	27,000	27,000	27,000	27,000	27,000	3 week/virtualized machine/year X 3 machines (Loaded admin cost $150k/yr)
Backup	14,000	14,000	14,000	14,000	14,000	15 mins/workday X 3 machines
Total Yearly Soft Costs	41,000	41,000	41,000	41,000	41,000	
Total Five Year Soft Costs	205,000					
Total Yearly Costs	126,200	52,100	52,100	52,100	52,100	
NPV Total Costs	254,864					

Figure 6-3:
A sample Project Cost Summary worksheet.

Virtualization Project Cost Summary

Category	Cost					Notes
	Year 1	Year 2	Year 3	Year 4	Year 5	
Current Infrastructure Costs						
Total Yearly Hard Costs	18,000	18,000	18,000	18,000	18,000	
Total Five Year Hard Costs	90,000					
Total Yearly Soft Costs	153,750	153,750	153,750	153,750	153,750	
Total Five Year Soft Costs	768,750					
NPV Total Costs	651,068					
Virtualized Infrastructure Costs						
Total Yearly Hard Costs	85,200	11,100	11,100	11,100	11,100	
Total Five Year Hard Costs	129,600					
Total Yearly Soft Costs	41,000	41,000	41,000	41,000	41,000	
Total Five Year Soft Costs	205,000					
NPV Total Costs	254,864					
Net Five Year Hard Cost Savings	-39,600					Total Five Year Current Infrastructure Hard Costs minus Total Five Year Virtualized Infrastructure Hard Costs
Net Five Year Soft Cost Savings	446,068					Total Five Year Current Infrastructure Soft Costs minus Total Five Year Virtualized Infrastructure Soft Costs
NPV Net Savings of Virtualization Project	386,204					96 Soft Cost Savings

Current Cost Structure / Virtualized Cost Structure \ Project Cost Summary /

The following list discusses what sections should be present in each of the spreadsheets. Keep the following in mind when mulling over how to apply the sample set to your own situation:

- ✓ **Show the financial implications across time.** Many times, a financial decision that doesn't make sense when looked at purely in terms of the immediate costs begins to make more sense when assessed with a longer time horizon. For that reason, listing the costs and benefits for yearly periods extending out through five years gives a much better picture about whether going forward with a virtualization project makes sense.

- ✓ **Include separate hard costs and soft costs sections.** In each of the detail worksheets, include separate sections devoted to hard and soft costs. Because hard costs are so much easier to identify — and are also somehow more "real" — list them first. For each of the categories of costs (for example, server maintenance), list the yearly amount for that category. You might need to list each item within each category (that is, for every server that's being considered for migration to a virtualized environment, list the annual maintenance costs for it). For each category of cost, create a summary line that sums the total for that type of cost.

- ✓ **The summary worksheet is the true kicker.** The summary worksheet should present an easy-to-understand, high-level picture of the two options: sticking with what you have and moving to virtualization. The summary worksheet should also present the comparison for yearly periods up to five years, enabling a quick understanding of the financial implications of the decision now and in the future.

- ✓ **Creating the spreadsheet with both detail and summary worksheets ensures that you've captured all the costs of the two options.** In addition, you can easily use the spreadsheet containing all three worksheets as the basis for the decision-making process. A clearly laid-out spreadsheet can help move discussions forward immeasurably. Documenting the two options — the previrtualization and the postvirtualization cost structure — might seem like a lot of work, but the upfront work of creating the spreadsheet shortens the decision-making process considerably.

What the example spreadsheet shows

Let me spell out again my assumptions of my sample project:

- ✓ Current server count: 20 (refer to the first note in Figure 6-1)
- ✓ Future server count (4 CPU, 16GB RAM): 3 (refer to the first note in Figure 6-2)
- ✓ Guest machines per server: 7 (20 virtual machines spread across the three new servers)
- ✓ Virtualization software used: VMware ESX Server (refer to the second note in Figure 6-2)

Right off the bat, you can see that I'm not being overly ambitious when it comes to loading my new servers with guest systems — the SunFire X4600 machines are described in Chapter 8 as being real workhorses built for heavy virtualization loads. At a seven-to-one ratio, the machines should be well able to handle the load. I'm also going to assume that I'll be training people immediately on the virtualization software, but I'll also continue such training in the future. This is a reasonable assumption because the staff inevitably turns over, and new employees need to learn how to administer the product.

From examining the Project Cost Summary spreadsheet (refer to Figure 6-3), I can tell that, in the short term, moving to virtualization is going to cost more than the current infrastructure. In fact, over the duration of the five-year time horizon I've used, it's more expensive to move to virtualization than to continue with what I have. Of course, I would likely need to replace the current servers even if I didn't move to virtualization, due to a typical equipment rotation policy, but I didn't try to include that factor in the calculation. If I had, the hard costs numbers would probably swing to a virtualized infrastructure benefit. In any case, it's not a slam dunk that virtualization wins on hard cost payoffs.

Be prepared to justify every one of the assumptions in your financial projections. Having good evidence — being able to document the current cost structure and projected virtual machine loads, for example — is an excellent way to raise everyone's confidence in your project; conversely, not being able to back up your numbers is a quick route to project cancellation.

If you look at the final three entries in Figure 6-3, it's clear that most of the benefits of the example virtualization project result from reduced administration tasks based on managing fewer pieces of hardware. If you were presenting this financial analysis, it would be important to be ready to back up your assumptions about increased administrative efficiency because that's where most of the savings occur. Being able to cite internal experience or external authorities would make the justification much easier.

The assumption that the current machines can be carried forward with only maintenance costs for the next five years might not be realistic. Many IT organizations have a three-year refresh cycle for hardware. If that were the case in this example, one of the five years would have a large outlay for new hardware, which would significantly change the Total Yearly Hard Costs of $90,000. To replace 20 servers with fresh machines — even lower specification hardware typical of the "one application, one server" environment — would cost upwards of $40,000, which would certainly change the total hard costs for the Current Infrastructure Costs and would make those costs roughly the same as replacing them with three workhorse servers, thereby changing the Net Five Year Hard Cost Savings move from negative $39,600 to about $0.

What could I have done to make my case stronger for the project? Well, if you look at the Virtualization Project Cost Summary (refer to Figure 6-3), the Virtualized Infrastructure Costs indicate that the biggest factor causing the virtualized project to be more expensive in terms of hard costs is the cost of the new servers. I could examine whether I could support ten guests per server, thereby foregoing the need for a third server. Many organizations are able to support more than ten guests on the class of hardware I selected (see the case study in Chapter 8), so the move from three to two Sun machines is certainly justifiable. Such a move would also reduce total power required for the virtualized system, further increasing savings.

Don't treat your initial analysis as if it's etched in stone. Based on the numbers you develop, re-examine your project assumptions. You might find additional ways to improve the financial benefits of your virtualization project.

If my hypothetical company were fortunate enough to be located in the Pacific Gas & Electric (PG&E) service area, I could take advantage of its rebate program, as described in Chapter 5. That program would have returned an additional $5,550 to the company, based on PG&E's rebate of 50 percent of the first year's energy savings. Although not an enormous amount, every little bit helps. If you pursue virtualization, be sure to check whether your local energy provider has a similar program in place.

My financial analysis also leaves out exogenous factors that might make the virtualization decision more critical. For example, if the company was experiencing rapid growth but had a completely filled data center, the cost of moving to virtualization would pale in comparison to the expense of expanding the data center, which might run $50 million or more.

The Cost-Benefit Bottom Line

This chapter walks you through the process of creating a financial justification for a virtualization project. Although many people feel they don't have the time to go through a financial projection exercise, creating such a justification can actually *save* time. This is because having a thought-out set of financials speeds approval of the project by the organization. I can't stress enough how quickly a spreadsheet can become the document of record in discussions and how quickly people rely on it to form their opinion of the virtues of virtualization. Don't be afraid to invest time in creating a spreadsheet about your virtualization project; it can create an unstoppable momentum for your project.

Chapter 7

Managing a Virtualization Project

*I*n earlier chapters of this book, I dutifully go over all the broad, conceptual issues — what virtualization is, how it works, the business case for virtualization, and what technologies and applications of virtualization are actually available. Now it's time to get cracking, put the pedal to the metal, get a move on, hammer down, *[insert appropriate cliché],* and go do some virtualizing.

It's the classic move from Understanding to Doing. In this chapter, I bring together all of the different topics I've been harping on and wrap them up with a pretty bow. In practical terms, that means giving you the info you need so that you can choose which virtualization technology will work best for you. Your choices — if you need a reminder — are

✔ **Operating system virtualization:** By providing an emulation of a complete operating system, this form of virtualization offers an excellent opportunity to partition applications into their own containers (that is, applications are presented with a virtual operating system that reflects the underlying operating system).

✔ **Hardware emulation:** By emulating the underlying machine, hardware emulation enables organizations to mix and match operating systems and application versions, thereby achieving great flexibility in virtualization deployment.

✔ **Paravirtualization:** You can achieve very high performance by pursuing the paravirtualization route, albeit with some complexity and limitations due to virtual machine and hardware restrictions. (*Paravirtualization* is a lightweight virtualization technology that does not emulate hardware, but instead coordinates access to hardware resources for the guest operating systems.)

I also discuss how to choose a virtualization application profile for your server virtualization project. Your choices are

- ✔ **Server consolidation:** Moving many physical servers onto fewer physical servers by converting the physical servers into virtual machines through a process called physical-to-virtual (P2V) migration.

- ✔ **Simple failover:** Ensuring better application availability by using virtualization software to rapidly restart crashed virtual machines.

- ✔ **High availability:** Protecting the application infrastructure by using virtualization software to automatically migrate virtual machines from one physical server to another in case of hardware failure or resource limitation.

- ✔ **Load balancing:** Using two or more virtual machines located on separate physical servers to ensure that physical server load doesn't degrade application service levels.

- ✔ **Clustering:** Coordinating the work of two or more virtual machines located on separate physical servers to ensure maximum application uptime and avoid interrupted service due to virtual machine or hardware failure. Because the clustered systems can be run as virtual machines, it is no longer necessary to maintain dedicated hardware, thereby making clustering more efficient and cost effective.

- ✔ **Server pooling:** Using virtualization software to coordinate a number of physical servers and the virtual machines they host as if the entire collection is one large resource, or pool, of servers. This enables IT organizations to allow the virtualization software to manage placement and monitoring of individual virtual machines based on the resource needs of the virtualization machines and the utilization rates of the underlying hardware.

Chapter 3 has much more on the three virtualization technologies as well as more detailed coverage of the various virtualization application profiles.

By the end of this chapter you'll have an understanding of how to travel your virtualization journey. So sit back, relax, and watch the landmarks of your virtualization project slide by.

Understanding the Virtualization Life Cycle

Despite what many vendors of virtualization software, products, and services claim, you can't achieve implemented virtualization through a simple purchase, after which you sit back and watch the savings mount. Although virtualization is an excellent technology that will be ubiquitous in the future, it still represents change in infrastructure and management, which, in my experience, always requires a methodical approach to achieve success.

Therefore, the right place to start your virtualization journey is with the virtualization life cycle — an overview, if you will, of all the steps necessary for a successful virtualization project.

If you look at Figure 7-1, you can see a graphical representation of a virtualization project. It might surprise you that a virtualization project doesn't start with selecting a product, but rather with looking inward. Without understanding what you're trying to accomplish and, crucially, the way your IT department is organized, you're less likely to be successful; worse, you might actually select products that will cause your virtualization project to fail — and you definitely don't want *that*.

The virtualization life cycle recognizes that the move to virtualization extends far beyond installing some new software in the data center. Implementing virtualization requires a thorough rethinking of your current operations, a new vision for your virtualized infrastructure, a plan of how to get from the existing infrastructure to the new one, and a method for operating the new infrastructure once it's in place. Virtualization changes the way you do information processing, and the virtualization life cycle helps you manage the transition.

The Virtualization Lifecycle

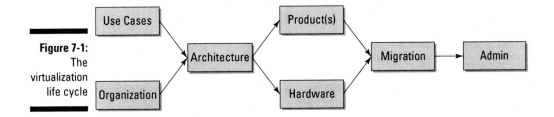

Figure 7-1: The virtualization life cycle

The following sections describe the three phases of the virtualization life cycle, and they provide brief descriptions of the tasks contained in each phase. Later in the chapter, I go over each task in more detail so that you can create your own action plan for your virtualization project.

Planning your virtualization journey

If you take another look at Figure 7-1, you can see that the virtualization journey begins with a planning phase that covers a number of separate tasks.

✔ **Use cases:** Define how you'll be using virtualization.

✔ **Organization:** Determining how your IT department is organized is critical because your virtualization solution simply has to align with the way your IT organization does its daily work; otherwise, you face the problem of your technology and your daily work routines operating at cross purposes.

✔ **Architecture:** You design the technical architecture of your virtualization solution based on your use cases and your organizational structure.

These tasks, to mix a metaphor, provide the foundation for your virtualization journey. The research you do in the planning phase helps ensure that your implementation will provide the right functionality and use the right products. It's tempting to jump right in to installing products, but your project is more likely to be successful if you do the up-front research.

 Planning is where you set the stage for a successful virtualization project. A key part of planning is making sure that all the politics of your project are worked out. Getting your ducks in a row might seem like a funny phrase, but getting everyone lined up behind your project is crucial to success. Spend the time on lobbying everyone now to avoid trying to placate everyone later.

Implementing your virtualization solution

After you've done your research and made your choices regarding your virtualization implementation, it's time to implement your virtualization infrastructure. In this phase, you address two elements of your virtualization solution:

✔ **Products:** The research you've done and the architectural decisions you've made will dictate which virtualization products are most appropriate for your solution. In this step, you evaluate and choose the product you'll go forward with. Chapter 3 covers the technologies and products you select from.

✔ **Hardware:** Likewise, your research and architectural decisions also dictate what kind of hardware you need to use. In this step, you select the hardware you'll move forward with. Chapter 8 covers the types of hardware that are available to use in your virtualization project.

This is the phase where things "really happen." New software is installed. New machines are wheeled into the data center (and really, it's great to unpack all those new boxes and drag out shiny new hardware!). People rush around muttering new technical terms. This is a phase you'll really enjoy.

This is also the phase where the money gets spent. While it might seem like this is the fun part (after all, who doesn't like to play with new toys), this is also the part where projects run into trouble. If people aren't prepared for the costs of the project, they might experience "sticker shock." Be prepared to justify why you're asking them to spend money on virtualization.

Operating your virtualization solution

Everything in the virtualization life cycle up to this point has been about getting ready to go live with a virtualized infrastructure. This operating phase of the virtualization life cycle is all about getting your virtualization project up and running. This phase has two key milestones:

- ✔ **Migration:** All of the physical servers that you aim to migrate to virtual environments aren't going to move themselves! This step is all about how you actually accomplish the transition from a collection of physical servers to a set of virtual machines running on a small set of virtualization servers.

- ✔ **Administration:** After everything is up and running, it's tempting to think the work is over. But, just as the old physical infrastructure required constant monitoring and management, so does the new virtualized infrastructure. This step addresses how you manage a virtualized environment on an ongoing basis.

This, of course, is the least sexy phase of virtualization. In fact, it can seem like a slog — especially the administration. After all the excitement of new hardware and software and the thrill of migration, administering the machines seems like, well, like what you used to do.

It's true that the end state of the virtualization journey leaves you managing an infrastructure, which seems not unlike what you used to do. The difference, of course, is that you are managing a more efficient environment with fewer panics due to crashed systems or hardware outages — so if you can live with an administration regime with fewer fire drills, you might actually enjoy this task more than you used to.

Migration and administration are often afterthoughts in a virtualization project, addressed in a reactive mode when problems arise. Don't wait until your virtualization solution is implemented to begin thinking about how you'll live with your virtualized infrastructure on an ongoing basis.

I'll say it again: Virtualization is a journey, not a product, despite what all the software and hardware sales reps tell you. The key to successful virtualization is careful planning and methodical implementation.

Creating Your Virtualization Plan

If you talk to a random sample of people who've implemented virtualization successfully, you'll repeatedly hear one theme: They *planned* their projects. By contrast, if you speak to a sample of people dissatisfied with their virtualization projects, a common theme is that they jumped right in, convinced themselves they couldn't wait to get started, bought the latest product and loaded it up — and then sat back and waited for magic to happen. This latter group can often be found implementing their second virtualization project — but this time planning for how they'll move forward, reinforcing the old joke "why is it there's never enough time to do it right, but there's always enough time to do it over?"

Remember that the planning phase has three high-level tasks:

- **Identifying your use cases:** How do you plan to use virtualization in your infrastructure?

- **Evaluating your organizational structure:** Given the way you're organized, how will that affect the manner in which you implement virtualization, and crucially, how will that affect which products you'll consider implementing?

- **Creating your architecture:** Given the output of the previous two steps, design your virtualization architecture, select your products, identify the necessary capacity for your project, and create an overall implementation plan.

Identify your use cases

How do I apply virtualization? Let me count the ways. Well, there's multiple hosting of applications in identical operating systems emulated by operating system virtualization; there's hosting of mixed OS virtual machines to achieve lower server counts; there's using virtualization software's ability to monitor and automatically restart virtual machines to achieve higher rates of infrastructure uptime; and don't forget achieving lower operations costs through the use of virtualization software to create pools of virtual machines. Chapter 3 discusses the different applications of virtualization technology extensively and outlines the pros and cons of each type.

Identifying your use cases means identifying your objective(s) for using virtualization. This task might be more difficult than it sounds, but it's vital that you think through what you want to achieve through the use of virtualization technology. The great danger is that you might hurriedly select a product and, only after implementing it, find that you have additional requirements that you can't accomplish with the product you've selected.

For example, you might decide to get started with virtualization by using VMware Server. It's an excellent product and is available for free. After you've implemented a large number of instances of the product, you discover that you need higher virtual machine density — in other words, you need to load more virtual machines per individual server hardware than you can achieve with VMware Server. (*Remember:* VMware Server offers hardware emulation on top of an existing operating system. The overhead of going through multiple layers of software reduces performance, which, in turn, reduces the number of virtual machines a given piece of hardware can support. Also, it doesn't manage resource scheduling or allocation either, as it depends on the underlying OS to perform those functions.)

You might think, "So what? It was free, wasn't it? I can just purchase ESX Server from VMware; it installs on bare metal, so I'll increase performance levels, and get the higher VM density we want." That's true, to a point. However, that attitude overlooks the fact that you might have ordered other equipment to run the virtualization software on or to integrate with the hardware the virtualization software runs on. For example, you might have purchased Host Bus Adapters (HBAs) to install in the servers to connect them to network storage. If you now rethink how many servers you'll need because you want higher virtual machine density, perhaps you'll have surplus (expensive) HBAs that you no longer need. Even worse, the HBAs you purchased might have worked just fine with VMware Server, but are not on the VMware ESX Server Hardware Compatibility List (HCL) and are now useless — a complete waste of money.

Perhaps more important than wasted money is wasted time. If you've spent weeks or months implementing a virtualization solution that ends up being inadequate, you've delayed moving forward with a better solution — and you can't recover that time. In an era of rapidly evolving business conditions, throwing away time is irresponsible. And, from a personal perspective, wouldn't it be better to plan what your use cases are and select the right products, rather than have to admit to your boss that you made a mistake and need to start over?

Here are the items you should evaluate when identifying your use case(s):

✔ **Business problem you're trying to address:** What are you trying to solve by implementing virtualization? Are you running out of room in your data center? Do you have a distributed computing topology of identical servers running in remote sites that you'd like to centralize for management and upgrade purposes? Or perhaps your business is growing rapidly, requiring new systems, but you want to get off the "every 15 servers require an additional operations admin to manage the machines" treadmill. Maybe you're looking to virtualization as a way to implement that long-delayed disaster recovery plan. Whatever the problems you're trying to solve, it's important to identify, document, and confirm them with all parts of the organization so that you can have a common goal for your virtualization project.

✔ **Overall business requirements:** Not everyone has the same perspective on the issues facing the business. When identifying the business problem you're trying to address, be sure to poll representatives of every part of the organization. Although a Test and Development group might be delighted with the virtual machine density VMware Server provides, the Facilities group might require far higher density due to overall server growth projections and limited data center space. And Operations might have specific servers (such as high-performance database machines) that must not be put into a virtualized server due to performance requirements, so you'll need to plan for some number of nonvirtualized machines.

✔ **Potential future requirements:** Where is the organization going in terms of its technology? If the company is rapidly growing and expects to increase the number of applications and (even with virtualization) the number of servers but doesn't want to continue to increase operations staff to manage the virtualized servers, a virtualization solution that offers server pooling (or at least a growth path to server pooling) is necessary. Identify what virtualization capabilities you'll need in the future, and yes, be sure to include representatives from all parts of the company who are interested in the computing infrastructure.

✔ **Desired virtual machine density:** What kind of virtual machine load are you hoping to achieve? Given the total number of machines you need to migrate to a virtual infrastructure, the virtual machine density will dictate how many servers you'll need, along with the numbers of complementary products like Host Bus Adapters (HBAs). So, if you need to consolidate five data centers into two and you need to use virtualization to accomplish that, you can estimate how many virtual machines per server you'll need to support. Naturally, the number of machines a server can support is affected by its type and load, but desired virtual machine density gives you a starting point for your use case planning and might help eliminate some products due to inadequate scalability.

✔ **Desired management toolset:** Every virtualization product comes with its own management tool, and some are more comprehensive than others. But many organizations already have implemented a general systems management product, such as HP's OpenView or IBM's Tivoli. If you want to manage your virtualized infrastructure with your existing systems management product, identify that desire up front. Keep in mind, though, that the virtualization world is still in its early days, and many management tools aren't integrated with virtualization. Sad to say, this means that end users often have to perform manual integration between their existing systems management tool and the virtualization software via scripting. Many organizations end up using the general tool to manage the physical servers and the virtualization tool to manage the virtual machines. Not an elegant solution, but it's one that many end up with.

If you ask people for their use cases, they might not understand how to respond. If you ask questions like "how do you back up data from existing machines?" you'll get higher-quality responses. And, instead of asking "how do you want to manage system provisioning in the future?" you can ask a leading question like "what will your daily work be like after a successful virtualization implementation?" Forming the questions like this will encourage people to give more imaginative responses and give you better information about how your virtualized infrastructure really needs to work.

At the end of the use cases step, you should have a good read on how you'll use virtualization now and in the future. You'll also have an idea of how you'll want to manage it, as well as a rough idea of how many virtual machines per server you're aiming for.

Evaluate your organizational structure

I can hear you now: "What does my organizational structure have to do with my virtualization solution?" On the face of it, your question makes sense. Organizations are people, and virtualization is software, so the two shouldn't be interdependent. But, in fact, of all the factors that could irreparably harm your virtualization project, organizational issues are the most likely to torpedo it — because technical problems can always be solved, but people problems are often intractable.

When considering organizational issues, keep in mind these fundamental facts:

✔ **Keep your hands off "my" server:** Many servers in your infrastructure were installed with the old "one application, one server" mindset. (This approach to application topology is discussed extensively in Chapter 8.) As part of the original project plans for acquiring and implementing those applications, somebody somewhere acquired a server to host a particular application. Now, many end user organizations that might have originally funded the project hold the attitude that the server that runs the application is theirs because they funded the acquisition. ("The one who pays the piper calls the tune," in other words.) Telling them that you're planning to move the application off "their" server to become one virtual machine among many on another server might strike them as stepping on their territorial rights. I heard one CIO address this issue by stating he just doesn't tell the end user organization that its application is now hosted on a virtual machine. This approach might work for you, but keep in mind that if an end user finds out inadvertently that you've virtualized "his" server, it might cause friction.

✔ **Keep your hands off "my" server, Part II:** It's not just end users who hold a proprietary attitude toward server ownership. Those responsible for administering certain machines tend to develop an "ownership" perspective and might resist your efforts to move to a virtualized infrastructure because it will affect "their" machines. Turf battles can be incredibly bitter and can be fought over meaningless issues. (In fact, it's often been observed that the less important the issue, the more emotional the discussion.) It's vital to communicate early and often about virtualization initiatives and to present them in a way that demonstrates how virtualization will help operations in their day-to-day work. The question of day-to-day work raises another issue.

✔ **That's our Windows group, and over there, way over there, is our Linux group:** Many organizations have their operations staff organized along platform lines. In other words, there is a Windows operations group, a Linux group, perhaps a Solaris group, and so on. Depending on the organization, each of these groups might contain subgroups organized for administrative efficiency. For example, in a large shop containing hundreds of Windows servers, the overall Windows administration group might have one group dedicated to marketing applications, another to human resources . . . you get the picture. With this kind of organizational structure, your use cases might be affected in the following ways:

  • *Each of the groups might be emotionally committed to "their platform."* It's no secret that Windows and Linux are battling in the marketplace. Well, oftentimes that battle can extend into the relationships between technical personnel in organizations. I have seen a number of IT organizations in which the Linux administrators look down on people working on Windows as being technically inferior, whereas the Windows administrators feel the Linux folks are standoffish and arrogant. I've also seen other varieties of mutual misunderstanding, lack of trust and respect, and unwillingness to consider other perspectives. In situations like these, it's unwise to try and solve problems through a technical solution that requires groups with poor relationships to cooperate. It is far better to find a technical solution that supports the way you currently organize your work.

  Don't mix virtual machine workloads on individual servers. Attempting to mix workloads on a single virtual server might be a problem. If a single server has two different groups attempting to administer it (for example, both a Windows and a Linux operations group have virtual machines residing on the server), you might face turf wars or even simple contention issues over access to the machine. Consequently, many organizations segregate their workloads, locating all of one type on a set of servers and all of another type on a second set of servers. Should you decide to follow this approach, it will affect your use cases because segregating workload types doesn't lend itself very well to server pooling. (You can do it, but it's more complex in configuration and administration.)

- *Mixed workloads narrow the product choice options.* If you have a mixed workload and you want to use a common virtualization product across all hardware, your choice of product during the architecture step will be affected because mixed workloads don't lend themselves to being handled by specific operating system virtualization products. Consequently, you might find your product choice being steered toward virtualization products that can support different guest operating systems. Of course, it's possible to use different virtualization products to support different guest OS types. However, that requires you to implement and manage more than one virtualization product, raising issues of complexity and skill sets. In general, it's better to have your choice of virtualization product driven by your use cases and select a single virtualization product that can support all your use cases.

✔ **I don't know how to do it, but I'll give it a shot:** The skill sets present in your organization are important to understand. If you're an all-Windows shop, using a Linux-based virtualization product like Xen or one of the Linux distributions that integrate Xen might pose problems. You might want to consider Microsoft's Virtual Server — or maybe even wait for Microsoft Windows Server Virtualization.

✔ **I don't know how to do it, but I'll give it a shot, Part II:** The experience level of the operations personnel should also be evaluated. Many people are quite capable of doing rote administration work but aren't ready to take on managing a server pool. If you have a relatively low level of admin skills, you might want to choose your architecture to reflect them. At the very least, you need to consider sending people through training — and giving them a chance to practice. (I cover training issues in the later section, "Performing a pilot implementation.")

Don't overlook the critical importance of people in the virtualization life cycle. Anytime you introduce new technology, you impose change — which many people resist. Assessing the impact of virtualization on your organization is a good investment of time.

Select your architecture

If you've identified your use cases and organizational structure, it's time to take the next step: creating your virtualization architecture. When you create an architecture, what you're really doing is describing the ways you'll use virtualization; your expected application distribution (that is, where specific virtual machines will be located on individual pieces of hardware); what pieces of equipment, networking, storage, and such will need to be in place; and so on.

What you end up with after all this architecturing is a list of key virtualization requirements, a visual representation of your virtualization infrastructure, and a high-level project plan, which will be further fleshed out in the early steps of the implementation phase of your virtualization project.

Selecting your architecture is the key task in your virtualization journey. By bringing together your research on use cases and your organizational work processes, you can sketch out what your final virtualization infrastructure will look like. And, based on the decisions you reach during this task, you'll be guided in your choices of virtualization software, the hardware you'll use as a virtualization server platform, how you'll migrate your existing physical servers to the new virtualized environment, and how you'll ultimately manage your final virtual infrastructure. So it's easy to see that selecting your architecture is an important job that should be carefully thought through.

If you have questions about how you might design your architecture, the major virtualization vendors all publish white papers on their Web sites about the different ways their products can be used. While the white papers promote their products (naturally), by sampling them from several vendors you can get a good sense of common implementation architectures that have been put in place.

Here are the individual pieces of the architecture puzzle:

✔ **Review all the use cases identified in the Use Cases step, including any considerations regarding future needs that would extend current desired use cases.** It's important to draw together all the feedback you've received because the sum of the different use cases might require you to implement a more comprehensive solution than any one use case would require. Document the final use case scenario and ensure buy-in from all interested parties.

✔ **Identify infrastructure implications of your use cases.** If you conclude that you definitely need to reduce operations costs caused by managing hardware, you're probably going to need to look at server pooling. That will cause you to look at certain virtualization products and reject others as inappropriate for your desired use case. Also examine whether your final use case scenario carries implications beyond the server virtualization software itself. For example, if you decide to implement multisystem failover architecture, you need to implement complementary storage virtualization to ensure that virtual machines that automatically migrated to another physical server as a result of some kind of failure are able to reach the same storage available when they were on the original server. Document your decisions about overall infrastructure design.

✔ **Decide how you'll organize your virtual servers.** Which of your current physical servers will you virtualize, for example? And will the resulting virtual machines be all of a single type (such as Windows) or do you want to virtualize different types of systems (for example, both Windows and Solaris)? If the latter, identify each type of server you'll virtualize. Recognize that some of your existing infrastructure might not be suited for virtualization or might impact your choice of products in the implementation phase of the life cycle. For example, do you have HP-UX systems (Hewlett Packard's own flavor of the Unix operating system) that you need to virtualize? If so, your product pool will be much smaller to select from because the major virtualization products don't support HP-UX; for that, you'll need to use a product from Hewlett Packard or choose to leave those servers in the current physical arrangement. If you want to run a multitype virtualization infrastructure, will virtual machines be segregated by type, with each type confined to one or more machines, or will you mix and match according to another scheme? Document your server organization decision.

✔ **Establish your hardware requirements relating to redundancy.** Redundancy refers to having enough hardware resources to avoid any problem relating to hardware outages. The danger of having only a single resource of any type in an infrastructure is that, should that one hardware resource fail, your entire virtualized infrastructure will be stopped dead in its tracks. The vulnerability to outage based on an individual hardware resource is referred to as single point of failure (SPOF) and is a very bad thing. There's a lot of discussion about hardware and SPOF in Chapter 8.

✔ **Create a chart of your overall virtualization architecture.** This chart doesn't have to be fancy, but it needs to include all the main system requirements and elements you've established through the first four steps of this task. You should note the physical requirements of each element (such as a physical server or SAN switch). So, for example, if you've decided to implement redundant hardware resources to avoid SPOF, each physical server should be labeled with its hardware requirements, such as "dual network cards," to indicate the capabilities required for it. The purpose of this chart is to capture the logical design of your virtualization infrastructure. Just putting this together is a valuable exercise because it will force you to examine your assumptions and choose what your final solution will look like.

✔ **Obtain approval of your overall virtualization architecture from all interested parties.** This is where your architecture chart will come in handy. As the old saying goes, a picture is worth a thousand words. An unfocused discussion about virtualization in the abstract would move forward much more quickly with a chart of the draft architecture available for review. This step is absolutely critical for the following reasons:

> *Identify shortcomings.* It will help you identify shortcomings or incorrect assumptions in your architectural design. With many people reviewing the proposed architecture, questions or issues that might have surfaced only after implementation can be identified much earlier, when they're easier to research and solve.

Address concerns. People issues are most likely problems to derail your virtualization project. By having everyone affected review the architecture, this enables you to hear and address everyone's concern early in the process. Perhaps more important, even if you cannot or choose not to modify the architecture to address a particular individual's feedback, just the act of consulting with them is likely to mean they'll be much more positive about the virtualization project. Giving people the chance to be heard is a vital tool in obtaining support. Don't dismiss the importance of giving everyone a chance to review the architecture; it will pay off in the end.

I can't emphasize enough the value of creating a chart of your proposed architecture. Pictures make it much easier for people to understand the future virtualization architecture. Moreover, pictures make your project more "real" and make it easier to generate commitment from everyone. Invest the time in creating a visual representation of your future infrastructure. It's well worth the effort.

After you've completed all these tasks, you're ready to move forward into the implementation phase of the virtualization life cycle. You might have to further modify your architecture based on additional requirements that pop up. (It's amazing how only *after* you're moving forward with a decision that someone new comes along with more information to add.) What's great is that with all of your work on use cases and organizational structure behind you, it will be easy to see where any new requirements will affect your architecture, and you can quickly update it.

Implementing Your Virtualization Solution

Okay, okay. You've done your planning. Now you want to move on to the exciting stuff: deciding which products to buy and then doing some hands-on work.

The important thing to keep in mind is that this phase is where the rubber meets the road, which is to say you're about to commit to a particular virtualization solution and most likely make a financial investment. Up to this point, you've been researching your virtualization options. Perhaps you've done a little experimenting with some free downloaded virtualization software. Now you'll start to spend money, so you want to get it right.

The implementation phase of the virtualization life cycle can be broken down into the following steps.

1. Confirming your planning assumptions and conclusions.

2. Selecting your virtualization software product.

3. Selecting your virtualization hardware.

4. Performing a pilot implementation.

5. Migrating to the new environment.

6. Administering your new virtualized infrastructure.

Each of these steps is described in the following sections.

Confirming your planning assumptions and conclusions

Yes, an agreed upon plan was the output of the planning phase of the virtualization life cycle, which you just completed. That's already done, right? So why would you confirm your plan again?

Just as the old saw has it, a good carpenter measures twice and cuts once. (Sorry about the pun.) The reason good carpenters follow that practice is to avoid making an incorrect measurement, sawing some wood, and then finding out that it's the wrong size, necessitating using another piece of wood — wasting both time and money.

The difference between a carpenter and you is that rather than wasting a board by a mismeasurement, which might cost $50, an incorrect virtualization plan, depending on the products you decide to use, might waste tens or hundreds of thousands of dollars. So inspecting your plan a second time with a keen eye is a good idea.

During your reinspection, you should go over the plan a second time with key project participants and sponsors, communicating that you're about to begin moving forward with the project. The prospect of real money being spent often raises people's interest level and focuses their attention on the project. Be ready to answer more questions and more detailed questions. If you've been having regular meetings, this is the time to make sure everyone attends and is present to agree to move forward with the project.

Your plan review should confirm all of your use cases and organizational assumptions and confirm the correctness of the architecture you designed based on those assumptions. If you find out any new information during this step, use it to update your plan and then go back through the process of getting buy-in from key participants and partners.

Now you're ready to select the products you'll use in your virtualization infrastructure.

Choosing your virtualization software product(s)

Based on the requirements laid out in the plans you just confirmed (see the preceding section), you can now move forward with choosing a virtualization product or products. If you're wondering why there's a plural listed, instead of just assuming you'll choose one virtualization product, remember that virtualization can be applied in many ways. Some of the applications require products beyond virtualization software. For example, if you move to multimachine failover, you need to look at virtualized storage, which requires additional hardware and software. (This goes to show how important it is to define your use cases and applications *before* you start ordering.)

How can you decide which products are the right ones for you? A good way to move forward is to match your use cases against the list of virtualization applications outlined in Chapter 3, where I outline each use case type and note which virtualization products can be used for that use case.

If you take a peek back at Chapter 3, you'll note that, as you move to more complex use cases, your pool of potential products becomes smaller and smaller. Although you have several options for simple virtualization use scenarios, as the requirement for better uptime and more sophisticated failover strategies increases, the number of virtualization products that are appropriate shrinks. Also, you'll undoubtedly find that as the capability of the virtualization software rises, so does the price.

What if you find more than one virtualization product that satisfies your use case scenarios? How can decide which one to select? Flipping a coin wouldn't be the way to go. Here are several items to consider during your decision process:

✔ **Evaluate application software support.** No one buys virtualization for virtualization's sake. The end vision is to run application software more efficiently. Consequently, a critical factor in virtualization software selection is support for your important applications. If you want help when it comes to asking the right kinds of questions, check out Chapter 5, where I describe how to evaluate the level of application support for a given virtualization product. Clearly, the virtualization product that provides the best support environment has a significant advantage.

Today, that winner might very well be VMware, but other virtualization products are catching up fast. The best way to handle this issue is to construct a table with critical applications in rows down the left side and with each potential virtualization product in columns across the top. If an application vendor provides full support for its application running on a particular virtualization product, put a check mark in the corresponding box. The virtualization product with the most check marks will be your favored candidate.

✔ **Evaluate the cost.** A decision about what's best often can change when financial resources are taken into account, which is why most folks fly coach and don't drive Mercedes. Although your use cases and application support evaluation might point toward one product, "is it afford-able?" is a key question. I've worked with companies that created scenarios about how they would move to virtualization and implement their virtualized infrastructure, and then they had to discard them when they realized concrete financial realities. (If you want to understand how to do a financial evaluation of a virtualization solution, take a look at Chapter 6.)

✔ **Run more than one virtualization product through a pilot.** If more than one product seems viable after the previous two steps, consider putting them through a pilot program. (Pilot programs are described a little later in the chapter.) If the products under consideration are very similar and cost about the same, doing a pilot for all of them probably isn't that important. Because there isn't much difference, the downside of choos-ing one over another is pretty small. Performing a dual (or triple) pilot is more critical if you find significant differences between the products available. For example, VMware's DRS and Virtual Iron's product offer roughly the same functionality, but one is roughly 80 percent less expen-sive than the other. At that level of cost difference, it might be worth-while to evaluate both in a pilot to see whether the less expensive product meets your needs.

Your virtualization product choices are affected by the hardware you'll be using to host and integrate with the virtualization software. VMware ESX Server only supports certain hardware products, whereas Xen-based paravir-tualization requires modified operating systems — unless you have physical servers containing the latest virtualization-enabled chips from Intel or AMD. Therefore, it's important that you conduct your software selection and your hardware selection in parallel and cross-reference your decisions to ensure that the total package will work correctly.

After you go through your evaluation exercise, you'll have no more than one or two candidate products for your virtualization project. At this point, you're ready to select hardware.

Choosing your virtualization hardware

Choosing virtualization hardware is one of the most important — and tricky — decisions you'll make during the course of your virtualization project.

Many organizations make a blithe assumption that they'll reuse their existing hardware, invest a little in virtualization software, and then sit back and watch the savings mount. That might not work.

The primary issue with the reuse scenario is figuring out what virtualization capability you'll have if you reuse existing hardware. Many of the servers in today's data centers were purchased with a "one application, one server" mentality. These servers were perfect for running with the loads typical of that mentality: cheap, easy to purchase from half a dozen vendors, and easy to install and maintain. However, in a virtualized infrastructure, those machines encounter significant drawbacks, primarily focused around the lack of sufficient resources to perform robust virtualization. These cheap and cheerful servers lack sufficient memory capacity and available slots to provide production-quality virtualization support. If you plan to use virtualization as a key component in your software infrastructure (as you should), using appropriate hardware is fundamental, and you should fully understand all of your options and choices. (You can read about virtualization hardware in more detail in Chapter 8.)

Capacity planning

One thing to keep in mind is that you'll need to select hardware that's capable of supporting the load capacity assumptions you made in the Architecture step of your virtualization life cycle. Although a good input into these assumptions is the claims of the vendor, you should also validate these claims in your pilot program. After all, it's not unheard of for vendors to make claims for their products that aren't borne out in real-world circumstances. Moreover, every environment is different, and establishing the requirements of yours is really the only important thing, no matter what the vendor asserts.

This brings you to a task that you might not be that familiar with: capacity planning. This task has fallen into disuse over the past few years as the price of hardware has plummeted. *Capacity planning* refers to the process of analyzing total load and calculating what hardware should be purchased to ensure full utilization while avoiding insufficient capacity to meet peak requirements. Capacity planning was discarded in favor of buying new hardware if loads increased beyond the carrying capacity of existing hardware. Of course, what accompanied that approach was the unfortunate side effect of underutilized hardware, overstuffed data centers, and skyrocketing energy costs.

The move to virtualization in an attempt to increase hardware utilization rates brings you full circle to the old discipline of capacity planning. Capacity planning is particularly important if you want to use some of the more sophisticated applications of virtualization (high availability, for example) that require storage virtualization. With so many more components in the virtualization infrastructure, selecting hardware for the entire architecture and ensuring that every part of the infrastructure is capable of supporting the expected loads is extremely important; this is because the lowest-capacity component of the infrastructure becomes the limiting factor of the total system throughput. In other words, one low-performance component imposes its limitations on the entire virtualization infrastructure, even if every other component has very high capabilities. Consequently, reviewing the capacity of each component is vital.

By querying your hardware vendors and doing some Internet research, you should get a rough estimate of the capacity of each component in your proposed architecture. By mapping the capacity of hardware to the requirements you derived from your use cases, you should be able to develop a good idea of what type of equipment you'll need. So, for example, if your use cases indicate that the peak network throughput of the number of virtual machines you're planning to load on an individual server comes to 600MB per second, you know that you'll need that level of network capacity in your servers.

By performing this kind of analysis for all the components in your architecture, you can document your hardware requirements, which will direct you toward specific hardware products.

Getting help

Does the topic of capacity planning seem daunting? Never fear. There are a couple of products available that you can use to perform capacity planning for your virtualization infrastructure.

One comes from a company called PlateSpin. PlateSpin is better known for its physical-to-virtual (also called P2V) software, which is discussed in Chapter 9. PlateSpin's PowerRecon product, though, is a planning tool that includes capacity-planning capabilities, and is capable of working with products from VMware, XenSource, Microsoft, and Virtual Iron. PlateSpin offers several versions of PowerRecon, including a version for free. To learn more about PowerRecon, go to www.platespin.com/products/powerrecon.

Another product is available from VMware itself. VMware Capacity Planner does just what it says. Naturally, it is limited to working with VMware products. Also, it must be obtained through a VMware partner that is certified to use the product. Nevertheless, if you're building a complex VMware ESX Server-based system, it might very well be worth considering using VMware Capacity Planner. You can find out more about the product at www.vmware.com/products/capacity_planner.

Even if you don't take advantage of capacity-planning tools, all is not lost. You can check the support forums of the vendors to see what kind of results other users have gotten in terms of hardware capacity. VMware has started user groups that can be a rich source of real-world experience. And, of course, there's always the technical person's best friend: Google.

Cost justification

The flip side of capacity planning is budgeting because cost usually directly correlates with hardware performance. While running through your hardware options, you should keep a running budget for each architecture option. (You can use the spreadsheets from Chapter 6 to help you do this.) This enables you to understand the overall costs for each set of choices you have for implementing virtualization.

In any case, when you move forward to get authorization to actually purchase your software and hardware choices, you'll undoubtedly be asked to justify your selections and might be queried about whether you considered other options. Having a concrete set of documentation on the different options that were considered, along with a list of pros and cons for each option, can be enormously valuable in gaining approval for your final choice. (For more information on how to create a financial analysis of your virtualization project, please see Chapter 6.)

With the selection of your virtualization software and hardware products behind you, you're now ready to roll your sleeves up and do some actual technical work. Are you ready?

Performing a pilot implementation

Like capacity planning, formal pilot implementations have fallen into disfavor over the past few years, discarded in favor of informal, agile systems development. Can you say "we don't have time to really do anything formal" and the ever-popular "we can't afford to do a pilot"? The latter phrase is a particular favorite of mine because it demonstrates a "penny wise, pound foolish" attitude that invariably imposes larger long-run costs than would have been invested in a pilot program.

As you can tell, I'm a big fan of formal pilot programs. They're absolutely critical for key infrastructure technologies like virtualization. Simply put, if the wrong choices are put into production, you won't have just one application that doesn't work right; rather, every application will be affected. In today's computer-intensive businesses, putting complete system performance at risk like this is unacceptable. You might ask, then, what is a pilot implementation?

Is your management unsupportive of pilot programs, viewing them as "throwaway efforts?" Many organizations are more supportive of projects called prototypes, seeing them as sort of mini-me versions of the final implementation — kind of a rolling start on the real rollout of the project. As Shakespeare said it best: "A rose by any other name would smell as sweet." My advice is to cheerfully call it a prototype and treat it like a pilot program.

A *virtualization pilot* is, essentially, an implementation of a proposed architecture with an aim of gathering valuable information about the proposed production architecture, confirming the accuracy of assumptions that went into product choice and capacity planning, and modifying the architecture to incorporate any discoveries from the pilot.

Here's how you should go about performing your virtualization pilot implementation:

✔ **Select a representative subset of your final production environment.** A pilot is valuable only to the extent that it accurately reflects the final production environment. Doing a pilot program with only the easy systems to virtualize (or without stressing the infrastructure with performance-demanding applications) won't give you good insight into what your true virtualization experience will be. Worse, performing a low-quality pilot implementation can create an overly optimistic perspective on virtualization with the potential for problems further on down the line. Choose pilot systems with an eye toward ensuring they're an accurate sample of your final set of systems.

✔ **Install a mini-production environment, including both hardware and software.** This means implementing a complete representation of your complete architecture. If you're planning to use a SAN for virtual machine storage, be sure to install a small version of your selected SAN solution or carve out a small slice of your production SAN to use for your pilot. As you run through your pilot, you might find out things about the infrastructure that are at odds with your expectation. For example, your selected SAN solution might not have the total throughput needed or it might not integrate well with your current backup processes. Be sure to use the same virtualization hardware and software products you'll eventually use in production. Don't be tempted to use a lower-level product in the hopes you'll learn enough from it. You won't.

If you're planning a significant rollout of virtualization that will require lots of new hardware purchases, you might be able to talk the vendor into letting you borrow enough hardware to perform your pilot. Even if you have to purchase the equipment for your pilot, you might be able to convince vendors to give you lower pricing based on the fact that you'll eventually be ordering lots more.

✔ **Migrate your pilot systems.** When you have the virtualization infrastructure in place, move your current systems into it. You have several migration options: manual installs, vendor-specific automation tools, and third-party automation tools. (See Chapter 9 for more info on this task.) It's a good idea to try more than one migration approach to see what works well for you. Don't be surprised if the migration is harder and less methodical than you expect. Be sure to keep good notes on your migration experience as they will be invaluable as you perform the big migration necessary to move to a production environment.

✔ **Manage the pilot implementation.** When you have the pilot infrastructure up and running, exercise the systems with representative workloads. Perform regular transactions. Run regular reports. The objective is to run the pilot as though it's a real production environment, so the testing you perform should mirror what these systems do while in production. Watch and document the following three key areas during the pilot.

- *Manage individual virtual machines.* Each virtual machine should be similar to what it was like when it was a physical system. Therefore, examine how running virtual machines is like and unlike running the same system in a physical environment.

- *Monitor individual and overall virtualization performance.* Every virtualization product provides some management mechanism. Some are more comprehensive than others. For your pilot implementation, use the virtualization management products you're considering and get a feel for how easy or difficult, how comprehensive, and how informative they are. (More information on management options is available in Chapter 10.)

- *Perform regular backups.* In production, making sure that data is safe and can be easily restored is incredibly important. Use your pilot program to ascertain whether the virtualization products you're evaluating can successfully back up your data. More important, evaluate how well the virtualization products map into your current backup process. Many organizations find that virtualization simplifies backups because virtualized storage is often part of a virtualization project, but you must assess whether that's true for your organization.

A pilot program is designed to be a bounded experiment to gain knowledge. There's always a temptation to move the pilot directly into production. That's an option, and perhaps it's one that you should consider if appropriate. However, moving something into production imposes far higher expectations about performance, support, and so on — and if you're not prepared to meet those expectations, the move can actually harm the perception of virtualization because people will assume the problem is with the technology rather than the situation.

A better approach is to set a bounded timeframe for your pilot program. During the period of the pilot implementation, carefully document your experiences with the implementation. Identify any problems that were puzzling or required intervention. Pay attention to what kind of support you received from your vendors (and if you use outside services for your implementation, how the service providers supported you as well). Have regular weekly meetings to evaluate the pilot's progress and any issues that have arisen. Of course, also note any upside surprises — stuff like better performance than you expected or easier migration than forecast.

It's important for you to assess the pilot's overall performance against your assumptions about your virtualization architecture. Assess these key questions.

✔ Were you able to achieve the virtual machine density you expected?

✔ Did migrations go better or worse than envisioned?

✔ Did your virtualized operating systems and applications function correctly?

✔ How well did your virtualized operating systems and applications actually perform?

Validate all your architectural assumptions against your actual experience. Create a list of areas in which your assumptions were met and areas in which the pilot implementation fell short. For the areas where the pilot fell short, create a mitigation plan to ensure these shortcomings don't carry over into a production environment, where they might cause serious problems.

After the conclusion of the pilot, perform an official debriefing with attendees from all the organizations that you involved during the use case work you did earlier. Make sure that everyone is included. Review your pilot program's assumptions, the representative sample of applications you migrated into the pilot, how the migration went, how management of the virtualization solution was accomplished, and relevant feedback, both positive and negative. Highlight areas in which the pilot fell short of your project assumptions and explicitly address how you'll mitigate the problems in the production system.

Some of this material might seem repetitious, but don't worry about that. Even though you've been tracking this virtualization stuff like a hawk, most of the attendees at your debriefing probably haven't given a thought to the project since the last time you spoke to them — and they've forgotten everything you discussed. A review brings them back up to speed and ensures a common framework of understanding. Your debrief review also gives you an opportunity to control the discussion and influence its outcome.

You spend all day, every day, working on your virtualization project. For everyone else, it's one out of a hundred things to think about. Keep that in mind when you explain for the hundredth time why you've set something up a certain way or why you believe you can achieve eight-to-one virtual machine density.

The goal for your pilot debriefing session is to reach agreement on the next step. Assuming your pilot outcome is positive, you should receive a go-ahead with approval to begin implementation of your production environment, including software and hardware purchase. You should also reach approval on moving forward with the migration of physical production servers.

Migrating to your production virtualization environment

Okay, the bad news is that migration is definitely the heavy lifting part of the virtualization life cycle. Moving to the new virtualized infrastructure will be a challenge, so you might as well acknowledge that fact — and put your game face on.

Moving production systems requires careful planning to ensure that the systems are successfully migrated while imposing the least possible downtime. (The goal is no downtime at all, of course.) It's unlikely that your production systems won't be down to some extent, so the key goal of planning is to minimize migration time.

You should have some experience with moving systems from physical to virtual (so-called P2V in virtualization parlance) from your pilot implementation. The difference is that your pilot efforts probably were fairly relaxed; after all, if you messed up something, you could go back and do it over, even if it took additional time.

In production migration, by contrast, you have much less room for error. You'll be under tight time constraints, with pressure to guarantee that all data is accurately brought across. Good thing you performed that pilot where you experimented and discovered the best and most efficient way to perform system migration, eh?

As I mention in my discussion of pilot implementation (see the preceding section), you have three migration options:

- ✔ **Vendor-specific migration tools:** Depending on the virtualization product you've chosen, the vendor might provide P2V tools that you can use. For example, VMware provides a tool called VMware Converter to migrate systems to VMware's virtualization software. One thing to keep in mind about these tools is that you must assess which operating systems they'll convert. VMware Converter supports migrating only Windows machines, not Linux. This limitation might not be a problem for you, depending on your use cases, but it's important to recognize. In general, migrating Windows machines is typically easier than migrating Linux machines, due in part to Windows systems having a more standardized file system configuration. In any case, you should evaluate whether your vendor has migration tools available.

- ✔ **Third-party tools:** Several vendors out there provide P2V tools. PlateSpin is one well-known company in this area. Because the migration companies focus on just this one aspect of virtualization, their tools might provide fuller functionality for your purposes. PlateSpin provides a free migration-analysis tool that is designed to help you perform capacity planning. As you might expect, this tool provides data that can easily be used as input to migrating your systems via the PlateSpin migration tool.

✔ **Manual migration:** This is the hardest option in terms of work because it requires reinstalling all software and performing a backup of the data on the physical machine and restoring the data on the new virtual machine. Although doing manual migrations in a pilot environment might have been alright because you had only a few systems, attempting to do manual migrations with dozens, hundreds, or even thousands of systems makes manual migration repugnant.

Far better solutions are the preceding automated options in this list. Keep in mind, however, that the automated solutions sometimes (perhaps often) prove inadequate to handle every server. Automated solutions typically fall down in more complex migrations (which is, of course, just where you desire them the most!). A good policy is to attempt automated migration options first and turn to manual migration only when necessary.

Whatever mode of P2V migration you select, don't forget that it's not enough to migrate the operating system, software components, and application. You always have data to consider as well. When migrating data, keep the following in mind:

✔ **For file-based data** (that is, data files that reside in regular files on the hard drive), you can migrate the data via one of the automated migration solutions, assuming that a useful P2V migration tool is available. Otherwise, you'll need to back up the data and restore the backup onto the virtual machine's file system.

✔ **For data contained in a database,** you have a couple of options. You might be able to use one of the automated P2V products to transfer the database data storage. If not, you'll have to use the database's backup mechanism and move the backup to the new virtual machine and restore it into the new database.

Because the migration process needs to reduce the overall amount of system downtime, it's really important to have a migration plan, with every step tested and documented. When it comes time to do your migration, 90 percent of the work should be rote execution; only exceptions should require evaluation and intervention. It's worth doing a dry run with your instructions to validate their clarity and effectiveness. Whatever you do, don't attempt to migrate in a hurried fashion, because that could lead to execution problems and thereby cause increased system outage. (For more information on P2V migration, see Chapter 9.)

Administering your new virtualized infrastructure

The final step in the virtualization life cycle is managing the infrastructure on an ongoing basis. Administering the infrastructure falls into the "last but not least" category due to its importance. If your virtualized infrastructure can't be managed efficiently, all the putative financial benefits in the world won't make up for the problems you'll experience daily.

This is especially true due to the hard-won system management battle that has gone on over the past two decades. Not so long ago, IT organizations had little choice but to manage their infrastructures by hand. If a machine needed a configuration change, someone had to go to the machine, log onto the console, perform the change, and then save the modified configuration. It's easy to envision how labor-intensive that is, particularly given the explosive growth in the total number of systems discussed several times in this book.

Early attempts at system management involved IT administrators creating their own tools via scripting languages, shell scripts, and so on (and, by the way, there's still plenty of this approach being used even today). This approach has some drawbacks, of course. For one, it depends on having staff that can understand how to interface with the different systems well enough to write tools to monitor and control them. Building a tool is always more difficult than using one, which means that many organizations didn't have the right talent on board to create their own tools.

Another drawback is that every IT organization writing its own system management tool ends up with a tool specific to it. It bears all the cost of developing and maintaining the tool.

Finally, it's very inefficient to have your own tool because any time you add staff, the new employee has to learn your system, thereby imposing a learning curve. And, of course, if the person who did the tool development leaves, you have no one to maintain and improve the tool, leaving you high and dry.

Clever software vendors spotted an opportunity in this system management situation and created system management software products. Common system management products include HP's OpenView, IBM's Tivoli, and CA's Unicenter.

The commercial vendors can spread their costs across many customers, thereby reducing the cost for any particular user organization. The vendors can afford to invest in understanding how to integrate every important hardware and software product with their tool. And user organizations that implement one of the commercial products can hire people already acquainted with the software they use, reducing the learning period for new employees.

One significant drawback to the commercial system management products is that they're expensive; in fact, many smaller IT organizations find they can't afford to purchase the products. To address the cost issue, several open source system management products have been developed, although they typically present other issues, primarily in the area of completeness of implementation and ease of use.

So how does virtualization affect the world of system management, with its assortment of home-grown, expensive commercial, and inexpensive open source products?

In a phrase: Virtualization adds complications.

First off, the commercial system management products are just beginning to incorporate management of virtualized systems. Their approach primarily has been to treat virtual machines just like physical machines and to monitor and manage the same things as always: performance levels, software availability, and so on.

However, managing a number of virtual machines individually isn't the same as managing a collection of virtual machines and treating them as one large resource to be managed as a whole. In this regard, the commercial system management products have not yet begun to address virtualization itself. Certainly the commercial systems have no mechanism to support more advanced virtualization like failover or server pooling; the systems have always left that kind of capability to other software products that provided specific functionality — application vendors' own clustering products to provide high availability functionality, for example.

All of the virtualization products themselves have management systems, which vary in their completeness. VMware, as you might expect, has the most comprehensive management mechanism, befitting the leader in the field. The less established virtualization products like Xen have more rudimentary management systems. (On the other hand, they're far less expensive than VMware, so there's something of a tradeoff between cost and comprehensiveness.) Something else to keep in mind is that the virtualization vendors' management products manage only their own products. Although this is quite understandable, if you use more than one virtualization solution, you'll be faced with needing to use more than one management tool for your virtualized infrastructure.

Nevertheless, as a user, you're faced with the challenge of deciding how to administer your virtualized environment. What can you do in a world where established management products don't yet fully support managing a virtualized environment and where virtualization software management products address a virtualization environment but don't attempt to address the entire IT infrastructure? Here are some possible solutions.

✔ **Accept that you'll use more than one tool:** One option is to recognize that you'll need to use more than one administration mechanism for your virtualized environment. Although it's not desirable, it certainly can be done. This dual administration situation is likely to be temporary, as the major system management players definitely want their products to be capable of administering a complete infrastructure, whether physical, virtual, or a mix. The move to administering virtualization is likely to be gradual, with the initial administration capability being the ability to manage a collection of individual virtual machines on a physical server. More advanced functionality (such as server pooling) is likely to come much more slowly and might, in fact, never really be implemented.

✔ **Postpone virtualization until your existing management tool supports it:** A second option is to wait to move to virtualization until your favorite system management product is upgraded to administer virtualized environments. Although this approach definitely reduces the burden of needing to train staff on a new administration product, it also has the effect of significantly postponing the use of virtualization. This option is probably not an option for all but the most conservative of IT organizations because the financial benefits of virtualization are so large.

✔ **Create your own management solution:** A third option harkens back to the days before system management software was available. Remember how some IT shops rolled out their own management software by creating scripts? Well, today some IT organizations are creating their own integrated virtualization and general system management software. They can achieve this because both the virtualization management and system management products offer interfaces called APIs (an acronym for Application Programming Interface) as well as SDKs (an acronym for Software Development Kit) to enable end users to write programs that can control the management software.

These IT organizations have combined the two different management software products by writing "glue" code (glue because the code permanently attaches two separate pieces of software; a weak pun, but technologists aren't necessarily known for their robust sense of humor).

Essentially, these glued systems enable IT administrators to execute commands on the general system management software that call into the virtualization management software and cause it to perform certain virtualization administration tasks. Therefore, the overall administration of the entire IT infrastructure can be done through the general system management product.

One challenge this glued virtualization management mechanism poses is that it confronts the IT organization with issues it faced before the availability of the general system management products: the need to be able to write tools to manage systems, which tends to be much more difficult than merely using tools to manage the systems. Although writing glue code isn't nearly as difficult as writing an entire management product, as was formerly required, it isn't trivial, either.

Also, writing one's own glue code still poses the same issues IT organizations faced when doing their own custom system management software: the need to absorb all the development burden and cost and the need to provide training and absorb the learning curve time of new employees.

You probably have questions about virtualization management that go beyond general issues of availability and overall mechanisms. Your questions probably revolve around managing specific virtualization products and what options there are for them. I go into more detail about specific virtualization management tools and how to use them in Chapter 10, so check there for answers to your more detailed questions.

Open source glue

One way forward in the whole virtualization management mechanism mess involves a relatively new development in the software world: open source software. Open source software is distributed with a very liberal license that encourages sharing. The distribution also includes the source code for the software product itself. This enables end users to access and modify the product's source code themselves.

The open source framework can help organizations with what I've described as their "glue code" issues because one organization can write some glue code, make the code available to another organization that wants to download the product and is willing to live with the license conditions, and allow that organization to modify the received code and use it internally.

Open source licenses allow organizations that have obtained and modified source code to then further distribute the modified code (this is called *redistribution*) to others so that they can take advantage of both the original functionality of the product as well as the improvements created by the second organization.

With this kind of mutual improvement, open source users can have their cake and eat it, too. They can custom create certain functionality, but with redistribution and modification rights, others can contribute additional functionality, making it possible for organizations to gain the benefits of custom code while circumventing the need to be the sole support for the product.

It is very likely that open source versions of glue code to integrate system management products with virtualization management products will be created and made available for download and improvement. Frankly, this is a very exciting development made possible by the growth of open source. Even five years ago, the thought that open source would be the mechanism for reducing the burden of custom code would have been ludicrous. However, with the rapid rise in the availability — and adoption — of open source, it's almost a certainty that IT organizations will have the option of custom integration of their virtualization infrastructure into their system management tool while avoiding the high cost of self-developed code.

Chapter 8

Choosing Hardware for Your Server Virtualization Project

*O*ne of the clear benefits of virtualization as a technology is that it makes hardware use more efficient. By abstracting the relationship between the operating system and the underlying server hardware, virtualization enables multiple operating systems to operate on a single server, thereby more efficiently using the hardware.

Virtualization is particularly attractive today, given the increasing power of machines powered by commodity x86-based chips from Intel and AMD. (The *x86-based* part of the name comes from the fact that they're based on designs that descend from a chip whose name ended with 86; the *commodity* part stems from the fact that vast quantities of the chip are sold each year.) Every year or so, these companies deliver a new generation of chips that provides twice as much power as the previous generation. Instead of running the same old software on more and more powerful machines, virtualization ensures you can use more of the total capacity of the machines by increasing the overall software load on them.

The next question, of course, is exactly *what* hardware you should run your virtualization software on. In a curious way, virtualization makes your hardware choice more important than ever before because it ushers in a world that's more complex than the old "one application, one server" world that made selecting hardware so simple. Also, you have a number of options of what type of hardware to select, dictated in part by what type of virtualization software and use profile you'll be putting into production. Finally, you should be aware of upcoming improvements in the hardware you'll be using as your virtualization platform so that you can begin to plan for the future.

This chapter provides a guide to help you understand how you should decide what hardware your virtualization software will run on and what factors to take into account during your decision-making process.

Taking Hardware Seriously

The typical practice of IT operations in the past has been "one application, one server." In other words, for every significant application, the IT organization dedicated a piece of hardware and an operating system to it. You can see where this is going: If you have 300 applications, you have 300 servers.

But why would the IT organization arrange the data center in this fashion? After all, all modern operating systems are capable of *multitasking* — that is to say, running multiple applications at the same time, doling out access to the underlying resources according to a scheduling algorithm, and ensuring that every application gets its fair share.

Here are a number of reasons for the historical practice of "one application, one server":

✔ **It's simple.** There's never any question about what's running where. Every server is identified as serving a particular purpose. And, because applications usually require particular versions of operating systems, it's much easier to dedicate a machine per application, thereby avoiding a typical problem confronted when trying to share hardware among applications: application A requires version 3.1.7 of an operating system, including certain patches, whereas application B requires version 3.1.7 of the same operating system with a different set of patches, whereas application C requires version 3.1.8 of the operating system.

Actually, this description is a simplification of the scenario an IT organization usually confronts. Applications ordinarily require a whole set of underlying software (for example, databases, application servers, and Web servers), each of which needs to be installed and configured in a certain way. Given the combinatorial challenge of keeping all these requirements straight, it often seems much simpler to give every application its own machine, which ensures that its server can be tuned just right for the application's specific requirements. So, overall, it's simpler to put every application on its own dedicated hardware. Of course, over time, this tends to cause server sprawl — machines multiplying faster than rabbits on an island with no predators — but it seems simpler at first.

✔ **"One application, one server" ensures there's never any question about resource contention.** Particularly in the past, when servers weren't so powerful, it wasn't easy to guarantee that applications sharing a server would each get enough processing power to ensure quick response, necessary scalability, and enough reserve processing power to respond to spikes in application demand. Indeed, so underpowered were machines that when one application received extra demand, others would often be starved of processing cycles. Following a "one application, one server" rule reduces the likelihood of resource contention — and, of course, if you have poor application performance due to resource contention, then people contention isn't far behind. To avoid arbitrating between irate users, IT organizations often find it easier to give every application its own machine. This problem of underpowered servers isn't much of a problem anymore, given how powerful machines have become, but the practices appropriate to a long-gone generation of machines live on.

✔ **"One application, one server" aligns with company policies and politics.** Many IT projects are initiated and funded by the business units that will actually use the resulting application. Part of the project plan usually addresses hardware requirements and might include procuring hardware to run the application. Business units that have funded a project that purchased hardware often have a proprietary attitude toward the equipment; in other words, they think of the server as "theirs." Proprietary feelings being what they are, funding organizations don't usually like to share "their" machine. Although this attitude made some sense in the days of low-powered servers, it's not really rational today, when "their" server might be taxed only at the 10 or 15 percent utilization level while running "their" application.

Another reason why "one application, one server" is used is that it makes chargeback (charging business units for the IT services they use) much simpler. Dividing up the cost of a single server among several different organizations is difficult and likely to lead to a series of heated discussions as the business units complain they're being charged more than they should be, based on their use of the overall machine resources. It's far simpler to give every business unit their own machine, even though it's kind of wasteful of computing resources.

Overall, moving beyond the "one application, one server" paradigm would be rational, given the power now available in hardware. Rational isn't the same as realistic, however, and this attitude continues unabated, despite no longer being necessary. Incidentally, this territorial approach toward machine "ownership" is often a barrier to successful virtualization projects, so it's good to keep in mind if you're working on one.

Don't think that such territorialism is solely felt by business units; many IT organizations have different groups or departments that also think of servers as "theirs," which can cause problems for virtualization projects. In fact, this can be a bigger problem with IT organizations than with business units because IT groups are much more aware of machine topologies and much more likely to know if "their" machine has been moved or is being shared, and therefore they're more likely to put up a fuss. Of all the reasons for continuing the "one application, one server" practice, this is the least logical but the most powerful.

✔ **Assigning a single application per server ensures good isolation of applications.** If you run multiple applications on a single server, you can suffer from applications affecting one another. For example, if one application is upgraded and needs the machine rebooted for the upgrade to take effect, guess what — the other application has to be restarted as well, whether convenient or not. Even if you manage coordinating the management of coexisting applications, you can be blindsided by the impact one application might have on another. Should one application crash and take down the operating system, any other applications running on the server would also be taken down.

This situation of one application's crash taking down other applications isn't that common on Unix-based machines. The Unix operating system (and its spiritual descendent, Linux) was designed from the ground up to provide good application isolation and to carefully partition user applications from the operating system, ensuring that an application crash couldn't affect the underlying operating systems.

However, the reliability of Windows-based servers, particularly early versions, was, to put it kindly, much less stable. Consequently, to ensure that applications couldn't affect one another, the default practice in most shops has been to install only a single important application on a particular server. In that way, despite the potential for application problems causing systems to go down, the overall robustness of the IT infrastructure was enhanced through maintaining redundant hardware.

None of the preceding reasons are appropriate in today's hardware environment. Servers are now so powerful that running a single application on them is extremely wasteful of processing power and leads to server sprawl. Obviously, an architecture like virtualization that can more efficiently use the power of today's servers makes a ton of economic sense.

If your organization uses the "one application, one server" approach, examine whether that approach still makes sense during your virtualization planning process. You might find that you're working according to assumptions no longer applicable in today's computing environment.

Just having more powerful machines doesn't solve the issue of version control and patch levels nor does it do away with the need for application isolation. If an application is badly written and runs on a crash-vulnerable operating system, having more powerful hardware underneath it all offers no protection. Something else has to be added to the mix — and that something else is virtualization. Virtualization is uniquely suited to address a slew of issues facing corporate entities while enabling organizations to take advantage of powerful commodity servers. By hosting multiple operating systems on a single piece of hardware, better use is made of the machine resources while still isolating the applications within virtual machines, ensuring that problems with one virtual machine won't affect another.

Running multiple virtual machines on a single server can cause a different sort of problem though, as the next section makes clear.

The multiple-eggs-in-one-basket syndrome

If you decide to load multiple operating systems onto a single server, it stands to reason that doing so makes all the hosted applications loaded on those systems vulnerable to a hardware failure. In a way, virtualization can increase the hardware risk profile of an organization, because more applications rely on a single piece of hardware.

In the old "one application, one server" world, if a server developed a hardware problem that took the server out of commission, only one application was rendered unavailable. With virtualization, multiple applications — 5, 10, even 20 applications — can all be dependent on one server. That server presents a risk — a single point of failure (SPOF). If that machine goes down, numerous groups of users can be unable to access the applications necessary for their work.

Consequently, it's easy to see that virtualization raises the hardware risk exposure for organizations. This explains why organizations that begin *server consolidation* — moving a number of operating systems from individual servers to a single server — rapidly begin to explore more advanced uses of virtualization like load balancing and system redundancy, as described in Chapter 3. And, as organizations move to the more sophisticated uses of virtualization, they begin to consider virtualizing their storage as well as using clustering to ensure data access.

The need to move beyond "one application, one server" and the awareness of the risks of SPOF mean that hardware selection becomes more important for the virtualized enterprise. Living with the SPOF characteristics of commodity servers was acceptable for the "one application, one server" world because the number of people inconvenienced by a hardware failure wasn't that large. Continuing vulnerability to SPOF needs to be rethought in the world of "many applications, one server," because many more users will be inconvenienced due to a hardware failure. Beyond this critical issue, of course, lie the more common issues of what type of server is best suited for virtualization, along with the need to understand how virtualization affects the key resources that comprise a server: processor, memory, network interfaces, and storage.

Remember the term SPOF. It stands for single point of failure and indicates something you want to avoid — by using virtualization failover or implementing server pooling, for example — as you move to virtualization. Any SPOFs increase the risk of system availability, and SPOF is much more dangerous in a virtualized world because so many more systems rely on a single piece of hardware; without a strategy to deal with hardware SPOF, you're facing unacceptable levels of risk.

The Big Four resources of servers

In the old days, project planners consulted with the hardware wizards of the IT organization, outlining storage requirements, hourly and daily transaction volumes, response requirements in terms of screen-loading times, and so on. Taking all this information in, the wizards reviewed their loading charts, cast spells, recited incantations, and then consulted with hardware vendors, eventually issuing a recommendation about what hardware should be purchased to effectively run the project application. Capacity planning was particularly important because hardware was so expensive; if you purchased a machine that ended up having only 50 percent of the necessary capacity, you might have just bought an $80,000 doorstop.

In those times, capacity planning was particularly frustrating because it was executed with the vision of a static world. Machines were so expensive that you never wanted to buy more than you forecasted you'd need. Unfortunately, the real world is anything but static, and application loads are notorious for increasing well beyond what planners envision. So, the old days were littered with expensive, outgrown machines made obsolete by the rapid growth of users and transactions.

Because of the onward march of Moore's Law, which refers to the yearly doubling of processing power offered by computer chips, most organizations have long since left behind the traditional practice of capacity planning. Commodity economics has meant that inexpensive machines have plenty of processing power available for the average application. If you're running a server at only 15 percent of capacity, it's unlikely that any resource will become a bottleneck in terms of server performance. Consequently, most organizations have discarded their loading charts, forgotten their incantations, and sent their capacity-planning groups off to a retirement home.

Guess what? Virtualization makes capacity planning relevant once more. As you load servers more heavily, you're likely to use all the capacity of some part of the server, whether processor or network card, which then throttles the overall performance of your system. In other words, if one hardware element of the system hits its maximum capability, the system has reached its maximum performance, even if other hardware elements still have capacity in reserve. The term *bottleneck* describes a situation in which one element is constraining overall system performance.

You must account for four key resources in your virtualization hardware planning. Depending on the numbers of virtual machines you plan to host on a particular piece of hardware, as well as the profiles of the applications you run in those virtual machines, you can estimate your hardware needs. This estimation enables you to select the proper hardware platform for your virtualization infrastructure.

So, what are these key hardware resources?

Processors

For many years, the central processing unit (CPU) was the primary point of comparison between machines. Through the various generations of chips (such as Intel Pentium, Pentium III, and now Intel Core and even Core Duo), the relentless focus was on the raw increase in processing power. People bought machines based on how many megahertz or gigahertz the machine's processor had.

Today, that discussion has become more nuanced. Because increases in processing cycles (that is, how many megahertz or gigahertz the processor operates at) increase the overall power required by the processor, energy use has become an important point of comparison among processors. The increased power consumption of chips increases the internal operating temperature of the computer, which can lead to component failures. In addition, the heat thrown off by the processors needs to be cooled via air conditioning, which uses even more power.

In part, this focus on energy efficiency has led to the recent development of multicore processors by AMD and Intel (and, for that matter, Sun, with its SPARC chips). Because these processors pack fewer transistors into a given space, they consume less power, throw off less heat, and require less air conditioning.

Modern processors are so powerful that, when used in the "one application, one server" mode, they loaf along at 10 or 15 percent utilization. (I've actually seen far lower utilization rates quoted; one company I talked with found a large number of machines in their data center operating at less than 1 percent capacity!) If used in a virtualization setting, though, it's likely that you'll begin to use more of a processor's capacity. However, the good news is that if you use a recent-generation machine, the processing power available to you is high enough that the processor is unlikely to be the performance bottleneck on the system.

At the time of this writing, quad-core processor machines were widely available. It's easy to see where this is heading, based on Moore's Law — soon you'll see 8-core and 16-core processors, and eventually you'll have multihundred-core processors.

Generally speaking, processors are the least likely bottleneck for your virtualization hardware. And, should you require more processing power than a typical 1U pizza-box server provides, a new generation of machines delivers much more processing power. (The term "1U pizza-box server" refers to a computer designed to fit into a data center rack; pizza-box servers are about 2 inches high and about 19 inches wide and deep — they resemble the boxes IT people's favorite food comes in.) Your server options in this regard are discussed later in this chapter, in the section "Choosing Servers."

It's not easy to know how much processing power your new virtualized server will require. Comparing the processing load an application represents on an old machine with the load it will represent to a new generation machine is, as the old saying goes, like comparing apples and oranges. An application that consumes 15 percent of the load on an old Pentium III machine is definitely not going to consume 15 percent of a new dual-core machine's load. That application will probably consume no more than 1 or 2 percent of the new machine's processing capacity.

Today's processors are much, much more powerful than those of just a few years ago. Never assume that processor loads are comparable across different generations of hardware. Look at Chapter 6 for some tips about assessing processor loading.

Beyond the question of how much raw processor power you'll require, you're going to need to address the SPOF issue. In other words, how can you avoid a situation where a processor failure would bring down a set of virtualized guests? One way to address this is to use servers with multiple processors, thereby ensuring that some processing will go on even if one processor fails. Admittedly, servers with multiple processors are more expensive than their single-processor brethren, but they provide protection against machine shutdown due to a processor going on the blink.

Another factor to consider with regard to processors is the fact that the latest generation of processors from Intel and AMD are designed to assist in virtualization. By offloading some of the virtualization processing from software to hardware, the performance of the virtualization solution improves. The virtualization-enabled processors go by the name of Intel-VT and AMD-V. If you're planning to run Windows virtual machines in a Xen-based virtualization environment, virtualization-enabled chips are a requirement. This is another example of why it's important to choose your virtualization product and your hardware together, to ensure compatibility in your overall solution. See the last section in this chapter, "But Wait, There's More: Future Virtualization Hardware Development," for a more detailed discussion of the exciting hardware developments available today and in the future.

Network cards

The network card (usually called the NIC, for Network Interface Card) in a server provides a critical service: It connects the machine to the world outside the machine, whether that world is bounded by the confines of the data center or encompasses the entire Internet.

Today's servers come with a network card preinstalled as part of the machine's motherboard. The NIC is typically a 10/100 megabit card, meaning it can operate at two different speeds, depending on what the rest of the network can handle. Data center infrastructures are slowly being upgraded to 1,000 megabit (or 1 gigabit, which is the term I'll be using), and many higher-end servers now include a gigabit NIC. And, on the horizon, courtesy of Moore's Law, are 10-gigabit cards and network infrastructure devices.

In terms of raw performance, there's typically enormous headroom when using an NIC. Put another way, network cards rarely create a bottleneck in system performance in the "one application, one server" world.

Nevertheless, NIC performance is something to consider when looking at virtualization capacity planning. Because you're loading a number of systems onto a single piece of hardware, all of them share the total network capacity of the NIC (or NICs) in the machine. A server that's completely adequate in terms of network performance while supporting a single operating system might not have enough network capacity if 12 guest systems are running on it.

One rough rule for calculating your total network throughput capacity requirement is to examine each of the physical machines that you're planning to migrate to a virtualized environment. Figure out how much traffic each of the machines is putting onto the network. Sum the average traffic of each machine to determine what the average network traffic will be from your virtualized server. Sum the maximum traffic of each machine to determine what the absolute maximum traffic will be from your virtualized server. This tallying gives you at least a ballpark figure for the amount of network capacity you'll need for your virtualization hardware.

Summing the average loads from the machines you plan to virtualize gives you the bare minimum of network capacity you need to have on your virtualization hardware. Summing the peak loads tells you the maximum capacity you need if all virtual guests pump out their maximum traffic at the same point in time.

So, if you sum the maximum total network load and it comes to 700 megabits per second, and your virtualization server has a single gigabit Ethernet card, you're covered, right? In the sense of network capacity not likely to be your virtualization bottleneck, yes.

On the other hand, using a machine with a single NIC exposes you to SPOF risk. If that network card goes belly up, you have a bunch of virtual machines that can't communicate with the world. So, it seems clear that you should have at least two NICs, even if you don't plan to saturate one NIC with any of your network traffic.

You can configure your virtualization software so that it uses the two NICs equally, which offers load-balancing benefits, which improves overall system performance modestly.

Okay. Two NICs will cover it. Well, not exactly. You might need to take additional NIC requirements into account. VMware's ESX Server demands a separate NIC to be used solely for its management subsystem. Running ESX Server on a system with two NICs would still leave you exposed to SPOF risk.

Consequently, if you're planning an ESX Server-based virtualization infrastructure, three NICs would be the minimum you should use in your server.

NIC planning for ESX Server implementations can get even more complex than just outlined. Many organizations separate a server's virtual machines into different groups and have the groups talk over different network cards to separate network switches, all in the interest of avoiding SPOF. Furthermore, some organizations keep another NIC in reserve to be used for virtual machine migration between servers. As you can see, it sometimes seems you can't have enough NICs in your servers!

This raises a different kind of capacity issue: the capability of your hardware choice to physically support the number of devices you need for your virtualization infrastructure. A 1U pizza-box server might have enough network capacity based on your load calculations, but it might offer only a single NIC. You can possibly add another NIC with a plug-in card, but should you be planning to use ESX Server, you're still one NIC short of what you really need.

You can address this issue of physical device capacity in more than one way. I get into the details of server selection later, in the "Choosing Servers" section, but the short answer is that a new generation of hardware servers that's coming onto the market is designed for virtualization and has sufficient physical capacity to work well in a virtualization infrastructure. What's important to keep in mind is that you need to consider more than just raw throughput numbers in your capacity-planning exercise.

Storage

The first word in data processing says it all. Computer systems are outstanding at generating gargantuan mountains of data. Adding virtualization into the mix compounds the situation: Your virtualization hardware is likely to require very large amounts of hard drive storage.

It might seem this is a moot issue, given the enormous growth in hard drive capacity over the past few years. One terabyte (1,000 gigabytes) drives are available cheaply. Just load several of them into your server, and you should be good to go, right? Well, not quite. Just as with NICs, the storage picture is a bit muddy.

The first thing to determine is how much storage you require. This is fairly straightforward. Sum up the total storage used on all the physical servers you're going to move to a single virtualization server, and that sum tells you your total storage requirements. Assuming that amount of storage fits into the available storage capacity on the server, you should be in good shape.

One thing to keep in mind is that many inexpensive servers can hold only two local drives. The usual term for local drives is DAS (short for Direct-Attached Storage, to highlight the fact that it's directly connected to the hardware). If your hardware can handle only two DAS drives, you're limited to a maximum of two terabytes on those servers. Should you decide to store your data in RAID (redundant array of inexpensive disks, which prevents SPOF by using multiple disks to create a duplicate copy of critical data), you'll get more data security at the cost of less overall storage. Therefore, it's certainly in the realm of possibility that the total storage requirements of your virtual guests might exceed your local storage capacities. So you might need to consider options other than just locally hosted storage — options that provide more storage than can be installed on the server.

Keeping all your storage on DAS might not be a good idea for other reasons as well:

✔ DAS data is available to the machine it's located on, but it generally isn't accessible to other machines on the network. It's possible to make DAS drives available through file access protocols like NFS (Network File System), but that generally isn't a desirable solution because of performance issues.

✔ Large drives can present problems due to the length of time it takes to access data. If you want really high performance from your disk access, you often have to use smaller drives and employ sophisticated data layout mechanisms regarding data striping (essentially, how data is organized internally within the drive). This kind of sophisticated arrangement is generally not possible with DAS — you usually have to move to a different form of storage, referred to as Network-Attached Storage (NAS) or Storage Area Network (SAN).

NAS and SAN storage mechanisms can be as simple as a specialized piece of hardware that can physically contain a number of drives and make them look like one humongous drive. (This simple arrangement is sometimes rather quaintly referred to as JBOD, or just a bunch of disks.) At the other end of the spectrum, very sophisticated SAN arrangements can have multiple pieces of hardware, each with a number of drives, offering virtual partitions of varying size and allowing partitions to be dynamically resized. SANs can also allow new drives to be swapped in dynamically to increase overall storage capacity.

Because these storage mechanisms decouple storage from particular hard drives, these mechanisms provide *storage virtualization,* which is important for virtualization after you move beyond simple server consolidation. As you create a pool of virtualized servers and migrate virtual machines among these servers, it's vital to enable a virtual machine, no matter where it's located, to access its data. Therefore, as you move through your virtualization life cycle journey, you're likely to begin to consider storage virtualization.

The physical access medium to store and retrieve data from more advanced storage options such as NASes and SANs is different than the mechanisms used for DAS access. Instead of using a local disk controller, these mechanisms have specialized hardware devices that are put into the server that speak to the network connecting the server and the remote storage hardware. These specialized hardware devices, which conceptually resemble NICs, are referred to as HBA (Host Bus Adapter) devices. I discuss NAS and SAN storage in further detail in Chapter 11; for now, just concentrate on the server hardware implications of your storage options.

HBAs resemble NICs in that they speak to networks, but they resemble NICs in another way as well: They're quite literally cards that can be inserted into the server's motherboard. And, just like with the card capacity of typical 1U servers, you can easily run out of card slots, especially if you want to avoid SPOF risk with your virtualized storage, as you most assuredly do.

The question of storage medium choice is critical and needs to be answered early in your planning. Depending on your virtualization product choice, you'll be directed toward one storage type or another, so be sure to review the storage options of the virtualization product you're considering.

If you decide to go the VMware ESX Server route, you have one more decision to make — the kind of external storage. You basically have two choices: Fibre Channel and iSCSI. They're two different protocols that offer similar capabilities. Fibre Channel is the most established, whereas iSCSI is a late arrival that offers some intriguing advantages.

Fibre Channel is a high-performance protocol that is widely used in the storage industry. (And, by the way, it's *Fibre,* not the more logical *Fiber.* I guess Fibre looks more sophisticated.) The primary drawback to Fibre Channel is the fact that it is a specialized protocol, which necessitates a dedicated network to carry its traffic as well as special switches to interconnect all the different Fibre Channel devices. In addition, because it uses this protocol, it can't use a standard NIC, thus requiring dedicated HBAs to be installed on the server. This, of course, has implications for your server choice because you should have three storage interfaces for ESX Server to avoid SPOF risk.

The iSCSI interface, however, uses standard Internet Protocols (IP — which explains the *i* in front of the SCSI) to transfer data. This means it can run over your standard Ethernet network to communicate between a server and remote storage. And, in fact, it can do this communication via the NIC already installed on the server.

Just because it can use the NIC, however, doesn't mean it should. Mixing performance-sensitive data traffic with the regular traffic on your network might not make sense. After all, you don't want your production machines to vie for network throughput with someone downloading a large presentation file. Because of network contention issues (explained in the earlier section, "Taking Hardware Seriously"), many organizations that use iSCSI segregate the traffic in the network by subnetting their network into an iSCSI-specific subnet and a normal traffic subnet. On the network side, you can accomplish this subnetting via *smart switches* — network devices that segregate traffic according to how they're configured — but on the server, the need to communicate to two different subnets requires dedicated iSCSI NICs. In other words, if you configure the network cleverly to separate the two types of traffic, your server needs to be able to address the separate subnets. You can usually communicate to the separate subnets through installing an iSCSI-dedicated NIC on the machine. You can see where this is going, right? You need two or more slots to support iSCSI NICs to avoid SPOF risk, depending on what virtualization product you end up using.

iSCSI is a protocol that has specialized functionality in order for the different parts of an iSCSI network to communicate. The server sending or retrieving data is known as the initiator. The NAS or SAN storage device is known as the target. Software is required on the different devices so that they may serve as either initiators or targets. The iSCSI NIC cards can be different than standard NIC cards. Because of the large amounts of data that can be communicated in an iSCSI environment, iSCSI NIC cards contain specialized chips that offload network processing from the server's main processor, which improves data throughput. All in all, iSCSI is simpler (and much cheaper) than Fibre Channel, but simpler is not the same as simple!

As you think about what storage mechanism to use for your virtualization infrastructure, keep in mind that your decision will impact what server hardware capabilities you'll need. Always re-examine your server selection in light of your storage choice.

As you begin to consider more complex storage options for your virtualization infrastructure, you'll need to carefully evaluate your server (that is, your server hardware) choices. Although traditional 1U pizza boxes can certainly run virtualization software, creating a robust virtualization infrastructure might force you to consider higher-end hardware. Your choices in this regard are described in the "Designed for virtualization: The new generation of servers" section, later in this chapter.

Memory

In terms of the four key server resources necessary for virtualization, memory is last, but certainly not least. In fact, memory is usually the critical resource for virtualization, and you need to really focus on it in your virtualization planning. This is because memory is the most common bottleneck for virtualization performance and is usually the least flexible resource in terms of hardware.

Figuring out why memory is such a critical resource is pretty much a no-brainer. Just think about the number of times you've complained about sluggish performance on your personal computer. What's the diagnosis nine times out of ten? Too little memory. And what's the prescription? Add memory.

If you don't have enough memory in a machine, the processor is forced to swap data out of memory and onto disk so that it can bring other data into memory to operate on it. Because accessing data is so much slower if the data has to be fetched from disk, insufficient memory really bogs down a machine. Essentially, the tradeoff is between amount of memory and overall system performance.

Modern servers typically come equipped with one or 2GB (gigabytes) of memory, which is more than enough for most application loads, especially when the server is being used in the "one application, one server" mode.

Virtualization changes all that, however. Because a server can support five, ten, or even more virtual machines, what was a perfectly adequate amount of memory to support a single operating system can now fall far short of what is required for good performance.

Obviously, a key question is how much memory you should plan to allocate for each virtual machine. Unfortunately, the answer to that question depends on several factors.

If a virtual machine is processing lots of data, it requires more memory. Conversely, if it doesn't operate on much data, it can get by with much less memory. A common example of the latter is a virtual machine dedicated to serving as the organization's DNS server. (DNS stands for Domain Name Server, which translates machine names into IP addresses.) Although DNS is an absolutely vital service, it's very lightweight in terms of the amount of data operated on. Many organizations migrate infrastructure services like DNS, directory services, and so on to virtual machines. This enables them to put all infrastructure services on a single piece of hardware; the lightweight processing loads of the services don't require much in the way of hardware resources.

Is there a general rule for how much memory to dedicate per virtual machine? If you talk to five different people, you'll get five different recommendations. Some maintain that each virtual machine should have access to as much memory as it would if it were running as a single operating system on a physical piece of hardware: 2GB of memory. I've heard others maintain that they can run high-data-load virtual machines with only 512MB (megabytes) of memory; some people run infrastructure services like those described in the preceding paragraph with as little as 256MB of memory. In my discussions with organizations considering virtualization, I recommend they plan for 1GB of memory per virtual machine.

Your choice of virtualization product affects how much physical memory your server requires. Xen requires that the total amount of memory allocated for the virtualization software itself (what Xen calls the hypervisor) and all virtual guests be equal to or less than the total amount of physical memory available on the machine. If you attempt to start a guest and its assigned memory would cause the total allocated memory to exceed the physical memory on the machine, the start operation fails with an error. So, if the physical memory available on a machine is 2GB and you allocate 512MB for the hypervisor and 512MB for each guest, you can support the hypervisor and three guests.

VMware is somewhat more forgiving than Xen. It allows you to overallocate the physical memory on the machine, meaning you can allocate more memory than is actually physically present on the server. On the other hand, this overallocation can cause performance to suffer as disk swapping of data occurs, so you might face performance issues while the system is running, rather than confronting them upon guest startup, as with Xen.

It's too early to know how memory will be handled in the upcoming Microsoft Server virtualization capability, scheduled to be released shortly after Microsoft Server 2008 comes to market. Given the importance of memory for both Xen and VMware, should you decide to begin working with the virtualization functionality in Microsoft Server 2008, be sure to evaluate your memory requirements carefully.

The virtualization hypervisor requires a certain amount of memory. Each virtual machine will require memory — the amount can be varied, but trying to run a virtual machine with very low amounts of memory can harm its performance as data is swapped out to disk repeatedly. Also, some of the hypervisors add additional memory to that allocated for the hypervisor itself as each virtual machine is started. All you have to do is simple math in adding up all the memory commitments, and it's easy to see that you can rapidly require more memory than is supported by a typical 1U pizza-box server. For the answer to this dilemma, read about the new generation of hardware focused on virtualization, which is described next.

The big four resources — the story so far

In the preceding sections, I devote a good deal of page real estate leading you on a tour through the four resources you need to evaluate when you plan the hardware aspect of your virtualization project. As part of the tour, I impart quite a few tips as well as a few touches of conventional (and unconventional) wisdom. Said tips and wisdom gravitate around the following key decision areas you need to consider when planning hardware:

- ✓ **Your virtualization product:** Depending on what virtualization product you decide to use, you might be forced to choose one type of hardware resource over another. For example, should you decide to use VMware's ESX Server as your virtualization product, you'll probably use external storage for your virtual machines, which will definitely affect what hardware choices you make.

- ✓ **Your risk profile:** Although you can certainly use commodity servers as virtualization platforms, they might be limited in their ability to support redundant hardware resources, important to avoid SPOF risk. If you want to increase the robustness of your virtualization infrastructure, you need to consider more sophisticated (and expensive) servers.

- ✓ **Your processor:** Although the processors in most servers are incredibly powerful, if you plan to support many virtual machines on a single piece of hardware, you need to be sure you're using the latest generation of multicore processors. In fact, you might need to consider using servers that support multiple processors. Multiple processors also protect you against SPOF risk. If part of what's driving you to virtualization is energy costs, using the latest generation of processors is sure to reduce your power needs.

- ✓ **Your NIC cards:** Most NICs are plenty powerful and unlikely to be saturated by the network traffic posed by virtualization. However, using redundant NICs will protect you against SPOF risk. In addition, your choice of virtualization product might affect your NIC planning because ESX Server requires a dedicated NIC for its management functionality. And if you plan on using VMware VMotion to enable live migration of virtual machines, yet another NIC is required.

✔ **Your storage:** Storage is probably the most complicated resource in terms of planning. Although Xen (and VMware Server) can use DAS, with ESX Server you're likely to use external storage. You have two primary types of external storage available — Fibre Channel and iSCSI. Your choice dictates what type of hardware access mechanism you need to use. Both types usually push you to use external storage adapters other than the NIC included with your server. These external adapters, known as HBAs, require card slots, which affect the type of server you need to use. Naturally, good practice dictates avoiding SPOF risk, thereby affecting the number of HBAs and card slots your hardware will need.

✔ **Your memory capabilities:** Memory is *the* key resource and the one most likely to affect the performance of your virtualization platform. Your choice of virtualization product affects the amount of memory you require for your hardware, with the proviso that memory availability can significantly impact system performance because inadequate memory forces the machine's processor to swap data on and off physical disks.

Okay, you have a few factors to keep in mind as you do your hardware planning. Time to check out some real-world server solutions that (hopefully) will stand up to your rigorous scrutiny as you lay down the foundation for your virtualization platform.

Choosing Servers

Deciding what kind of server to run your virtualization solution on requires a careful assessment of your requirements regarding the big four hardware resources.

There are three general types of hardware platforms available for your server choice. Each comes armed with pluses and minuses. It's easy to reuse your existing 32-bit servers, but you'll pay a price in functionality and the number of virtual machines that can be hosted per server. Another alternative is 64-bit servers, which have more processing horsepower, but might not be able to scale in terms of the big four resources. Finally, you can look to the new generation of virtualization-ready servers that provide awesome virtualization capability, albeit with a larger price tag and additional complexity. Let's consider each server type in turn.

Reusing your existing 32-bit hardware

One option you have for your hardware choice is sitting right in front of you: your existing 32-bit servers. They're called 32-bit servers, by the way, because they manipulate data in 32-bit chunks. Prosaic, but accurate.

Because many of your servers are currently underutilized, it's possible to migrate the operating systems and applications from several machines onto one underutilized physical server. This allows you to get better utilization from one machine and remove the others from your data center. In this way, you can reduce your overall server count significantly.

It's important to evaluate the servers you might repurpose as virtualization servers to see how well they meet the hardware requirements necessary to provide a robust infrastructure.

Many of the servers present in today's data centers are four or five years old. Although their performance and reliability are certainly sufficient for a "one application, one server" mode, the average server probably falls short in terms of offering the hardware resources required for a production-level virtualization server.

In particular, most pizza-box servers (remember, the flat machines that resemble the cartons that techies' favorite dining choices are delivered in) fall short in these aspects:

- ✔ **Network connectivity:** Pizza-box servers traditionally have a single NIC with 10/100MB throughput. Although sufficient for typical application loads, this throughput might not be enough if four or five virtual machines need to share the available bandwidth. Furthermore, most pizza-box servers have only a single NIC, providing inadequate single point of failure (SPOF) risk protection as well as being inadequate for VMware ESX Server minimum requirements.

- ✔ **Storage:** Pizza-box servers usually can support two DAS drives, which, depending on the storage needs of the guests, might be adequate to provide enough storage. However, if the total storage requirements exceed the maximum amount of DAS available or if the infrastructure design of the organization dictates virtualized storage — a storage option where data is stored on an external device — the machine might not have enough card slots available for the HBAs.

- ✔ **Processor:** The processor is least likely to impose a performance bottleneck for a 32-bit machine. However, if too many virtual machines are installed on the server, it might be possible to overload the processor in the machine.

✔ **Memory:** This is the most likely bottleneck and the primary reason 32-bit servers don't provide a satisfactory hardware platform for a virtualization infrastructure. The maximum memory a 32-bit machine can address is 4GB; however, many pizza-box servers support only 1GB or 2GB of memory. Whether a server supports the theoretical maximum of 4GB or has an actual limit below that amount, the memory on the server limits how many virtual machines can be supported on the server. Depending on the virtualization product you use, you might be physically limited to a certain number of virtual machines — or you will suffer performance penalties if you try to exceed a recommended guest-to-memory ratio. (See the section "The Big Four resources of servers," earlier in this chapter, for more on memory issues.)

Given the limitations of 32-bit machines, they aren't a good choice to serve as virtualization host hardware for production-level infrastructures. However, all is not lost. These machines can serve very usefully in circumstances where their inability to host large numbers of guests or production-level applications isn't a drawback.

Examples of situations for which 32-bit servers are well suited include

✔ **Software development:** Developers often have to set up an infrastructure of several machines to develop software: a Web server machine, an application server machine, and a database server machine. (The fact that three machines are used causes this arrangement to be referred to as a *three-tier architecture.* Those seeking academic preciseness might prefer the term *N-tier* to acknowledge that additional tiers might contain other servers.) Although creating this environment is critical to ensure programs can be developed in an environment similar to the one they'll run in, using physical machines for development tends to be wasteful of resources. This is because it's expensive to purchase separate machines for every developer, but even more so because the load on the machines is usually trivial: Developers want to test functionality, not run big loads. For this reason, virtualization on 32-bit servers is increasingly being used in development environments.

✔ **Quality assurance:** Just as developers usually need to reproduce the physical environment their products will ultimately run in, quality assurance (QA) engineers also need to test whether the products run properly in those environments. Furthermore, QA engineers often have to test products in multiple configurations. For example, a QA engineer might need to test a product with several versions of the Apache Web server to ensure the product works against all of them. Similar to the software development situation described in the preceding paragraph, dedicating numerous machines to QA engineers is wasteful and time consuming. Using virtualization enables QA to efficiently test applications with a minimum of setup time and with a minimal amount of hardware.

So, don't throw away your 32-bit servers as you begin your virtualization trek; just acknowledge that they might not be appropriate for all virtualization scenarios and focus on using them where their limitations aren't a problem.

Using 64-bit servers

Unfortunately, 32-bit servers suffer significant limitations in terms of their ability to act as the physical underpinnings of a production virtualization environment, as spelled out in the previous section. Particularly in terms of memory, 32-bit servers just don't have the resources for a demanding environment.

On the other hand, over the past few years, a new generation of servers using 64-bit processors have come to market. (They're called 64-bit processors because they manage data 64 bits at a time, double the amount of 32-bit processors; a side effect of this is the fact that they can manage much larger amounts of memory.) This effectively removes any practical limitation on the amount of memory a server can contain, although the theoretical amount of memory that can be addressed is way beyond what any machine could, practically speaking, make use of.

Both Intel and AMD offer 64-bit chips, and there's a decent chance that some of your servers might be 64-bit-chip based.

Given the fact that 64-bit servers don't present the same memory size issues of 32-bit servers, does that mean that the 64-bit route is the solution to the question of what type of server to use in your infrastructure? Yes — and no.

Certainly, 64-bit machines *can* hold sufficient memory so that memory would no longer be a bottleneck for your infrastructure. On the other hand, many servers containing 64-bit chips are, in effect, 32-bit designs with a more powerful processor. Although that's somewhat better than the same design with a 32-bit processor, it still might not have all the necessary capabilities that a production-level virtualization environment requires. To use an analogy, it's like having a car with a turbocharged V8 engine, but with a three-speed transmission: Much of the power of the engine is wasted because of an inability to usefully apply the power through the drivetrain of the car.

Many 64-bit machines support no more than 4GB of memory. Those machines that *can* go higher than 4GB tend to top out at 8GB. That's definitely better than a 32-bit machine that holds only 2GB of memory, but it still imposes limitations on the number of guests the server can support, even if the 64-bit processor is plenty powerful enough to support more.

Moreover, the physical architecture of a 64-bit server might be no better suited for virtualization than a typical 32-bit server. If a 64-bit server lacks sufficient card slots for needed HBAs or NICs, the machine presents a risk for a production virtualization environment.

Blade servers: A 64-bit alternative

You have another 64-bit option for servers — one that might be a bit more attractive for use as a virtualization foundation: blade servers. Blade servers essentially extract the processing portions of a server out to a plug-in card while centralizing resources that provide infrastructure services. A typical blade server has a chassis that includes a power supply and network interfaces. These resources are shared by all the individual blades, each of which contains a processor, memory, and (perhaps) storage. Depending on the specific blade system and the customer's desire, some blade systems will offload storage from DAS on the blade to virtualized storage somewhere in the data center.

The move to blade computing is driven by the desire to gain more processing capability in a given amount of physical space. Sounds like the same desire as that driving virtualization, eh?

A blade server is a multi-U box, often 9U. (Yes, 9 times higher than the 1U pizza-box servers described earlier — think of them as really, really deep-dish pizza-box servers.) In it, individual blades (each of which contains a processor, memory, and possibly storage) are inserted vertically into a blade slot. If you've ever inserted a PCI card into your home computer, you instinctively understand how this works. The number of blades that can fit in an individual blade server varies, but as an example, Hewlett Packard's p-Class blade enclosures can each support up to 16 blades.

What's attractive about blade servers, beyond the fact that they provide more computing for a given amount of rack space, is that they provide more cost-effective redundancy for system resources like networking and power.

If you consider the importance of avoiding SPOF risk by having multiple power supplies, networking cards, and storage HBAs (discussed in

the "Multiple-eggs-in-one-basket syndrome" section in this chapter), you can see that the cost of providing two of everything for every server can mount up fast. Blade servers, by contrast, can spread the cost of redundancy across multiple processing blades, thereby reducing the overall cost of avoiding SPOF. For example, providing redundant power for 16 blades requires only two power supplies, far lower than the 32 power supplies that would be necessary if 16 individual servers were installed, each with its own redundant power.

The blade enclosures are clever in terms of network connectivity. Each blade achieves network connectivity through its connection with the blade slot, whereas the blade enclosure multiplexes all the network traffic from all the blades onto a couple of cables. This reduces the overall number of cables, which, beyond making for neater data centers, makes infrastructure management easier because there are far fewer cables to keep track of.

Each blade is truly a server in its own right, with its own system resources like a processor and memory. Consequently, it's easy to use blades as virtualization servers, and many organizations are exploring using blades as their chosen platform for virtualization. Of course, many blades are still architected with the assumptions of their more traditional brethren, and they still retain limited memory capacity, which is the most typical performance bottleneck for virtualization.

Blades are a relatively recent arrival in the data center, and many organizations are just beginning to consider how they might use blades. They're worth a look as you begin to put together your virtualization plan.

Consequently, it's important to look at more than just the raw capabilities of the server's processor when evaluating 64-bit machines for your environment. You might have machines (or be considering purchasing machines) that have a powerful processor but lack other critical resources. On the other hand, many 64-bit machines that are incapable of serving as production virtualization hardware platforms are fully capable of fulfilling the development and QA roles discussed in the previous section. And, with the price of 64-bit machines plummeting, you have no reason not to use 64-bit machines in these roles.

Designed for virtualization: The new generation of servers

Most of today's servers have been designed with the assumption of "one application, one server" as their guiding principle. Virtualization has now come along and knocked that assumption for a loop. This situation leaves the average organization with a set of unpalatable choices:

- ✔ **Use the existing servers,** with the severe hardware limitations that significantly restrict the ability to scale virtualization.
- ✔ **Acquire modern 64-bit machines** that, unfortunately, still don't provide the hardware capability to take full advantage of virtualization.
- ✔ **Explore the use of blades,** which address some of the SPOF risks of redundant hardware resources but still don't provide complete virtualization hardware capability.

Fortunately, a new generation of hardware is just now coming onto the market that addresses the shortcomings of the current crop of servers. One might say this generation is designed for virtualization from the ground up.

To take one example, check out the Sun Fire 4600. It's a single server in a 4U box. (Yes, it's about halfway between a 1U and a 9U server in terms of height, kind of a calzone-sized server. You can see that an IT army marches on its stomach.) However, it's architected to hold up to eight dual-core AMD Opteron processor chips. In addition, it supports up to 128GB of memory, with enough card slots to enable redundant networking and storage interfaces. A machine like this can easily support more than 20 virtual machines (VMs) and can conceivably support as many as 100. Pricing starts at around $20,000.

IBM makes a similar, although lower-end offering available in its System x3550. Priced at less than $2,000, this 1U server holds up to 32GB of memory and offers a single dual-core Intel Xeon processor. Certainly, this machine would be capable of running ten VMs and could scale beyond that while offering each VM sufficient resources to achieve more-than-acceptable performance.

Using the new generation of servers

To provide a concrete example of how the new generation of servers delivers real virtualization capability, here's an example. A subsidiary of Siemens, New Energy is an energy consulting and software company. It faced a common problem: running out of space in its data center, coupled with skyrocketing power and air-conditioning costs.

Using a Sun Fire X4200 server and virtualization software from VMware, New Energy was able to consolidate 18 1U servers onto a single 4U machine. Power consumption went from 14,000 watts to less than 600. And the temperature in New Energy's data center immediately dropped by over 10 degrees. In addition, additional capacity remains on the machine, providing headroom for future growth in computing needs.

As this example shows, the capability of the new generation of hardware is impressive indeed.

Making the Hard Hardware Choices

The decision about what hardware to use as the computing platform for your virtualization infrastructure is a difficult one. To make your decision easier, I've included a table (Table 8-1) that lists each type of server, including pros and cons for each type as well as the best use for each of the types.

Table 8-1	Your Hard Hardware Choices		
Type of Machine	*Pros*	*Cons*	*Use*
32-bit	Might already be present in your data center; ready to be repurposed; inexpensive	Limited expansion of critical resources like memory and card slots	Low-density virtualization, Development, QA
64-bit	Might already be present in your data center; ready to be repurposed; inexpensive; able to address larger amounts of memory, thereby potentially able to support larger number of virtual machines	Often limited to 4GB to 8GB of memory; typically lack enough card slots to support sufficient NICs and HBAs	Medium-density virtualization, Development, QA

(continued)

Table 8-1 *(continued)*

Type of Machine	Pros	Cons	Use
New Generation Servers	Can support large amounts of memory — 32GB to 128GB; many card slots hold additional NICs and HBAs; contain latest generation of processors that are virtualization enabled	Expensive in comparison to 32-bit and 64-bit pizza-box machines; require new system administration skills	High-density virtualization

As the 32-bit row in Table 8-1 indicates, repurposing existing hardware is attractive for a number of reasons. It doesn't require additional budget, and the machines are already on hand, making it easy to get going. However, most existing servers were built for the "one application, one server" world and lack the resources necessary to provide a high-quality virtualization infrastructure.

The row describing 64-bit machines indicates they can provide better performance, but many of them were designed using the "one application, one server" mindset. The recent 64-bit blade servers mitigate many of the limitations of these machines by providing easy redundancy of key resources like power supplies and network interfaces, but they still suffer from key limitations in the area of total processor capability and, crucially, memory capacity.

For high-density virtualization, you probably want to consider the new generation of server hardware, which is described in the last row of the table. This new generation of virtualization-ready servers, like the Sun Fire machines, can contain huge amounts of memory and provide enough card slots to support any virtualization product. Keep in mind, however, that considerations beyond raw virtualization capability are important as well.

You might have a preferred hardware vendor that doesn't provide this type of virtualization-ready hardware. Introducing new hardware into a computing infrastructure will require training to allow your employees to be able to manage it efficiently. And, of course, you'll need to ensure your chosen applications are certified and supported on your possible choice of hardware.

Your choice of hardware is important, particularly because virtualization raises SPOF risk. Carefully think through all factors relating to hardware before embarking on a production virtualization project.

But Wait, There's More: Future Virtualization Hardware Development

From the description of the new generation of virtualization-ready servers, hardware manufacturers clearly are getting involved in the game. The new generation of servers removes many of the limitations of older servers in terms of their suitability to support production-level virtualization.

However, additional hardware developments that are on the horizon will further improve the virtualization capabilities of servers.

Virtualization-enabled chips

One of the drawbacks of processor chips is that they, too, have been designed for the "one application, one server" paradigm. Actually, it would be more correct to say they've been designed for a "one operating system, one server" paradigm. In other words, these chips assume a single operating system has been set up to access the hardware resources of the processor, so there's no need to arbitrate among multiple systems attempting to access a common resource such as a hard drive.

Consequently, to enable multiple guest OSes, the virtualization software must be extremely clever to coordinate access to system resources while still allowing the central processor to think only one operating system is actually accessing them.

What if, instead, the chip was designed from the get-go for a "multiple operating system, one server" paradigm? The virtualization software wouldn't have to perform so many clever tricks, and many operations that are currently performed in software could instead be performed in silicon, which is always much faster.

In fact, that vision of processor support for virtualization exists today. Recent chip releases from both Intel and AMD contain virtualization support. Intel's virtualization-capable chips are labeled Intel Virtualization Technology (usually referred to as Intel VT), whereas AMD's counterpart chips are known as AMD Virtualization (usually referred to as AMD-V).

This virtualization capability offers performance gains while also enabling the Xen-based hypervisor to support unmodified guest operating systems. VMware also plans to take advantage of these new types of chips in an upcoming release.

If you're considering purchasing new hardware for your virtualization infra-structure, I strongly recommend you ensure that your server choice contains this new type of chip. These chips are the future of virtualization, and it doesn't make any sense not to take advantage of them.

More efficient memory

Just as virtualization software must be very clever to coordinate access to the processor, it must likewise perform similar tricks to coordinate access to memory to ensure that each virtual machine only uses memory assigned to it. Requiring each memory access to go through the virtualization software imposes significant overhead and, correspondingly, reduces performance.

In the near future, that overhead will be reduced considerably through a new technology that addresses this memory inefficiency. Without going into details, this technology will allow a virtualization hypervisor to dedicate a portion of system memory to a particular guest VM at VM initiation, and thereafter allow the VM to directly access the memory without needing to go through the virtualization software. The virtualization overhead will be restricted to the startup phase of the guest VM rather than being imposed for every memory access.

Both AMD and Intel have plans to deliver this functionality. AMD refers to its version of the technology as Nested Page Tables, whereas Intel calls its version Extended Page Tables. (It would be too tough for them to use a common term for similar technology, right?) The Page Tables memory technology should be available sometime in 2007 and begin to show up in production servers shortly thereafter.

Faster networking for virtualized machines

It wouldn't do for virtualization support to be moved into processors and memory access but leave out networking, would it?

NIC cards are being upgraded as well to better support virtualization. Rather than forcing the virtualization software to supervise every network interaction, the new cards are able to handle multiple clients accessing a single NIC. Similar to the Page Tables arrangement described in the preceding section, the virtualization software cooperates with the NIC during virtual machine initiation to assign dedicated NIC resources to the guest, but then it doesn't need to be involved in subsequent network interactions. The overall goal of virtualization networking is to bypass the virtualization software for most networking and thereby improve performance.

Virtualization on devices

Is there anywhere that virtualization can't be applied? I discuss server virtualization, client virtualization, and storage virtualization — what about *device virtualization*?

What is device virtualization? *Device* is a fancy term for a small piece of hardware, often special purpose, which is a computer. What is a common device? You might have one in your pocket in the form of a mobile phone.

Virtualization on devices is a hot topic, and virtualization on mobile phones is white hot. Why? Well, because it's a computer, your mobile phone can run programs. Today, most of those programs are installed by the phone manufacturer or the service provider who delivers service. By the way, the circumstances of who delivers phone service and who decides what programs are installed vary widely throughout the world. For example, in Europe, most phones are purchased directly by consumers who then decide which carrier they'll use for service, whereas in the U.S. most phone purchases are subsidized by the service carrier, which controls what's on the phone.

Because the phones are computers, it's possible that additional programs not originally present on the phone can be installed. From the perspective of the consumer, it's obviously very desirable to be able to add new programs to the phone in order to get the best experience from the device.

On the other hand, there are complications regarding consumer-installed programs. Because mobile phones interact with the mobile phone network, there are strict limitations on them in terms of their transmittal power, transmission frequencies, and so on. Consequently,

manufacturers have a reluctance to allow consumer-installed applications on mobile devices out of concern that the applications might manipulate elements of the device that must follow government regulations.

Furthermore, many carriers have established relationships with content providers. For example, Verizon has the Vcast service, which provides content from ESPN, CNN, and even from music providers. Clearly, these providers want to protect their content from being manipulated (that is, copied, or as the music companies say, stolen) by other applications.

Nevertheless, the momentum toward mobile device user customization is unstoppable. How can the interests of the different parties be reconciled? Virtualization to the rescue!

Several companies have developed virtualization software that can run on mobile devices. Their products are something like a mini-hypervisor, capable of running different virtual machines that can isolate applications in one virtual machine from interacting with an application in another. One virtual machine can be made available for user-installed applications which can be prevented from accessing basic phone functionality such as the software that controls device power as well as other applications delivering content.

From the perspective of the user, all this wizardry is hidden. The virtual machines controlling the phone and the content are invisible. Through the use of virtualization software, the device is able to support these conflicting goals without imposing additional complexity upon the user.

A few of this type of NIC cards are available today, but allow me to pull out my crystal ball and predict the future: Soon every NIC card intended for industrial use will include this capability, and this capability will be a natural part of virtualization infrastructures.

Better device support in virtualized systems

One drawback to virtualization is that it is typically difficult to enable virtual machines to address devices like graphics cards or sound cards. As you might expect, this is because the hardware architecture is designed as though only one operating system will access these devices; in a virtualized environment with multiple virtual machines, there's no way to coordinate access to these devices. Well, the folks at Intel and AMD are busily solving this problem as well. Upcoming releases of their products will include Intel's Virtualization for Directed I/O and AMD's IOMMU to enable easy device access for virtual machines. This functionality should really improve the capability of virtualization, as it will make the world of virtualization much more flexible and capable. Look for it soon, coming to a machine near you!

Part II
Server Virtualization

In this part . . .

The leading application of virtualization is server virtualization, and this part focuses on it. Although it might seem that *everyone* is implementing virtualization, the reality is that most IT organizations are just now coming to terms with what their server virtualization plans should be. If you're in the "making up your mind" camp, this part is for you.

I first discuss how to decide whether virtualization is right for you. Surprisingly, not everyone should take advantage of virtualization, despite what the vendors say! It's important for you to analyze your environment and organization to determine whether it makes sense to move forward with virtualization.

Part of any virtualization decision should be an analysis of the costs and benefits of the technology. Chapter 6 goes into detail about how to perform a cost-benefit analysis, as well as all the different elements to pull into your calculations.

Every virtualization implementation should be managed properly, and many aspects of a virtualization project need to be kept in mind. Chapter 7 shows you how to manage your virtualization project efficiently and keep you sane.

Finally, one of the most important decisions you'll make about your virtualization infrastructure is what hardware you'll run it on. Many exciting developments in the hardware arena are related to virtualization, and I explain them all to you in Chapter 8 so you can make an informed decision about your hardware platform.

Chapter 9

Migrating to Your New Virtualized Environment

*D*id you ever see any of those funny work-related cartoons designed to poke fun at the sometimes-infuriating, always-chaotic environments that all workplaces tend to be?

One of my favorites depicts a project manager standing in front of a whiteboard. You see a bunch of jumbled boxes drawn on the whiteboard's left side, illustrating the disorganized present situation; on the right side, you see a neatly arranged set of boxes indicating the project outcome: a well-ordered, calm, efficient system.

In the middle of the whiteboard you see a big cloud labeled "then a miracle occurs," indicating that *something* happened to transform the incoming mess into the outgoing superorganized outcome; the implication being that no-one could foresee how the mess was going to be fixed.

The theme of the cartoon is that it's easy to see the unsatisfactory present and easy to envision post-project perfection, but the stuff in the middle is where the challenge lies.

As you've probably realized, that "challenging middle" part is pretty good shorthand for what awaits you when you take the virtualization plunge.

Everyone recognizes the messy, inefficient sprawl that is typical of today's data centers. And everyone responds with oohhhs and aahhhs to the beautiful vision of a data center with virtualization — orderly, cost effective, energy efficient, and much easier to manage. The rub comes when thinking about how to transition from today's data center reality to tomorrow's virtualization potential. In a word, how do you *migrate* from today to tomorrow? That's what this chapter's all about.

Moving from Physical to Virtual: An Overview

Don't feel alone in wondering how you get from here to there — from today's machine-choked, underutilized data to tomorrow's smaller, more efficient, virtual, machine-enabled, smooth-running data center. The entire virtualization industry recognizes that the move from physical to virtual systems is both critical and challenging. In fact, the industry has a term for this migration: P2V, for physical to virtual.

That neat term, P2V, however, is something of a misnomer. When the industry uses the term, it's referring to the transformation of an existing system, consisting of an operating system and application(s), into a virtual machine (VM) format and installing that VM onto an existing hypervisor. However, the process of migration encompasses much more than this transformation, although that is the key event in a P2V migration.

When vendors refer to P2V, they mean a product that will convert a physical server into a virtual image. However, server conversion is but one piece of a successful migration project.

There are three phases to a successful migration:

1. **Preparing the environment for migration.**

    Before you start boxing up stuff to move to a new house, you always try to get rid of the junk you no longer need first. (No sense in carting junk to your new home, right?) In a system migration, you should do the same. For virtualization to succeed, you need to clean up the existing physical systems before migration takes place.

    Part of preparing the environment means having the new virtualization infrastructure in place, and getting that done properly is a must-do item. Key items here are installing new hardware, taking care of the necessary infrastructure, and procuring the virtualization software itself.

And, to continue the moving metaphor a bit further, part of any move is packing properly. The corollary in virtualization migration is to ensure that you have your current software systems prepared and backed up prior to the migration.

2. **Migrating the existing systems.**

This is the part of migration that the industry refers to when it uses the term P2V, and getting this right is absolutely fundamental to a successful virtualization implementation.

What's interesting about the term P2V is that it sounds so neat and clean, but, as you discover later in this chapter, it's a neat term that means very different things, depending on the nature of your virtualization project. Also, depending on the nature of your virtualization project, you might be reduced to manual migration, which doesn't sound very neat or clean at all!

3. **Putting the new virtualized infrastructure into production.**

If you've done your planning and migration properly, turning up the new virtualized infrastructure should be as easy as pie. Although this is true, it's important that you understand what it will take to actually begin running your new virtualized infrastructure.

Only by successfully executing all three phases of migration can you be certain that your move from today's sprawling data center to tomorrow's squeaky-clean virtualized environment will go smoothly. But, rest assured, a successful migration doesn't require a miracle — just careful planning and methodical implementation.

Getting Ready to Move: Preparing the Virtualized Environment

It seems like three is a lucky (or at least an important) number, and just as migration has three phases, preparing a migration involves three tasks:

✔ Prepare existing systems for migration.

✔ Prepare the new virtualization servers that the old physical servers will be running on.

✔ Implement any new infrastructure that is needed for your new virtualized environment.

I go over each task in succession in the next few sections.

Preparing existing systems for migration

The moving-to-a-new-house metaphor I use earlier in the chapter postulates that preparing your existing systems for migration is something like the cleanup you do at the house you've been living in when you're getting ready to move to a new place to live.

Getting your existing systems shipshape will make your migration much more successful. A little work at the start of the project shortens the duration of the overall effort.

The place to start is to understand the terminology of migration. The existing system that will be moved via P2V is referred to as the *source* for the migration, whereas the new virtualization server is referred to as the *target* for the migration.

So why do you want to clean up the source system prior to migration? It's important to prepare the source so that when it is installed on the target there will be no issues in production. Certain things that are present in a running physical server can cause problems if you put them into production on a virtualization server.

What kind of things am I talking about? The following list gives you a good idea:

- **Hardware-dependent software:** If the physical server has specific hardware attached to it — a tape backup system, for example — that won't be present on the new virtualization server, it's critical that the software be removed. Otherwise, you'll come up with software that tries to execute and puts out error messages when it can't run properly, can't find drivers, and so on and so forth. Such a state of affairs will be a nightmare to sort out — and you don't want to be sorting out such things when you're in the midst of an off-hours migration project.

  Removing hardware dependencies is particularly important if you're moving to VMware because its hardware emulation model requires that the hypervisor contains the system drivers. Unless VMware certifies that it supports whatever hardware you have attached to an existing physical server, you'll run into big problems during migration. So be sure to yank any hardware-dependent software from the physical server prior to migration.

- **Unused and/or obsolete software on the system:** Systems, like houses, tend to collect a lot of junk over time. When it comes to software, applications that were once important but now abandoned, extra installed versions that were used for testing but are no longer needed, or applications that were installed for evaluation purposes but never put into production are all just extra bits that are unnecessary and should be removed. Take a look at the process tables of the running system and see whether there are any applications you don't recognize; examine unrecognized apps and remove them as appropriate.

Part of cleaning up involves what I consider to be standard maintenance tasks. Don't think you can blow off such tasks just because you're raring to get this migration project underway. So be sure to

✔ **Bring the operating system and application(s) current by applying updates and patches:** You probably have an existing process by which you apply updates and patches, but you're probably still working out how you'll do the same process in your new virtualized environment — so get your existing systems shipshape before migration. There'll be plenty of stress when you do the virtualization cutover, so why add to it with another task that you can take care of beforehand?

Getting your systems updated and patched to the right level is important at any time, but it's vital when you're moving to a virtualized environment. You don't want to be solving two types of problems when you put virtualization into production — one type caused by the inevitable problems of moving to a new infrastructure and the other caused by running a system at the wrong patch level.

✔ **Back up your applications and data:** Let me repeat: Back up your applications and data. The aim of virtualization is to make your life easier, and nothing makes it more difficult than something not being right and having no way to recover to a known, safe state. Although there are tools to aid in the P2V migration — tools discussed later in this chapter — they are by no means foolproof, and they might not be available at all for some of your systems. If no P2V option is available, you need to do a manual migration, and pristine backups are necessary for that migration option. In any case, even if your P2V migration goes smoothly, until you have a virtualization backup solution running, a backup of the source physical system is the only option available if something goes wrong and you need to recover everything. So — back up your applications and data. (Is there an echo in here?)

Preparing the new virtualization servers

Your source is ready, so now you need to prepare your *target* (the new virtualization server). Fortunately, this is probably the most straightforward step of all in the entire migration process.

The physical servers that the virtualization hypervisor will run on must be made ready prior to installing the virtualization software. Installing them should be relatively straightforward because hardware is hardware and a server is a server. One thing to keep in mind, however, is that VMware supports only certified hardware configurations, so you need to be sure that you're installing the right type of hardware for it, if you do decide to go with VMware as your chosen virtualization platform.

As Chapter 8 describes, a new generation of virtualization-oriented servers, which are significantly different than the 1U pizza-box servers typical of today's hardware environment, is being made available by hardware manufacturers. (They're called pizza boxes because that's what they look like: flat square boxes for the delivery of a significant link in the techie food chain.) So you might have to familiarize yourself with a new hardware type to be sure you're installing everything associated with virtualization properly. However, if you've done a pilot implementation, you'll have planned for — and addressed — any hardware restrictions imposed by your virtualization product or any new twists presented by a new type of hardware.

Common software installation scenarios: The manual path

After your new hardware is in place, it's time to install your virtualization software.

Fortunately, the virtualization vendors have really worked hard to make their products relatively easy to install. You can look at Chapters 12 through 14 to find out how to install several virtualization products. VMware's ESX Server and Virtual Iron's product are, thankfully, no longer in the rocket-science category when it comes to installation. And, of course, the container-type virtualization products from Sun and SWsoft are application-level products and therefore straightforward to get up and running. (Container-type virtualization, also known as operating system virtualization, extends the base operating system on a machine to provide virtualization environments that *contain* — thus the name container — applications in segregated execution environments. Installing any of these virtualization products on a single machine is easy, provided you follow the instructions closely.)

Deciding on your hardware is one of the most important decisions of your entire virtualization project. Be sure to research your hardware choices thoroughly before embarking on implementation. Particularly critical is the memory available in your virtualization servers because memory is the most common bottleneck for virtualization scalability. (Disk capacity and disk controller capacity are the next most common performance bottlenecks.)

Common software installations: The automated path

But what if you want to install a bunch of systems at the same time? After all, a multiserver infrastructure is likely when you implement a production virtualization environment. Is there any way to avoid hopping from machine to machine, installing software like a demented bunny?

In a word, yes. In fact, you have a few options.

✔ **Software management products:** If you have a software management product in place (something like HP's System Insight Manager; see Chapter 10 for more information on this and other products), you might be set. Software management products usually have the ability to install software onto multiple bare-metal systems — "bare metal" meaning that the server hardware has no software installed other than the firmware BIOS.

There are pros and cons to these products, as discussed in Chapter 10. One factor to take into account is their expense, which is significant. Another factor is that these products are themselves notoriously difficult to get installed and running properly — so if you don't already have a sophisticated system management product installed and working, you might find that, by installing such a product, you've jumped from the frying pan into the fire, software installation-wise.

In general, a good approach to take with the software management option is to consider using it if you already have such a system implemented. If you aren't already using system management software, it probably doesn't make sense to start now, merely to address installing your virtualization software. Even if you have system management software installed and want to consider using it, check to be sure that your particular product supports installing virtualization hypervisor software.

The products that fall into the software management category are products like HP's OpenView, IBM's Tivoli, and CA's Unicenter. Ask yourself whether your organization is already using them and how easy it would be to use them for installing virtualization software; even if you answer the two questions with "yes" and "easily enough," find out whether you can use the product to install your virtualization software. Because of how much work it takes to get one of these system management products installed and configured properly, system administration groups are often extremely reluctant to change them, fearing that attempting to do so will tumble their system management house of cards. If you do go this route, test it before attempting full-scale implementation.

✔ **Customized management products:** Other available products are a bit more focused in scope than the software management products — especially when it comes to automated installation. These products have the ability to deliver customized versions of products, certain configurations, and so on. Furthermore, you can configure them to control the automated updating of products with patches, bug fixes, and so on. Because they are task focused, these products generally are less complex to install and less expensive to purchase than the general system management products, although they aren't necessarily either simple or cheap.

There are certainly such customized products out there on the market —
Symantec's Veritas Provisioning Manager and Levanta's Intrepid would be
two examples. One issue to be aware of if you want to consider this type of
installation product is whether it supports your virtualization product —
they tend to be targeted at operating systems rather than virtualization
software. However, with the growing popularity of virtualization, these
products are being extended to support hypervisor installation.

✔ **Prebooting:** If you want to use an inexpensive, straightforward automated installation solution — albeit one that requires more elbow
grease — try Preboot Execution Environment, usually referred to as PXE.
PXE — created by Intel — is a BIOS extension designed to allow
machines to boot from a remote system and then have an operating
system installed remotely. PXE works by extending the BIOS of the
machine upon which the OS will be installed, which then calls to the
installing system, which in turn installs an OS on the calling machine.

An advantage of PXE is that you can use it to install any kind of image, so
it's not limited to standard OSes. In fact, you can use PXE to install both
XenSource and ESX Server, so it's quite flexible. Microsoft provides a
PXE-based feature called Remote Installation Server, which will undoubtedly be extended to support Windows Server Virtualization.

The downside of PXE is that implementing it is, as the saying goes, "left
as an exercise for the reader," meaning you have to install and configure
the arrangement on your own. You can find good instructions on the
vendor Web sites or via Internet searches, so getting PXE up and running
properly shouldn't be too difficult. A number of the automated install
products (like Symantec's Veritas Provisioning Manager and Levanta's
Intrepid, noted above) are PXE-based, so you can save yourself money
and give yourself more control by using PXE directly.

Deciding whether to use installation automation software to get your virtualization software in place or to install it manually should be based on your
assessment of the tradeoff between the time (and money) of using an automated solution versus the time of doing the installations by hand. One thing
to keep in mind is that automated installation is much better at consistently
repeating a task, whereas manually doing installs, which seems easy and
quick, can easily lead to inconsistent installations. Inconsistency of configuration is an infamous issue when trying to track down problems, so the point at
which you decide to take on the overhead of setting up an automated installation arrangement should be quite low. If you're setting up more than four or
five systems, I recommend you consider automating the installation in some
fashion.

Install necessary infrastructure (hardware and software)

I wish I could tell you that getting your new servers and virtualization software in place is all you need to do, but the truth is that you might need to install additional hardware and software as part of your virtualization project. (The horror!)

For many organizations, moving to virtualization represents a change in the way they manage their systems. Because of the growth in computing over the past 15 years, many IT shops have never changed their basic system management practices — which means they're still using the same manual processes that have always been in place. It's easy to understand why: The marginal work required to add one new server is always much smaller than the effort required to implement new management processes, even though the net effect of the new processes might be to reduce the overall workload.

Moving to virtualization, however, gives an organization the opportunity to take a fresh look at how things are being done. Have backups been performed manually for each system or, if automated, in a fashion that creates separate backup data for each system? With virtualization, actions that seemed to make sense when being executed for physically different boxes might seem less logical when a number of systems all reside on one server.

You might also have to rethink your infrastructure based on the virtualization product you'll be using. VMware's ESX Server, for example, typically is implemented with shared storage, so the direct-attached storage that's common today will be discarded in favor of centralized storage of some type. (For more information about virtualization storage options, check out Chapter 11.)

Here are some types of infrastructures you might need to consider installing:

- ✔ **Backup software:** You can take a couple of different approaches to backing up virtual machines. One is to back up each machine individually, and the other is to centralize the storage of all the virtual machines and back up that centralized storage. There are even a couple of approaches to individual backups — the backup software can reside with the hypervisor, or each virtual machine can have its own backup software. No matter which approach you pursue, you're going to move away from physically putting tapes in drives.

- **Centralized storage:** As noted previously, ESX Server is commonly implemented with shared storage (that is, folks tend to drop Direct-Attached Storage, also known as DAS, in favor of a shared storage strategy). Even if you're using a different product, you might choose to use shared storage rather than DAS, seeing the move to virtualization as an opportunity to implement a more robust storage strategy. You have many, many options for storage, but one thing is for certain: If you're not using DAS, you'll be installing hardware and software. (Again, check out Chapter 11 for more on storage issues in a virtualization environment.)

- **Network infrastructure:** You might need new networking capability for your virtualized infrastructure. If you've moved to a Fibre Channel–based storage solution, for example, you definitely need new networking cables as well as HBAs (*Host Bus Adapters*, the interface cards that enable the server to communicate via the Fibre Channel protocol). Even if you're sticking with iSCSI-based storage, you might very well want to segregate the storage traffic on the network from other storage, which requires, at the least, network configuration changes.

   Moving to iSCSI often motivates organizations to migrate from their existing 100MB network to higher-capacity GIG-E Gigabit Ethernet, which, as you might expect, requires new network hardware. Furthermore, moving to a more sophisticated storage strategy usually suggests that folks have a bit more invested in uptime — as in the opposite of downtime, which is a very, very bad thing — which necessitates redundancy in infrastructure. Naturally, this means two (at least) of everything and a more complex connection topology.

Virtualization security

Does virtualization offer better security than the traditional "one application, one server" world, or does it present even more security threats? You can find viewpoints on both sides of the debate.

Shortly before I began writing this book, I attended a presentation on virtualization security, the primary theme of which was that virtualization is something to be scared of because it has, as the presenter mentioned numerous times, more "attack surfaces." Boiled down, this means that, because virtualization is software, there's more software present for security attacks to focus on. For this insight, consultants get paid big fees!

What security issues should you think about when you consider virtualization?

One thing to consider is whether virtualization truly presents new security threats or is subject to the same range of security issues present with regular operating systems. One school of thought, represented by the speaker at the presentation I went to, is that virtualization does present new security issues.

The countervailing argument to that perspective is the fact that hypervisors are much smaller pieces of code than typical operating systems, which include many, many functions having nothing to do with controlling hardware. For example, most operating systems ship with File Transfer Protocol (FTP) servers, which are notorious for being attacked by outside hackers. Hypervisors include none of these security-threatening features because they focus on the limited tasks necessary for controlling communication between guest virtual machines and the underlying hardware.

Another argument for the "more security threat exists" side is that, given the ease of creating new virtual machines, data centers will soon be inundated by a tidal wave of new systems, presenting a flood of security problems that will drown the operations staff. The countervailing argument to that is that because virtual machines can be created from images, it's actually easier to implement consistent security practices because a single image can be kept up to date with patches and used to clone new virtual machines, thereby ensuring that fully protected systems are distributed throughout the data center.

To my mind, this "tidal wave" security argument is particularly weak. If data center security relies on the fact that it's hard to provision new machines — meaning that any easy solutions that come along for creating machines are seen as a threat and must therefore be fought at every turn — something is seriously wrong with the security practices being used, and those should be fixed rather than relying on how hard it is to create new physical systems.

As you can see, I'm not especially supportive of the "virtualization creates new security issues" viewpoint. The benefits of virtualization far outweigh the threats, and many of the people trumpeting virtualization security problems just happen to be in the business of selling security products and/or services.

In one area, though, virtualization does pose some security issues that are important to address. Because hypervisors can allow virtual machines to communicate with one another without going through the corporate network (this is referred to as creating a private network for the virtual machines), hypervisors contain a network switch internally, implemented in software. This can pose a potential threat because system administrators can't view the network traffic — it's all carried internally within the hypervisor. If the virtual machines were physical machines, the traffic between them would be carried on the corporate network, and the traffic could be examined. The lack of visibility into the traffic between virtual machines (remember, this is in the private network case; if the virtual machines are communicating to each other through the company network, their traffic will be available for sniffing) could pose security issues because traffic carrying an attack from one virtual machine to another would be hidden.

I expect that virtualization providers will address this vulnerability in the near future to ensure that visibility into internal hypervisor network traffic can be accessed for analysis. However, for today, it remains a possible threat (mostly theoretical because no one has made public a real-world example of such an attack) that you should be aware of. Overall, I would say that you should be aware of security as part of your virtualization plans, but not to allow it to derail your progress. As I said, the benefits of virtualization far outweigh the security issues that have thus far been raised.

As you can see, just getting your environment prepped for migration can be a challenge in itself, requiring time, money, and expertise. It's absolutely necessary to do it right, however; otherwise, you run the risk of your transition to virtualization going belly up.

After you've gotten the virtualization infrastructure installed, it's important to test it to make sure it's working properly. In addition to operational testing, try some destructive testing — for instance, unplug a network cable and see whether everything keeps operating properly. It also makes sense to test some heavy loads to ensure that you have sufficient headroom in capacity to deal with peak loads.

Keep in mind that a move to a more complex infrastructure generally requires different IT groups to collaborate in order to implement an integrated solution. Although this sounds like a no-brainer, getting each of the groups to cooperate can be a challenge. Take a look at Chapter 7 for some tips on how to get everyone working together for the good of the project.

To achieve an efficient virtualization environment, many groups have to cooperate to ensure that all the different parts of the infrastructure are integrating properly. Be sure to include all the affected groups in your virtualization project team to avoid any last-minute glitches.

At the end of this phase, your infrastructure is virtualization ready. It might seem like a lot of work, but it's absolutely vital that you get this phase's tasks done correctly: This is the foundation upon which your virtualization infrastructure will rest. If the foundation isn't solid, your virtualization infrastructure will be fragile and subject to failure. So don't overlook this phase in your enthusiasm to get virtualized!

Migrating Your Physical Servers

You're now at the phase of migration that most people are thinking of when they discuss "migrating to virtualization." Before, you have a jumble of physical boxes, each with an OS and one or more applications running on it. After, you have a much smaller number of physical boxes, each with multiple OSes running, along with all the applications formerly hosted on separate boxes.

Although virtualization vendors use the term P2V to cover the entire migration process, P2V actually addresses only transforming physical servers into virtual machine images; the rest of the migration process isn't addressed by P2V products.

So, how do you go from Before to After?

Consider the Before picture. You have a number of individual operating systems, probably of different types, almost certainly of different versions, and definitely of different patch levels.

Running in each OS, you have middleware — a surprisingly poorly defined term meaning software that sits between the end application and the operating system — which offers different kinds of services to the application so that it can operate effectively. Examples of middleware include application servers, databases, and integration software.

Just as you have various OS configurations, you have the same issue with middleware — in spades. In addition to having a variety of products, versions, and patch levels, individual servers might have these products installed but configured differently — with files installed in different directory locations, configuration files set up differently, and so on.

Finally, of course, you have the applications themselves. Although it's tempting to think that only one instance of an application would be in existence, many applications are installed on multiple physical servers for load or redundancy reasons, and these applications might vary in terms of installation and configuration from one server to another.

Be careful when working with P2V software. This software also has the ability to do what is called *cloning,* which refers to making identical copies of a single virtual machine. Although this is an excellent feature for rapidly building duplicate systems, it's inappropriate for migrating a number of similar, but differently versioned and patched, systems; to achieve that, you need to use the P2V system migration feature.

In other words, it's common that every physical server is a beast unique to itself — and the challenge is to transform each physical server into a virtual machine, successfully preserving its unique characteristics while enabling it to run successfully in a virtualized environment.

You might ask, why do I have to do any complex migration at all? Why can't I just copy the file system of my existing physical server into the file system of the virtual machine and be done with it?

Well, if you've ever tried to copy a Windows installation from one machine to another, you have your answer: hardware inconsistencies. I once moved the hard drive from a dead laptop to another laptop. When I booted the machine up, Windows complained mightily that the hardware it was seeing was different from what it had before. I finally got it straightened out, but it was a hassle.

Virtualization is virtualization because it emulates hardware or redirects hardware calls so that operating system instructions can be intercepted by the hypervisor, thereby allowing the underlying hardware to support multiple operating systems. Therefore, each guest OS must be modified in order to successfully execute in a virtualized environment. Consequently, a simple copy of files won't work for system migration. The software must be modified so that it can interact with the underlying hypervisor.

Manual migration: The hands-on approach

The most obvious approach to successful migration is to treat transferring the OS and applications to a new virtual machine the same way you'd treat them if you were transferring them to a new physical server. This typically entails the following steps:

1. **Back up all relevant application data after shutting down the application.**

   Application data is the crown jewel of a system because, after all, that's why you have systems — to manage and manipulate application information; that's why folks call the field *data* processing.

2. **Identify all relevant OS, middleware, and application configuration settings.**

   This might seem like a trivial task, and something that should already be documented, but working systems often have lots of configuration settings that haven't been documented. The inability to identify proper configuration settings is the biggest problem for successful migrations.

3. **Install fresh copies of the OS, middleware, and application on the new server.**

   Yes, this is a time-consuming, repetitive, boring step.

4. **Configure the OS, middleware, and application on the new server.**

   This is extremely challenging because a lot of configuration information isn't available. Consequently, getting all the new software operating — and cooperating — properly can be a lengthy and frustrating process.

5. **Load the backed-up application data into the newly installed application.**

6. **Ensure that all data is cleanly loaded.**

7. **Pray that it all works properly.**

The process is extremely labor intensive. Moreover, it's fraught with potential for mistakes — manually entering all that configuration information provides many opportunities for mistyping. And trying to track down a problem due to incorrect configuration settings can be like seeking a needle in a haystack.

 Manual migration is labor intensive and mistake prone — but sometimes necessary. For example, VMware's P2V product doesn't support conversion of Linux systems. In fact, most P2V products focus on Windows and give Linux the cold shoulder.

Multiply this process by a large number of servers, and you have a nightmare outcome — massive disruption of the data center followed by tortuous debugging of formerly working-just-fine applications.

Say, whose bright idea was this virtualization thing, anyway?

Does a better and easier alternative exist? Yes — at least, there's an alternative that covers many migration scenarios.

Automated migration: Let software do the work

Repetitive, detailed work on computer files — hmmm, sounds like the perfect opportunity for someone to create a computerized solution. And, a solution is at hand: automated migration software.

A number of migration solutions are available to ease the work and to speed up the process of moving from physical to virtual. They all do pretty much the same thing:

- ✔ Copy the physical server files in their entirety: system, middleware, and application software along with application data.

- ✔ Modify the system software, replacing hardware-specific portions of the software with software that will interact with the resident hypervisor on the new virtualization server.

- ✔ Register the newly modified system with the resident hypervisor on the new virtualization server so that the new virtual machine can begin operating.

Actually, this process makes a lot of sense. The only parts of the overall software aggregation — the OS, middleware, and application products — that need to be changed are those that interact with the hypervisor; everything else continues to operate just the same as it used to. If that's the case, why go to the trouble of reinstalling all that software that will operate the same way in the new virtualized environment as it did in the old physical environment? Furthermore, why ask for trouble by attempting to reinstall all the old software and get it properly configured?

Okay, so it all sounds like a pretty good deal in general. But when the rubber meets the road, what options for P2V automation are out there?

You have three different sources of PV2 automation software:

- **Virtualization vendors:** Each virtualization vendor has created P2V software to make it easy to move existing systems into its virtualization solution. VMware offers VMware Converter; XenSource offers a P2V wizard as part of its product; SWsoft offers VZP2V; and so on.

  In an echo of the word-processor wars of a decade ago, many of these vendors also import image files for other vendors' products; if you have virtual machine images running on one hypervisor, another virtualization vendor's P2V product will import the original image and convert it to its own image format. ("V2V migration" might be a convenient way to think of this ability to import other vendors' virtualization image formats.)

- **Third-party virtualization P2V vendors:** Companies like Platespin (www.platespin.com), Leostream (www.leostream.com), and Invirtus (www.invirtus.com) offer tools to convert physical systems to virtual machines. Because their business models entail working with all virtualization products, these company's products offer import and export in all formats.

- **System management tools:** Companies such as HP — with its System Insight Manager product — and IBM — with its Director product — offer P2V functionality as part of their system-management suites, characterizing P2V as just one more aspect of total system life cycle management.

Although each P2V solution has its particular architecture and method of functioning, they all operate in pretty much the same fashion. Here's how it works:

1. A piece of server software scans the source system, analyzing its setup to prepare for migration.

2. The P2V software then copies the source file system, modifying it in appropriate places so that the source system can interoperate with the target hypervisor.

3. The software converts the source system into the image format of the target hypervisor.

4. The P2V software then installs the newly created image format on the hypervisor. Magic!

P2V solutions vary somewhat in that some of them require a separate physical server to run the P2V software on, whereas others install on the target system.

P2V software is an excellent aid for system migration. Be sure to evaluate your specific needs against the functionality of the P2V product(s) you're considering — in other words, be sure to read the documentation to confirm the product will address your needs.

What if you're cheap?

One of the themes of this book is that virtualization is bringing the cost of computing down. If you work through the examples of virtualization in Chapters 12 through 14, you'll see that there are even ways to use virtualization at no cost.

So it might stick in your craw to see a situation in which you can use virtualization for free, but need to pay for the P2V software to get your existing systems converted to virtual machines. Is there a P2V solution available at no cost?

Fortunately, you're in luck. Just as the shrinking price of software has caused virtualization vendors to offer versions of their products for free (albeit versions that have somewhat less functionality or scalability than their enterprise versions), the same trend has caused P2V providers to offer somewhat restricted versions of their products for free.

For example, VMware offers a free version of its VMware Converter, called VMware Converter Starter, for download. Now, VMware Converter does P2V only for Windows systems, so if your project is focused on Windows, you're in luck. Also, the Starter version doesn't support P2V for ESX Server, so if your target is ESX Server, you need to consider the Enterprise version.

But what if your target is XenSource's XenEnterprise? You can turn to one of the commercial vendors and pay for a P2V product. But remember what I said about the virtualization products offering import capabilities, a la word processors of a decade ago? Well, XenSource XenEnterprise offers the ability to import VMware image files. So one way to do a P2V of your Windows systems for XenSource's product would be to do a P2V conversion with VMware Converter Starter, and then use the XenSource import function to import the converted-to-VMware-format systems. Clever, eh?

Longer term, I don't think you'll have much to worry about. As the competition heats up among hypervisor vendors, each will recognize that it's in their interest to make it as easy and inexpensive to load systems onto their virtualization software, which is where they make their real money. I expect to see full-featured P2V software to become a free product, as vendors get in a race to stake out virtualization territory. And this makes sense, doesn't it? At one time, converters for documents were a separately priced product, until word processor vendors figured out that the important thing was to achieve dominance on the desktop — and making it easy to put documents into their format would help achieve dominance. At that point, document conversion software became a giveaway. I'm sure you'll see the same trend in virtualization.

As you begin to think about using a P2V product, one thing to consider is what source OSes you seek to convert. Most of the P2V products on the market are focused on converting Windows systems. Some offer support for Red Hat and Novell Linux but no other Linux systems, whereas others don't support Linux at all. In any case, Linux support by P2V products is quite recent. Therefore, depending on your particular circumstances, you might find that the available P2V products address only part of your migration needs. Certainly you need to research your options in light of your specific infrastructure.

The reason for this Windows bias is very understandable. First, Windows tends to be the primary type of system to be virtualized; most people consider Windows to be the critical platform to be virtualized.

Second, Windows systems are easier to convert. Windows systems tend to have a very consistent file system layout, with no confusion about where configuration information resides. Linux systems, by contrast, are much less consistent about how their file systems are organized and where configuration information resides. This Linux inconsistency applies within the product lines of individual Linux distributions, because file system layouts have been known to vary from one version to another. I noted earlier the challenges of Linux configuration files, which, as you can imagine, make it difficult for an automated solution to successfully handle conversions.

If you decide to use an automated solution, here are some things to keep in mind:

- **Analyze your source systems and match them against your potential automated solution.** Depending on your mix of source systems, you might be guided toward one automated solution or another. You can perform such an analysis by checking what your source systems are and then checking to see if those are supported by your favored P2V vendor.

- **Evaluate and test your chosen automated solution to ensure that it really performs as advertised.** There's a world of difference between what a vendor claims and what a product does! This evaluation can be performed as part of a pilot of your virtualization solution, which is the best place to test your favored P2V solution as well.

- **Evaluate your network topology.** Many of the P2V solutions replace drivers as part of the migration process. When it comes to network cards, your virtualization solution might require all of them to be on the same network subnet so that the updated drivers can communicate properly. Therefore, research your chosen P2V solution so that you understand its requirements and limitations with respect to network connectivity, data location, and so on.

- **Carefully consider whether you'll use all of the features of the P2V solution.** A couple of the vendors claim that their products will even convert a system while it's live (that is, in production). Even if I were confident that this would operate properly, I'd avoid attempting to convert a live system. The situation involves too many moving parts, and too many things could go wrong. Moving to virtualization is a significant initiative; if you can't develop a plan to take some of your systems offline during migration, perhaps they aren't good candidates for automated migration.

Speaking of which, recognize that some percentage of your systems will need to be migrated manually. P2V is a tremendous aid to migration, but it probably won't be able to do the entire migration task. Your goal is to minimize the number of systems you need to migrate manually. If you're planning to virtualize Linux systems, especially less popular distributions, you have to do some manual work. Be sure to allow time — plenty of time — for the right amount of manual migration in your project plan.

It might seem like a cliché, but it's important to recognize that migration is a vital process that requires attention and dedication. Although the Web sites of vendors breezily assure you that their P2V product will operate automatically, leaving you nothing more challenging than deciding between coffee and tea while you put your feet up on your desk, you're likely to have some manual work as part of the P2V process.

Moving to Production

When you have your new virtual machines installed, the next task is to get them up and running so that you can begin regular operations.

I can tell you right now that a flash cutover of all systems at once is a bad idea. Even though you've tested the systems in a pilot environment, you'll be putting the new virtual machines into production in a different environment, one which has lots of other systems running, with different network traffic patterns, and so on. Consequently, it's important to take a measured approach to your virtualization cutover.

Particularly important is to watch the load factors on your virtualization servers. Most organizations pursue virtualization as a way of raising server utilization rates, but going too high in utilization can be just as bad as running too low. Depending on what management approach you've decided on for your virtualized environment (see Chapter 10 for more information on virtualization management), keep an eagle eye on the management console as you begin turning up your new systems.

A good plan is to incrementally add new virtual machines to each virtualization server in a round robin fashion — that is, start a machine on virtualization server #1, start a machine on virtualization server #2, and so on until you've reached your last virtualization server; then start again by putting a second virtual machine on virtualization server #1, and so on. You get the picture. While incrementally adding machines, keep an eye on the management console to see how the machine is responding.

Of course, you can use the performance information within each virtual machine to track its response time to determine whether the machine itself is performing adequately.

If you've implemented an additional infrastructure (such as network switches or virtualized storage), you'll want to keep an eye on that as well, especially if it's new to your infrastructure.

Essentially, a cutover to a new virtualized environment is very similar to moving an existing system to a new physical server. The main differences are

- **There's additional software in the mix in the form of a hypervisor.** You need to track the performance of your systems as they operate in a virtualized environment, so you'll be tracking some extra things compared to a standard conversion.

- **Physical hardware conversions usually happen individually or in small batches.** P2V conversions, by contrast, can encompass much larger numbers of systems. So, careful planning for the cutover and sufficient staffing to track all the migrated systems are important.

One thing remains the same, however. The end of a successful cutover calls for a celebration: T-shirts, pizza, and your preferred beverage. Go for it!

Chapter 10

Managing Your Virtualized Environment

In This Chapter

▶ Seeing virtualization as a commodity

▶ Management: The new virtualization battleground

▶ Analyzing the two philosophies of virtualization management

▶ Deciding the right philosophy for you

*V*irtualization's move from niche to center leads to some very interesting developments, which I invite you to ponder. As virtualization moves to the center of your data center (if I may put it that way), one thing you'll need to strategize about is how you'll manage this new resident that has moved in. And you have lots of options; in fact, you might have too many options, because every virtualization product has several different ways you can manage both the product itself as well as the virtual machines it hosts. Of course, the right management option will depend on which of the many available virtualization products you ultimately choose.

Although VMware isn't the only solution, it has by far the largest market share today. With respect to how you'll manage those products, one important thing to keep in mind is that VMware comes in two flavors:

✔ **As an application that sits on top of the native operating system:** These VMware products (VMware Server and VMware Workstation, to be more precise) are added to an existing system that already has an operating system installed. You then install guest operating systems on top of the VMware virtualization software and interact with the guest operating systems as though they were native operating systems.

These products are aimed at desktop use and software development and test environments. They're easy to use and can use Direct Attached Storage (DAS). If you'd like more information, see Chapter 3, which describes virtualization technologies and applications.

> ✔ **As a virtualization layer that sits on "bare metal":** These VMware prod-
> ucts (VMware ESX Server and Virtualization Infrastructure 3, for example)
> are installed directly on a server, the so-called *bare metal,* without any
> intervening operating system. In other words, the virtualization software
> (also known as the *hypervisor*) is self-contained and capable of interacting
> with the underlying hardware without any help from a native OS. These
> products are aimed at running production systems in data centers.

Another trend discussed in Chapter 4 is the delivery of software as a *virtual
appliance* — a file image containing a preconfigured bundle of virtual
machine, guest operating system, and application, ready to be dropped onto
an existing virtualization hypervisor. End users love this concept because it
promises to get rid of lots of the error-prone manual work that comes with
installing and configuring myriad pieces of software just to get an application
up and running. Software vendors love this concept because it might reduce
the number of support calls they receive, because installation and configuration typically account for a large percentage of support requests.

If you look at these trends as a whole, it's obvious that they promise to shake
up the existing product and vendor hierarchy in the technology industry.
And change carries both threat and opportunity with it. Change threatens
to upset the existing market positions of dominant players, and it offers the
opportunity for new vendors to achieve dominance. And, so far, VMware has
been the beneficiary of the change represented by virtualization.

As you might imagine, the existing big dogs of technology, such as the big
application vendors and operating system vendors, aren't that happy that a
new market entrant threatens to muscle in at the head of the line. Crucially,
they worry that VMware will become the critical piece of software that end
users focus their attention on, instead of the current darlings of technology
planning — companies like Microsoft and Red Hat.

Consequently, the big dogs are responding to what they view as a significant
competitive threat posed by VMware. The most obvious method of responding is by providing their own brand of virtualization, bundled with the OS.

Because VMware products are actually quite good, it's not enough just to provide some token form of virtualization as part of the OS. After all, if the virtualization included with the OS is technically inferior, customers are still likely
to choose VMware. So if you can't win on technical merits, what do you do?

How about give your product away?

And that's just what the OS vendors are doing — bundling virtualization with
the operating system at no extra cost. Now the argument shifts to "why
would you use VMware, which will cost you a bunch of extra money, when
you can use the free virtualization delivered as part of the operating system?"

And free is a powerful argument, as you undoubtedly know.

Microsoft gives away its current product, Virtual Server, as a free add-on to its Server product. And Microsoft plans to include its higher-performance virtualization hypervisor in the upcoming Microsoft Windows Server 2008 product. In fact, because Microsoft is so intent on communicating the message that virtualization is just part of the product, it doesn't plan to give the capability its own brand name — it just refers to it as Windows Server Virtualization; in other words, just one part of the overall operating system.

The open source virtualization product called Xen is bundled for free with Linux distributions from commercial Linux vendors such as Red Hat and Novell.

I think you can see where this is going: The long-term trend in virtualization is free. Basic virtualization functionality is moving from a high-price offering to something available on every machine at no extra cost.

As a user, this is a trend you should celebrate: great technology trending to free. What's not to like?

For the operating system vendors, the trend makes sense. They can just bundle the virtualization functionality in with the existing commercial operating system offering. For the commercial virtualization companies like VMware and Virtual Iron, the situation is more challenging: how do you compete with free?

Managing Virtualization: The Next Challenge

Competitive pressures are pushing down the costs of virtualization. That's a given. Another trend associated with virtualization is that, because the technology makes installing and configuring new systems so easy, you'll probably put more systems in. Perhaps lots more.

And that brings you to the next challenge of virtualization: managing all those virtual machines. If it only costs a tenth as much as it used to in terms of hardware and administration to install and configure a new system, you'll more than likely increase the overall number of machines you put in — maybe not ten times as many, but at least two or three times as many. It just stands to reason that the previously high cost of getting new systems up and running deterred organizations from putting in very many. Now that the cost has dropped, that deterrence is gone, so more will be put in.

This principle is honored in economics as price elasticity, the maxim that states that, for most goods and services, demand goes up as cost goes down. Price elasticity predicts that because the cost of installing and configuring a system drops with the move to virtualization, organizations will implement many more systems. Put another way, because virtualization drops the overall cost of implementing new systems, system users will implement more inexpensive virtual machines than they would have implemented if their only alternative were expensive physical machines. Common sense, huh? Makes you wonder why people award a Nobel Prize in economics!

If you listen to many of the pundits in the virtualization world, you'll hear virtual machine price elasticity described as an enormous threat. You'll also hear the phrase "server sprawl" thrown about as something to be feared — how IT organizations are about to be inundated by new virtual machines and how IT organizations will lose control as they fail to keep track of all their machines. From this perspective, virtualization sounds like a plague that will make you long for the expensive, time-consuming world of physical machines.

Frankly, this strikes me as self-serving. Many of these Chicken Littles are opportunists who want to scare you so that you'll pay good money to consult with them on "best practices" or "developing a virtualization strategy."

On the other hand, it makes sense that managing two or three times as many systems might impose a burden on your administration staff. Although implementing a system is certainly faster and cheaper with virtualization, every new system, whether physical or virtual, does need to be monitored and managed. And developing a management strategy for your new, much larger collection of systems is part and parcel of an overall virtualization strategy. So, you can take it as a given that figuring out the right way to manage this new, larger collection of systems is going to be important for you as you implement your virtualized infrastructure.

Managing Free Virtualization

Downward cost pressures and increased demand have merged to create the new battleground of virtualization: management. If there's no money to be made in providing basic virtualization services and the likely pain point for users is managing the ever-increasing number of systems that will be implemented due to virtualization, there's money to be made by helping IT organizations manage their virtual machine collections.

As you might expect, this situation has created a feeding frenzy among virtualization vendors. The challenge for you as a virtualization consumer is making sense out of the mosh pit that is the virtualization management market. You must decide how you should manage your virtualized infrastructure today, and even more importantly, in the future.

The critical items for you to consider as you construct your management strategy are

- **Your virtualization solution:** Have you chosen a virtualization solution that will serve as the foundation for your virtualized infrastructure now and in the future? This is critical because your range of options varies based on whether you're pursuing a VMware or Xen solution and which version of these products you've selected.

- **Your hardware platform:** Do you have a favored hardware vendor that provides most, if not all, of your hardware systems? Depending on what hardware you use, you'll find that your management options vary.

- **Your location and destination on the virtualization journey:** Where are you on your virtualization journey, and what is your expected destination? Depending on how you expect to use virtualization, you'll need more or less sophistication in your virtualization management. Your likely destination in the journey will affect your choice of management platform.

You might feel it's impossible to know all the answers to these items, but keep them in mind because they'll guide you toward your virtualization management choice.

The first things for you to examine are the two competing philosophies of virtualization management. Think about which one you lean toward.

Virtualization Management: The Two Philosophies

There are two schools of thought about how a virtualized infrastructure should be managed:

- The predominant philosophy is that virtualization is this new technology that should be managed as a specialized resource.

- The lesser-established philosophy is that virtual machines are, well, machines, and should be managed just like physical machines — as part of the overall infrastructure of the data center.

Both philosophies have elements of truth to them, and which you decide to pursue depends on your view of virtualization — is it a game-changing technology, or is it an evolution of existing IT trends?

Virtualization as a specialized resource

The specialized resource perspective of virtualization emanates from virtualization vendors. The characteristic here is that virtual machines carry their own formats and require the knowledge of the vendor to manage efficiently.

This perspective is especially applicable as you move farther on the virtualization journey. If you plan to treat your virtualization capability as a server pool, with virtual machines assigned to whichever machine is the most appropriate, the software helping you with the distribution and management of the systems needs to have a deep understanding of the virtualization software. The management software should know how virtualization works, what system parameters affect the virtual machine distribution decision, and so on.

For VMware, which has a tight coupling between the hypervisor and the different hardware elements of its virtualization infrastructure — stuff like servers, storage, and networking — this argument is particularly compelling. After all, VMware understands what makes its software tick better than anyone, so, as one would expect, its virtualization management is the best at managing VMware.

For Xen, the situation isn't quite so clear-cut. Xen technology is included in Linux distributions, so the management of virtualization is distribution specific. For example, Novell SUSE Linux Enterprise Server (SLES) integrates Xen management into Yast, its general system management tool. Red Hat, on the other hand, provides a specialized virtualization manager called Virtual Machine Manager for all your virtual machine management needs. (See Figure 10-1.)

However, XenSource, the commercial sponsor of Xen, offers its own version of Xen, focusing on more highly sophisticated infrastructures with better management tools. Likewise, Virtual Iron uses the base Xen functionality as the jumping-off point for its product, which delivers a more sophisticated management of Xen. So choosing a Xen virtualization-specific management tool will most likely be guided by how you obtain the Xen functionality: If you obtain Xen via SLES, you'll most likely use Yast to manage your virtual machines, but if you plunk down some cold hard cash for the commercial version of Xen, you'll likely use XenEnterprise or Virtual Iron.

The specialized resource perspective of virtualization probably will direct you toward using the management provided by the virtualization vendor. The vendor, after all, knows its products better than anyone else and can deliver the most tightly integrated product set containing both hypervisor and management tools.

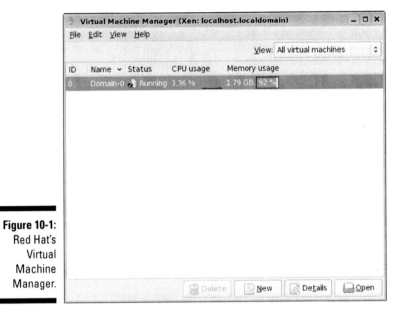

Figure 10-1:
Red Hat's
Virtual
Machine
Manager.

But what if you don't have that neat all-in-one virtualization product that can be managed by the virtualization vendor's management console? What if you're like everyone else and you've got a messy sprawl of multiple physical hardware types, with not one but several virtualization products? Then the best-of-breed approach that dictates "use the management solution the virtualization vendor delivers" will guide you to implementing several virtualization management products, which is a high-cost headache. What is your alternative if you live in the messy real world? For the answer to that, check out the next section.

Virtualization as an equal member of the data center

The alternative philosophy to "virtualization as a specialized resource" is the "virtual machines are just machines" perspective. Seen from this viewpoint, virtual machines are a resource that provides an operating environment, hosts applications, consumes networking and storage capacity, and needs to be managed just like their physical counterparts. This philosophy can be summed up as "if it looks like a machine, consumes resources like a machine, has to be kept up and running like a machine, and needs to be backed up like a machine . . . it's a machine."

This philosophy leads you to use a general system management tool that is able to manage virtual machines as one more type of IT resource. This perspective has a lot going for it: First and foremost it treats virtualization as an integral part of the infrastructure, one of a number of resources that need to be managed holistically in order to gain the most efficient infrastructure possible. This type of virtualization management is particularly attractive if you envision implementing virtualization extending from server to storage, because one management system can extend throughout your infrastructure.

As you might expect, this philosophy is pushed by the vendors of system management tools. They promise a nirvana of seamless systems all playing together, managed from one über-console. Doesn't that sound great?

If you're drawn toward this approach to virtualization management, check out products from HP (System Insight Manager), IBM (Director), and their large vendor brethren.

On the other hand, choosing this approach isn't without its challenges:

- **Expense and complexity:** System management tools are notorious for being expensive, complex, and very difficult to implement properly. So taking this route imposes additional costs and tasks on your virtualization implementation.

- **Vendors struggling to say up to date:** Although the system management vendors work very hard to keep their products up to date with respect to the underlying resources they manage, it's a difficult task to do, as you might imagine. When a virtualization vendor comes out with a new version of its product, its own management products are likely to support the new version immediately. The system management vendors typically lag supporting the latest releases from vendors by some period of time.

- **Incompatibility issues:** The system management products from hardware vendors usually support their own hardware more effectively than they support hardware from competitors. If you think about it for a minute, this makes sense. HP, for example, will know everything about HP systems and understand how to most effectively manage them, but its ability to manage, say, Dell machines, will be based on general information available from Dell.

How effectively do system management tools actually manage virtualization? Depending on who you talk to, you'll hear different things. Some people (especially the system management vendors themselves) maintain that they can fully manage virtual systems as part of a general management infrastructure. Others tell you that, to manage virtualization software by using the system management product, they had to do a ton of integration by hand, writing scripts to knit all the resources together to get a single view of all computing resources.

Making Sense of Virtualization Management

Okay, you have a lot of options. How should you decide how to manage your virtualization infrastructure?

I recommend you evaluate where you are in the virtualization journey, your current system management approach, and what your current and future mix of hardware looks like. These three factors will guide you toward one of the two virtualization management approaches.

Where you are in the virtualization journey

Perhaps the most important factor in deciding how to manage your virtualization infrastructure lies in what you're actually using virtualization for: Are you just experimenting, is this a pilot/departmental project, or are you talking production here? Each of these uses has distinct characteristics that carry implications with regard to how you manage the virtualization infrastructure.

✔ **Experimentation:** By definition, if you're in the experimentation phase, you're learning about virtualization. The technology is new, and you're probably trying to understand how it works. You're also probably trying to understand how your applications work in a virtualized environment.

In other words, your mind is probably reeling with a lot of new information. The important task to accomplish in experimentation is to get a deep understanding of virtualization. To accomplish that, it's critical to have as few variables as possible. If you attempt to evaluate system management tools as a part of your virtualization evaluation, your work will expand exponentially. Worse, if you run into problems, you won't be able to determine easily where the problem lies: Is it in the virtualization layer, the system management layer, or the integration layer that knits the two together?

✔ **Pilot/departmental:** Using virtualization in these environments is kind of a tryout for the production use of virtualization. If you look at Chapter 7, you see that the purpose of a pilot project is to understand the tasks and challenges you'll face in rolling virtualization out in your production environment, but in a safe learning environment. It's better to make mistakes and learn from them in a controlled situation rather than in your production infrastructure where any problem means lost money and productivity.

A departmental implementation is a bit different than a pilot system, but both affect a limited number of people and typically impose relatively low costs for a failure. Departmental implementations are often precursors of a production rollout and therefore often feature testing production-level elements. Specifically, production management techniques are sometimes used for departmental systems even though the scope of the system doesn't really call for them. Departmental systems offer the opportunity to try out production-level systems in a more forgiving environment.

Your management approach to virtualization in the pilot/departmental environment depends heavily on how you're likely to manage the systems in your production data center. If you use a sophisticated system management product as part of your production environment, it's critical to evaluate how well it works with your virtualization product *before* you put it into production.

✔ **Production:** This is the real deal, where every system has to be up and running as much as possible and problems have to be fixed as soon as possible. Most IT organizations have established processes regarding how they manage their production environment. Introducing a new technology into a production environment is stressful enough; trying to introduce a new management approach on top of the new technology might be the straw that breaks the camel's back. In other words, if you're introducing virtualization into your production environment, this is no time to try adding new ways of managing it as well. Stick to your established management techniques and processes. (You did test them during a pilot, didn't you?)

Where you are on the journey through virtualization affects how you'll approach managing your virtualized environment. Essentially, as the risk of problems rises, your tolerance for trying out new things should be lower. Get one thing working properly at a time before introducing something else.

Your current system management approach

Here's a key question for how you'll manage your virtualized infrastructure: How do you manage your current nonvirtualized infrastructure?

The vendors of system management software would have you believe that *everyone* uses their software to manage their production environment, but the truth is far different.

Many companies manage systems individually. The reasons for that vary.

✔ **Some want better control of individual systems.** Inevitably, if you insert a layer of system management software between the administrator and the managed systems, you lose some control and visibility into the system state. If you're managing a highly tuned environment, you probably don't want anything between the administrator and the individual systems.

✔ **Some can't afford system management software.** Did I mention the fact that system management software is expensive? Many companies can't afford or can't justify purchasing system management software, so systems are managed individually.

✔ **Some tried it but didn't like it.** Many organizations have purchased system management software and tried to implement it but found the complexity overwhelming and just threw in the towel. This has led to much system management software ending up as *shelfware* — meaning the software just sits on a shelf in a back room, forever gathering dust. The folks who requested the software just hope and pray that no one higher up ever asks, "What ever happened to that superexpensive system management software we bought that was supposed to make our lives so much easier?"

On the other hand, many organizations have successfully implemented system management software. Often these are larger companies that have the financial wherewithal to make an investment in training and integration in order to take advantage of the efficiencies of system management software.

As discussed in the preceding section, most IT organizations have an established method of system management, whether manual or automated via management software. How your organization currently manages its production environment should guide you toward deciding how to manage your virtualized infrastructure. I believe in avoiding too many balls in the air; virtualization is likely to be challenging enough without trying to impose a new way of managing systems as well. Therefore, if you have an established method of automated system management, you're probably better off using it to manage your new virtualized environment. If all you've relied on in the past is manual management of individual machines, you're better off using the management software that is part of your new virtualization product.

What your current hardware mix looks like

Most system management products do a better job managing the products that come from the same company as the management software itself. The result is that the management capabilities will vary by system in a mixed-hardware environment. Although the system management vendors probably won't state it too bluntly, they'd prefer that you implement an environment primarily made up of their products. Of course, canny IT organizations usually try and avoid letting one vendor's products dominate their environments precisely because they want to retain leverage. Every IT organization has its own solution for the tradeoff between efficiency and control.

Consequently, depending on how your organization has decided that trade-off, you might have a mixed-product environment that doesn't lend itself very well to a generalized system management solution. Therefore, before you make a decision about how you might want to manage your virtualized environment, take stock of what you have running in your data center.

Deciding on Your Virtualization Management Approach

Whew! It seems like a bunch of different factors to take into account with regard to managing your virtualized infrastructure, doesn't it?

Don't worry. I've created a handy table — Table 10-1 — that provides guidance about making your system management choice. By following the table, you can form a general idea of the best direction to take for your virtualization management approach.

Table 10-1	Virtualization Management Recommendations	
Virtualization Use	*Current System Management Approach for Production Environment*	*Virtualization Management Recommendation*
Experimentation	Not applicable	Use virtualization-specific management tools — you're in a learning mode, so explore all aspects of the virtualization product you're experimenting with.
Pilot/Departmental	No current system management tools in use	Use virtualization-specific management tools. Because no tools are being used in production, the virtualization-specific tools are what you'll use when you move to production.

Virtualization Use	Current System Management Approach for Production Environment	Virtualization Management Recommendation
	System management tools in use	Use system management tools as the primary management mechanism to assess your ability to manage virtualized environment in production. Consider performing assessment of virtualization-specific management tools to compare capability to currently used system management tools.
Production	No current system management tools in use	Use virtualization-specific management tools.
	System management tools in use	Use the old system management tools unless comparison of management tools performed during pilot phase and virtualization-specific tools assessed as significantly superior.

If you don't currently use a system management tool, you should lean toward using the virtualization-specific management functionality offered by the virtualization product. If you do have a system management tool in place, I suggest that you use that to manage your virtualized infrastructure.

The only exception to this guidance is if you're experimenting with virtualization. In that case, I recommend that you stick with managing your virtualization through the virtualization-specific tools because it's important to get exposed to all aspects of the virtualization product in order to thoroughly understand its capabilities.

Virtualization management is the next competitive frontier, and there'll be plenty of market noise about it. Just remember that after the dust settles, no matter what a vendor says, you'll be in charge of making your virtualized infrastructure hum. Don't accept vendor claims at face value; evaluate your virtualization management options and be sure to select one that aligns with the way you currently manage your infrastructure. It's vital that you manage your virtualized infrastructure effectively and efficiently to ensure you get the most from the technology.

Chapter 11

Creating a Virtualized Storage Environment

In This Chapter

▶ Looking at storage fundamentals

▶ Investigating your storage options

▶ Linking storage choices to different types of virtualization

▶ Evaluating your evolving storage needs

*O*ne of the most important decisions you'll make about your virtualization project is where to store virtual machine data. You have a number of options, each with positives and negatives. Moreover, the type of storage you use will affect your virtualization options; certain storage types will constrain your ability to continue further down the road on your virtualization journey. Of course, no storage decision is set in stone. You can always change where and how your data is stored, but it's better to understand all your storage choices before making a decision.

This chapter begins by describing the different types of storage available. It then moves on to describe how a virtualization solution interacts with storage. Understanding the relationship between storage and the different types of virtualization is important because, depending on which virtualization solution you choose, you'll be guided in one direction or another in terms of your storage choice. The chapter concludes with a discussion about how the virtualization journey — your virtual life farther down the road, as it were — can impact your storage choices.

Storage Overview

If you're like many (if not most) computer users, you've happily gone about your life without ever thinking of something called "storage." Oh, you might have used files. You might have even swapped hard drives in your computer. But storage?

Storage is a word used to describe methods of saving and retrieving data in all its forms. Nothing more, nothing less. However, you have many, many options for storage, and it's important to understand the different types of hard drive–based storage so that you can devise an appropriate storage strategy for your virtualization project.

With regards to hard drive storage, you have three options:

- ✔ Direct-Attached Storage (DAS, also known as *local* storage)
- ✔ Network-Attached Storage (NAS, a form of shared storage that resides on the corporate network)
- ✔ Storage Area Networks (SAN, another form of shared storage that uses a storage-specific network to carry data traffic)

Just as virtualization is awash with straightforward rules that have numerous exceptions, so too is storage. SANs now come with the ability to communicate over the corporate IP network, although many organizations choose to partition their IP network to separate data and storage traffic — see what I mean about exceptions?

Read on to find out more about them.

What the heck is DAS?

DAS is a TLA (three letter acronym — get used to them because storage is littered with TLAs) that merely describes storage that's local to a machine. In other words, DAS refers to one or more hard drives residing within a computer. There — now you can throw around your own TLA and sound extremely knowledgeable about storage. (Okay, okay, if you insist — DAS is short for Direct-Attached Storage.)

DAS is the most common type of storage because it's the easiest type to use and manage. Most computers come with at least one hard drive installed so that users immediately have someplace to store any data their applications create.

For applications to be able to write data into a file, a file system must be installed on the hard drive. Fortunately, the installation programs used to place operating systems onto computers are smart enough to format a hard drive and create the appropriate file system on the machine. Of course, if you buy a machine with an OS preinstalled, you'll never see the installer create the file system. However, if you work through any of Chapters 12, 13, or 14, you see an installer create a file system as part of the overall installation process.

The storage industry has done an amazing job over the past decade in creating ever-larger hard drives at ever-smaller prices. In fact, I've seen data that illustrates the fact that hard drive capacity growth has outstripped the technology industry gold standard of growth, Moore's Law. This law, named after Gordon Moore, cofounder of chip company Intel, posits that chips double in processing power every 18 months. Moore made this observation in 1965; despite all challenges, the industry has reliably delivered increased power right on schedule for four decades. But the storage industry has done even more, perhaps tripling capacity every 18 months.

I've certainly seen evidence of this growth. In 1995, I bought a hard drive with a capacity of 400MB for $600. In August of 2007, I bought a 250GB hard drive for $59 — 600 times the capacity for one-tenth the price. (Adjusted for inflation, it's probably more like 600 times the capacity for one-twentieth the price!) Isn't technology wonderful?

This increased capacity has meant that computer storage has increased unbelievably over the past few years. That's the good news. The bad news is that applications continue to generate more and more data at an increasing rate, leading to some definite problems, which I turn to in a moment.

In terms of technology choices, hard drives come in a few different flavors. Typical home computers are usually IDE based, which means they use the IDE interface protocol for data transfer. (IDE stands for *I*ntegrated *D*rive *E*lectronics.) IDE is being superseded by SATA, which stands for *S*erial *A*dvanced *T*echnology *A*ttachment and is another interface specification. Business computers often use Small Computer System Interface (SCSI, pronounced *skuzzy*) drives. SCSI offers greater scalability because you can chain more devices (such as hard drives) from a single cable. Furthermore, SCSI offers somewhat higher performance than SATA or IDE. (And IDE, confusingly enough, is sometimes referred to as PATA; I mean, really, don't these engineers have anything else to do with their time?) However, SCSI drives are typically more expensive than SATA or IDE drives; consequently, consumer computers and many small business computers now use SATA or IDE drives, whereas larger computers use SCSI drives.

Drive capacity has grown dramatically, but so has application data generation. In 2003, 5 exabytes (each exabyte is 1 million terabytes) of new data were created and stored by computer users throughout the world. A recent study by the Enterprise Strategy Group predicted that governments and corporations will store over 25 exabytes by the year 2010. Certainly, the trend of data growth within organizations is accelerating. The growth of data can be easily seen in one key statistic: In 2006, the storage industry shipped as much storage in one month as it did in the entire year 2000. The research firm IDC estimates that total storage shipped will increase 50 percent per year for the next five years.

What do all these big numbers mean? Just that, despite the best efforts of hard drive manufacturers, many computer users can't get enough storage capacity in a single server. Most servers hold one or two drives; with today's largest capacity drives at 1TB (terabyte), servers can handle at most 2TB of storage, which seems like a lot, but many business applications need even more. This insatiable demand for storage has caused the creation of a new storage offering, going under the general label of shared storage.

Shared storage

Shared storage is storage capable of being shared by a number of computers, thereby implying that the storage is typically *not* directly attached to any one server, but rather resides somewhere else in the data center. Now, this doesn't mean that a pile of hard drives is sitting over in the corner. Far from it — being located remotely just means that the storage is located in hardware other than the server itself.

There are basically three types of shared storage:

✔ **Network storage:** This term really refers to storage that resides on one computer but is used by another. If you've ever used a Windows network share on another computer, you've used network storage. A Windows share is listed on a Windows computer with a drive letter (F:, for example), and it can be used like any local file system. Another common type of network storage is the Network File System (NFS), which is a set of files exported by one computer and imported by another computer as part of its hierarchical file system (/nfsfilesystem/data, for example). Access to network storage usually goes across the standard corporate network, making it easy to install and use.

By the way, you might have noticed that network storage seems to contradict the premise of shared storage, which is storage located off of servers. Don't worry, network storage really is shared storage, but the fact that it resides on one server and is accessible by others is just another one of those exceptions I mentioned at the beginning of the chapter.

✔ **Network-Attached Storage (NAS):** This is storage that resides on a dedicated piece of hardware but is accessed just like the network storage options outlined in the previous paragraph. One of the advantages of NAS is that the hardware can be optimized for data storage and access, making NAS more efficient than vanilla network storage. A NAS device can be installed directly on the corporate network, and data going to and from a NAS device is carried by standard file access protocols like NFS and SMB.

This description makes NAS sound like a single system attached to the network, but in fact NAS has been extended to increase scalability and reliability. You can now get NAS solutions that transparently cluster several NAS systems together to avoid single point of failure (SPOF) issues, so that if one NAS system fails, a backup takes over the work immediately. (These more sophisticated NAS systems operate transparently to the user, although there's even more administrator work required to configure more complex NAS solutions successfully.)

✔ **Storage Area Network (SAN):** Unlike NAS, which uses standard data protocols over the corporate network, SANs use the block data communication protocol, which uses lower-level storage mechanisms than NAS-based systems to increase performance. Moreover, SANs use specialized network protocols over dedicated networks to further improve performance.

The most common type of SAN uses Fibre Channel (note the idiosyncratic spelling of Fibre) networks rather than the Ethernet-based networks used as the basis for corporate data networks. Fibre Channel traffic is usually carried on fiber optic cables, but — despite its name — traffic can also be carried on copper cables (again, an exception!). For the actual data communication, SANs use the SCSI interface described earlier in the chapter.

To communicate with a Fibre Channel–based SAN, a server can't use a standard network interface card, because such cards communicate using the old-fashioned Ethernet protocol. Instead, a special-purpose data communication device called a Host Bus Adapter (HBA) is inserted into the server. The HBA can communicate over the specialized cables and protocols used by Fibre Channel.

At the storage end of a SAN (that is, the place where the actual physical hard drives reside) is dedicated hardware that knows how to communicate with a Fibre Channel client. The hardware itself contains hard drives to store the data but also contains sophisticated software to perform data management wizardry with the data. Among other things, this software can spread the data across several hard drives (more on that in a moment); keep a redundant copy of the data in a separate location to protect against data loss; and perform transparent backup of the data. (In fact, SANs can do far more than these three things, but you get the idea — this is way beyond just reading and writing data.) Furthermore, additional pieces of hardware might be attached to the SAN device to hold more drives. All of this hardware is managed by the SAN device, which also provides a management interface to allow data administrators to control the SAN configuration and operation.

Often sitting in between the servers containing HBA cards and the storage device are one or more data switches, which are analogous to the network switches found on corporate data networks. These switches allow any server to talk to any SAN storage device. (Companies might have many of them.) Of course, the *switch fabric* (the term used to indicate the topology of the overall storage network) can do more than connect all servers to all storage, it can also be administered to limit certain servers to only certain SAN storage devices or to provide redundancy in data paths to avoid SPOF — as you can see, the switch fabric has a lot of configuration flexibility to support corporate data use practices.

A new wrinkle in SANs (and NAS, for that matter) is the rise of a new networking protocol called iSCSI, which uses the same SCSI data communication protocol but runs it over standard Ethernet. The iSCSI protocol doesn't require specialized cabling, and it can, if desired, be run on a pre-existing corporate network (although in practice a separate Ethernet network is strung so as to segregate standard network traffic from data network traffic). Because iSCSI uses standard protocols and runs on existing hardware, it's usually significantly cheaper than Fibre Channel alternatives, which explains the high level of interest in the protocol. Furthermore, because it uses existing equipment and protocols, there's no need for network administrators to learn new skills, which reduces operational costs as well.

Why use shared storage?

You might wonder why shared storage is used even though it's obviously more complex than DAS. Here are several reasons for using shared storage:

- ✔ **Limited scalability of DAS:** Although hard drives are growing all the time, a system might outgrow the maximum amount of data that can physically be stored on the locally attached drives. If you've ever installed a second disk drive in your own computer, you recognize the issue with DAS — there are a limited number of drive bays (physical drive holders) in the machine. It's easy to run out of drive bays in a computer, and then you're stuck — there's nowhere else to add additional drives. Because shared storage can handle many more drives, you can avoid the problem of limited data capacity.

- ✔ **Wasted data capacity of DAS:** A problem at the other end of capacity is the fact that many large DAS drives sit with very little data actually stored; this means storage capacity is being wasted. It's even possible to have a situation where one system has maxed out its DAS capacity while others sit with scads of wasted capacity. This is obviously inefficient.

- ✔ **Easier management of the organization's overall data:** Data is the lifeblood of organizations, and having it spread across hundreds or thousands of machines makes it extremely difficult to manage and keep track of. Shared storage allows centralized management of data.

LUNS and RAID

DAS uses the OS file system that has been installed on the local hard drive for its storage purposes. A hard drive on a local machine can be subdivided into sections called *partitions*. Although each partition is a separate piece of storage, the totality is owned and organized by the physical machine. However, in a shared data storage arrangement such as NAS or SAN, where a number of machines might have storage on a single device, you need a way to section off the data so that machines can have dedicated portions of the device's storage and be prevented from accessing storage assigned to another machine.

A scheme involving LUNs (Logical Unit Number; again, this protocol is obtained from SCSI) is used to keep the different pieces of storage on a shared storage device separate. Essentially, the LUNs are identified with a numbering scheme to assign specific areas of storage to one machine or another — this enables the storage device to keep the storage organized and ensures that systems don't write over one another's data.

Naturally, a file system must be installed on a LUN to enable the server to read and write file data to the shared storage device. Part of configuring a new operating system to work with a shared LUN is installing its file system on the LUN.

You might have identified a shortcoming — a single point of failure, or SPOF — in all these storage schemes. They're all based on hard drives, which, although quite reliable, can fail. All the smart data management in the world won't help if the hardware at the bottom of it all poops out.

To address the vulnerability posed by hard drive failure, the industry developed a mechanism to spread data across multiple hard drives so that the failure of a single drive wouldn't cripple access to the overall data residing on all the drives. It goes by the acronym of RAID, or redundant array of inexpensive disks. The *R* in RAID is critical to providing data invulnerability. Data is distributed *(striped)* and *mirrored* (two copies are created to ensure that even if one copy is unavailable the second copy can be used for data access) across individual drives with enough data about the data (known as *metadata*) to enable automatic recovery of lost data contained on any single drive that fails. The details of how RAID works aren't important; what is important to know is that RAID uses multiple disks to provide data durability. A number of different RAID types exist, known by numbers like 0, 1, 5, and 1+0 (yes, RAID types can be combined). While RAID is often used for local storage, it's almost a prerequisite for shared storage configurations — after all, why go to all the work of setting up shared storage and then face vulnerability due to simple hard drive failure?

By the way, the alternative to careful data management via RAID is to use what's known as JBOD, for just a bunch of disks, which I think is one of the funniest technology acronyms I've ever heard. (As for my all-time favorite technology acronym, it's definitely the image-scanning protocol know as TWAIN — the Technology Without An Interesting Name protocol. Who said technology people don't have a sense of humor?)

Setting up and configuring LUNs and RAID can be quite complex, but fortunately from the perspective of the OS using the storage, the actual mechanics are quite simple. The shared storage mechanism requires upfront work, but little work is required to use shared storage when it's up and running. Of course, administering a shared storage implementation involves significant ongoing work. In fact, a new administrative group, referred to as *storage administration,* is often created when shared storage is implemented. The job of storage administration is to make sure all that shared storage is configured properly and is kept up and running, that any modifications to storage arrangements are implemented properly, and that data is backed up properly.

Data redundancy

As data use has grown and the use of shared storage has become more common, IT organizations have recognized that any single point of failure (SPOF) in the entire data infrastructure presents an unacceptable risk. There's no point in implementing RAID if an HBA goes down and prevents a system from being able to communicate with its vital data.

Consequently, many organizations are implementing full redundancy throughout their storage infrastructure. This implies:

- **Redundant HBAs:** Having redundant HBAs ensures that data can always find its way off of a system. Naturally, this requires server hardware that has enough card slots to install at least two HBAs — or redundant Ethernet cards if iSCSI is being used.

- **Redundant switches:** Redundant switches ensure that systems aren't blocked when accessing storage. Servers are connected to duplicate data switches, thereby ensuring that, should one switch stop working, data can communicate across a second switch.

- **Redundant storage hardware:** Of course, you must have more than one piece of storage hardware to ensure that data is always available.

- **Redundant drives (RAID):** Because hard drives are the ultimate location of all the data flying through HBAs, switches, and shared storage hardware, it's critical that enough drives configured for RAID be available in each piece of shared storage hardware.

Furthermore, to achieve full system redundancy, it's not enough to ensure that the data is redundant. The server itself must be implemented in a redundant fashion, not to mention the need to have redundant network connectivity (yet more card slots required unless the server comes configured with duplicate NICs). Therefore, mission-critical systems often have duplicate applications running on duplicate servers, all of which need to be tied into the redundant infrastructure just described. Furthermore, to enable the duplicate servers to access the same LUNs, additional software known as *clustering software* is required to coordinate data access and preclude two different systems overwriting one another's data. In short, implementing full redundancy can be a significant project in itself.

Cost implications of storage

The cost of implementing storage can run from less than $100 on up to millions of dollars. DAS is clearly the least expensive solution, with expense scaling upwards as you move to more robust storage solutions that incorporate redundancy. Low-end shared storage like file servers aren't much more than DAS, but the cost of a full-blown Fibre Channel–based solution can be eye watering.

What's exciting about storage — with significant implications for virtualization — is that the cost of more robust shared storage, based on iSCSI, has been plummeting, with options available today that cost 90 percent less than what was available a few years ago. Robust shared storage, reserved for only the wealthiest IT organizations until the recent past, has now become attainable for nearly every budget.

Just as the cost of the storage solutions themselves has plummeted, so too has the cost of the storage infrastructure (such as data switches). New entrants to the market are delivering more cost-effective products, enabling redundant storage solutions to be created for thousands of dollars instead of millions. Of course, the reduced cost of the hardware doesn't negate the cost of managing a more complex environment, but overall, the news is good on the storage front. Robust storage is moving from custom tailoring to off-the-rack pricing, with no end in sight for the trend.

What this implies for you is that your virtualization storage decision now can be driven by what you need to accomplish rather than what you can afford. Examine your virtualization use profiles to understand what kind of storage is most appropriate for your environment. Based on the profiles, you can then seek out the most appropriate storage solution, assured that you'll probably be able to find a solution that works within your budget. To find out more about analyzing your needs, see Chapter 7.

Choosing Storage for Virtualization

Now that you have a good overview of storage and the different permutations available, which of these options can you use for your virtualization project?

Actually, all the options can be used with virtualization. The next few sections explore how each of the storage types might be applied with virtualization.

DAS and virtualization

Certainly, DAS is the easiest of the storage types. Part of installing a virtual machine is identifying where its storage is located, and nothing is easier than using local storage for a virtual machine's file system.

Here are common applications of virtualization that use DAS:

- ✔ **Quick prototyping:** If you're developing software, nothing is quicker than creating a virtual machine on your development machine to slap together a quick-and-dirty experiment. Local storage is the obvious way to go, because it's a temporary system.

- ✔ **Development and test:** These engineering tasks require repetitive set up and tear down of systems, for which local storage is ideal because it can be easily allocated and deleted. Furthermore, these tasks are often performed in circumstances under which access to the corporate network is impossible or inefficient; for example, many developers and QA engineers telecommute. By avoiding the need to connect to shared storage, development and testing can be done anywhere, anytime.

- ✔ **Small-scale systems:** Systems with low data requirements might not need the scalability or redundancy of shared storage. For example, many intranets aren't used very much, so they're good candidates to use local storage.

- ✔ **Static systems:** Applications that are primarily read oriented are good candidates for local storage; therefore, the scalability of shared storage is unnecessary. Many infrastructure applications such as DNS fall into this category. They use small, rarely modified data files as the basis for their operation, so local storage is perfect for them.

- ✔ **Virtualization pilot implementations:** As you begin experimenting with virtualization, local storage makes it easier to explore the ins and outs of the technology. Using shared storage for your pilot implementations would require involving other groups to obtain test space on shared storage. Also, because most shared storage is tuned for current production loads, any pilot work would necessitate additional equipment or at least additional configuration. I firmly believe that the more complex it is to attempt something, the less likely it is to happen; therefore, using DAS for pilot implementations instead of going the shared storage route makes a lot of sense. However, there's one large exception to this: If your ultimate production implementation will use shared storage, it's vital that you test shared storage during some part of your pilot implementation to ensure that you understand all the requirements of your virtualization solution.

On the other hand, DAS has real shortcomings when it comes to virtualization:

- ✔ **Limited total storage:** As noted earlier, most servers can hold only a couple of hard drives, which limits the total amount of storage possible on a typical server. If you put a number of virtual machines on a single server, they all have to share that limited storage, making it more likely that you'll run out of storage. And it's not easy to add storage to a DAS-based system.

✓ **Limited system scalability:** One of the most common ways used to enable additional system load today is to add more instances of the application. Referred to as *horizontal scaling,* which describes the fact that numerous peer machines host multiple copies of the application, this system scalability approach requires that all systems access common data. When it comes to virtualization, this means that virtual machines spread across physical servers must be able to access common data, which is difficult when you use DAS on a particular server. (Shared storage schemes like NFS can be used in this situation, but they typically impose unacceptable performance penalties in terms of system response times.)

Another scalability limitation has to do with the input/output (i/o) of DAS. Most servers have a single disk controller, through which all the system's data must pass. If you have a number of virtual machines, all reading and writing, it's easy to saturate the capacity of the server's disk controller and end up *i/o-bound* — stuck waiting for the computer to hurry up and compute, which means you'll have to put off being *home-ward* bound just a tad longer.

✓ **Limited system flexibility:** If a virtual machine uses DAS, it can run only on the machine the DAS is installed in. If the machine goes down for any reason, the virtual machine can't be migrated to another machine, because it won't be able to access its storage, which is located on the DAS in the down machine.

✓ **Administrative complexity:** With large numbers of virtual machines accessing individual DAS storage, it's difficult for administrators to know what storage belongs to what virtual machine. By contrast, a LUN-based shared storage scheme clearly identifies which storage is associated with which virtual machine. This complexity extends to backup because it's difficult to know whether a particular virtual machine's files have been backed up properly.

Overall, virtualization vendors report that most organizations use DAS when they first get going with virtualization, but that most don't stick with DAS when they go into production. VMware estimates that no more than about 25 percent of VMware-based production systems use DAS. Likewise, Xen users reflect this same phenomenon: pilot/prototype with DAS, deploy with shared storage.

Shared storage and virtualization

The description of shared storage earlier in the chapter makes it clear that shared storage offers much more scalability and flexibility at the cost of complexity.

How can you know whether shared storage is a good bet for your virtualization project? The following sections discuss some key applications where shared storage would make sense for a virtualization implementation.

System cloning

Rather than keeping individual virtual machine images on each server, ready to be instantiated as needed, it's often more convenient to keep the images in a central location, where they can be accessed by hypervisors throughout the data center. When a hypervisor needs to bring up a new, say, RHEL-based virtual machine, it goes to the central location and brings up a machine based on the system image stored there. Implementing system cloning also helps with security and system consistency because it's necessary to change only one system image, which is automatically used by all hypervisors when they bring up a new virtual machine based on that image. Because only one image is used, administrators can focus on making sure that image is configured exactly right, relaxed in the knowledge that the properly configured image will be automatically propagated to any virtual machine that starts up.

The alternative to system cloning is to store images on individual machines, which requires every machine's images to be kept fully patched and updated. Keeping track of images on a large number of machines is complex, labor intensive, and error prone. Shared storage is required to store cloned images.

Horizontal scaling

For applications that have been designed to scale by adding servers, shared storage is required. As new virtual machines are brought up, they need to be able to access the same data as other virtual machines that make up the total application. Shared storage is especially important for horizontally scaled applications where individual user sessions can migrate from one server to another as individual interactions between the user and the application occur.

As an example of such interactions, imagine a home-banking transaction in which you begin by entering your ID. Based on that, the system returns a page asking what kind of transaction you'd like to perform. You choose Transfer Money. The system returns a page asking the From and To accounts as well as the amount to be transferred. You enter the accounts and the amount. The system then asks you to confirm your transfer transaction. You enter a confirmation. It performs the transfer and then returns a page indicating success (one hopes, anyway).

Just for a simple transfer, you have a number of separate interactions. If the system is architected properly, each of those steps can be executed on any available system, which lends itself to load balancing to ensure consistent response times; the alternative is to force a transaction to stay with a single system after it's initiated, which provides much less flexibility in terms of load balancing and system response times. To allow transaction sharing and load balancing, systems require shared storage, making it fundamental for horizontally scaled applications.

Large numbers of systems

As the number of virtual machines increases, keeping track of the individual pieces of storage associated with each machine becomes more and more difficult. Using LUNs and associating them with individual machines makes tracking storage much easier. It's also easier to ensure proper backup when storage is centralized in a shared (that is, off-server) location.

Mission critical

A mission-critical application is one that a company depends on to keep its fundamental business processes operating. For example, for a retail chain, the point-of-sale systems that handle customer transactions are mission critical — if they're not working, the company can't take in any money, which they, understandably enough, regard as really, really important. Mission-critical applications are architected to avoid any SPOF vulnerabilities. Certainly one of the areas that would be addressed would be data redundancy to ensure data availability. That would require shared storage; furthermore, it would require a storage architecture that has RAID, duplicate storage, a redundant storage network infrastructure, and so on. You get the idea: It's like Noah's Ark — two of everything, configured in a way that any one component's failure doesn't affect the ability of the system to keep working.

Naturally, this means multiple virtual machines running on separate servers. It also means that the machines must have access to shared storage so that if one machine goes down, other machines can continue to access the storage. For true application resiliency, the mission-critical application should operate in redundant data centers to ensure that failure of an entire data center doesn't shut down the company's mission-critical applications. (Failure to implement data center redundancy ruined many New Orleans companies that had implemented intra–data center redundancy.)

High availability/failover

High availability/failover refers to using virtualization to ensure that failure of an individual virtual machine — or the hardware underlying an individual virtual machine — doesn't cause an application to become unavailable. (High availability is often referred to as HA.) Hypervisors can be configured to constantly check the state of virtual machines; if one disappears because the system crashed, the hypervisor will automatically restart a new instance of the virtual machine. More sophisticated virtualization software can track the state of virtual machines spread across a number of physical servers; if one or more machines are no longer available because a physical server goes down, the virtualization software will restart a virtual machine on another machine.

HA/failover is a great use of virtualization because it makes system recovery much quicker and reduces the effort for system administration staffs. Just as horizontal scaling requires shared storage that can be accessed by any virtual machine operating on any physical server, HA/failover also requires shared storage.

Pooled virtualization

Pooled virtualization involves treating a set of physical servers, all running virtualization software, as a single virtualization resource. The user no longer has to decide where to place a new virtual machine; instead, the virtualization software, which tracks system load on each machine that's part of the pool, selects the most appropriate machine upon which to install the new machine, and then automatically installs it. This substantially reduces the effort system administrators need to expend keeping track of individual virtual machines, monitoring the current state of each server, and calculating where new machines should be installed. Shared storage is a fundamental prerequisite for virtualization pooling because it's never clear where individual virtual machines will be placed; without shared storage, you could never be sure whether a new machine would be able to access its data.

Storage and the Different Types of Virtualization

If you've selected your virtualization solution, what are your storage options? And, among the options you have with your virtualization solution, what's the best choice? You'll hate the answer, but it depends — on the solution, on your goals, and even on what storage solutions you have in place. In this section, you have a chance to look over the possibilities for every type of virtualization.

Operating system virtualization (containers)

Operating system virtualization uses libraries running on a base operating system to present applications with interfaces that isolate the applications from all others on the system. Popular with ISPs and other uses in which numerous identical operating environments are necessary, each container actually reflects the underlying operating system. Consequently, the containers have access to whatever storage option(s) the operating system itself has.

Containers aren't a true hypervisor, because they require a host operating system to be present on the underlying hardware. One might think of containers as a specialized type of application — one whose purpose is to host other applications and present them with the illusion of an isolated operating environment. (For more information on containers, see Chapter 3.) Containers hosting applications aren't typically mixed with applications running on the host system, because the scheduler of the host system would conflict with the scheduler for the operating system virtualization. In other words, in production, operating system virtualization usually runs by itself on the machine, with all applications running in individual containers. That way, the applications can all be managed by the container software, ensuring the fairest scheduling and best possible performance.

Containers are very well suited to DAS because operating system virtualization maps a pseudo-native operating system onto the actual file system structure assigned to each container. As an example, operating system virtualization might have a series of physical directories named `container1`, `container2`, and so on, all existing as subdirectories of a `machine` directory located in the root file system of the host machine. Each container would be assigned to an appropriate directory; however, rather than seeing the root directory of the container as `containerX` (where X is the appropriate number), the container would see its assigned directory as its own root directory.

Because one of the purposes of containers is to offer flexibility with respect to the operating environment, if the underlying operating system is attached to shared storage, containers can be shifted from machine to machine if desired. In fact, depending on the overall usage profile of the organization using the container-based applications, it might be necessary to use shared storage to provide expected uptime and availability.

Overall, operating system virtualization can use all types of storage; the choice really depends on the specific use profile of the organization.

Hardware emulation virtualization

Hardware emulation presents an emulated hardware interface to guest operating systems. Unlike operating system virtualization (where applications "believe" they're running in a separate operating system instance, but in fact are running in a container that presents a virtualized operating system), hardware emulation supports actual guest operating systems; the applications running in each guest operating system are running in truly isolated operating environments.

The guest operating system makes system calls to the emulated hardware. System calls that would actually interact with underlying hardware are intercepted by the virtualization hypervisor, which maps them onto the real underlying hardware. Hardware emulation comes in two flavors: In one, the hypervisor runs as an application on top of a host operating system; in the other, the hypervisor resides on bare-metal hardware and provides the entire operating environment for guest operating systems. The latter flavor of hardware emulation is used in production environments where the penalty overhead imposed by running a host operating system in addition to a virtualization software layer would be unacceptable.

One critical aspect of hardware emulation virtualization is the fact that the hypervisor is the be-all and end-all for the guest operating system — the hypervisor is all it interacts with. Consequently, guest operating systems have access only to whatever hardware interfaces are provided by the hypervisor. Crucially, this means that user organizations are limited in their choices of storage to those that have device drivers included in the hypervisor.

Naturally, hardware emulation virtualization supports DAS and standard NIC interfaces, making it possible for guest operating systems to communicate with shared storage that uses iSCSI interfaces. However, shared storage using Fibre Channel HBAs are limited to those devices for which drivers are shipped with the hypervisor. Put another way, hardware emulation doesn't provide the ability to add storage options by loading a new device driver. Also, it's not possible to upgrade to an improved driver made available by an HBA manufacturer; rather, the user must wait for an updated hypervisor to be released by the software provider.

Paravirtualization

Paravirtualization doesn't present an emulated hardware environment to guest virtual machines. Instead, it insets a software layer that controls access to the underlying hardware, acting like a traffic cop who controls which car is allowed to enter an intersection.

One distinguishing feature of paravirtualization is that it doesn't provide its own device drivers. It inserts a dummy device driver — called a *front-end* driver — in guest virtual machines. That front-end driver communicates with a back-end driver that resides in the privileged guest (known as `Domain0` in Xen and the Root Partition in Windows Server Virtualization). The privileged guest contains the actual device drivers for the underlying hardware, and it coordinates communication between the back-end drivers and the actual device drivers.

By using the actual device drives of the privileged guest, the paravirtualization provider doesn't have to ship device drivers in the software. This offers more flexibility in use because the paravirtualized system can take advantage of whatever hardware the privileged guest is connected to, rather than only whatever hardware the hypervisor is configured to work with. This also means that new hardware can be introduced into a paravirtualized environment because all you need for the hypervisor to speak to a new storage solution is for an appropriate driver to be loaded into the privileged guest.

Because of this flexibility, paravirtualized systems can integrate with every type of storage, requiring only that a storage solution have a driver present in the privileged guest. Most organizations that use paravirtualization begin by experimenting with it in a DAS environment, but move to some kind of shared storage when moving into production.

Storage and the Virtualization Journey

There's a hierarchy of data storage methods, both in terms of functionality and complexity. It can be challenging enough to decide on the right storage strategy for your chosen virtualization solution. A bigger challenge, though, is choosing a storage strategy that will evolve as your virtualization solution evolves over time.

This evolution, which I sum up in the phrase "virtualization is a journey, not a product," refers to the fact that organizations often find virtualization so useful that they extend the scope of their use of the technology.

It's very common for organizations to begin with a simple server consolidation project, with a number of physical servers converted into a like number of virtual machines. Simple and straightforward.

It's not unusual for such organizations to then recognize that they can use the monitoring aspects of their virtualization solution to check the status of each virtual machine, and, should one go down, to automatically restart it.

And, it's not a long step from that to configure the virtualization software to restart a virtual machine on a different machine should the virtual machine's original host system become unavailable.

You get the picture — a series of incremental steps, each relatively small and extremely logical, that brings you to a final location quite distant from your starting point. And, certainly, the final location is a very effective use of virtualization.

The challenge of this virtualization journey is that each step implies a more sophisticated infrastructure, particularly with regard to storage. Although DAS is perfectly appropriate for a simple server consolidation infrastructure, it's inadequate for an HA/failover infrastructure. Moving to HA/failover, although logical, carries with it a significant expense to upgrade the environment in which the HA/failover solution operates.

"Fine," you might think. "If I move to HA/failover, I need to implement shared storage." The larger challenge is the fact that as you move along the journey, you might find that you're upgrading the environment repeatedly, replacing equipment more than once, which is obviously a bad idea.

What is the right way to approach this journey, seeking to avoid repetitively purchasing storage products?

Although I can't guarantee that you'll never go wrong, here are some things to keep in mind while assessing your storage choices:

- ✔ **Initial migration is straightforward, but plan for subsequent migrations.** P2V migration software does a very good job of moving DAS storage associated with a physical system to whatever data storage mechanism is associated with your virtualization choice. After the data is located in a virtualized solution, though, you need to depend on your new storage solution to provide a data migration mechanism. Most of them have a migration option, but be sure to research them, because they might have limitations or (worse) carry an extra charge.

- ✔ **Seek products with an upgrade path.** The metaphor of a journey is an apt one in that you don't know exactly where you'll end up at the time you start your journey. Because of this, it's important to remain as flexible as possible in your storage choices. When examining a potential storage choice, try to understand what options you have if you decide to extend your journey. For example, should you move to NAS to support using shared storage, research whether the NAS solutions you're considering can support redundancy, which will be required if you move to operating an HA/failover infrastructure.

- ✔ **Look to the future for standards.** The world of storage is evolving rapidly as the onslaught of data continues to gush forth, demanding larger and more-effective storage solutions. When deciding on a shared storage solution, consider the trajectory of standards within the industry. The arrival of iSCSI for data communication is already having a dramatic impact on the storage industry, so be sure to evaluate it as one of your options when evaluating your storage choices. Likewise, look at what's happening in standards that would affect multisite redundancy; with costs coming down, this will become more important for IT organizations.

It's an exciting time for storage. New challenges, new standards, and added complexity as businesses demand more robust solutions that offer higher availability are all contributing to new solutions arriving in the market every day. Virtualization is causing IT organizations to move to shared storage; in turn, the functionality and flexibility of shared storage enable them to further extend their virtualization journey.

How cost effective is shared storage?

You might be thinking that I'm negative about the more sophisticated forms of storage — particularly SAN-based storage that implements redundancy — all because of the cost. It's true that implementing a storage solution that includes all the bells and whistles of performance, redundancy, and scale can add up to an eye-watering amount of money.

On the other hand, a pricy storage solution might not be that expensive in light of the overall financial benefit it delivers. Let me share one such example with you.

A large West Coast–based bank was faced with an unpalatable situation. Its remote site system infrastructure was based on a distributed architecture — every site had its own server, which allowed site autonomy. A new financial regulation came into effect, requiring that all financial data of the type stored in its distributed architecture be encrypted to ensure customer data privacy.

Unfortunately, the encryption software would need to be purchased for each site to encrypt the data stored on the local server. Moreover, the processing requirements of the encryption software were such that the existing hardware couldn't handle the load. Consequently, between buying more hardware and forking over for the encryption software for its distributed infrastructure, the company was looking at a project price tag of close to $35 million — a large investment, even for a large bank. The bank decided to research its alternatives to building out its current infrastructure.

One of the alternatives the bank explored was using a combination of hardware consolidation and storage virtualization. By migrating each of the remote physical servers to a virtual machine located on a few central virtualized servers — each using shared storage to efficiently store its data — the bank was able to avoid the purchase of additional remote servers as well as many copies of the encryption software.

When the project costs of moving to virtualization were tallied, the amount came to $3 million, which is less than 10 percent of the projected project cost prior to considering virtualization. Leveraging virtualization — particularly storage virtualization — made moving to a new centralized architecture a foregone conclusion.

So don't write off shared storage just because of its complexity or cost. Just remember that in the right circumstances, shared storage can be far more cost effective than other options. This example illustrates that the key to successful implementation of shared storage is finding the right use profile.

Part III
Server Virtualization Software Options

The 5th Wave — By Rich Tennant

"I'm not saying I believe in anything. All I know is since it's been there our server is running 50% faster."

In this part . . .

Key to any project is the whole "how do I get from here to there, and once I get there, what do I do?" issue. This part covers the very important process of moving your existing physical servers to a virtualized environment, as well as how to manage that virtualized environment when you have everything installed.

Deciding how you'll store and manage your data is important in any data center, and virtualization makes the question even more important due to the way it rearranges the physical infrastructure of the data center. I cover the different virtualization options for data storage, and provide some guidance about how to decide on the right storage strategy for you.

Chapter 12

Implementing VMware Server

*I*f you've been dutifully making your way through Chapters 1 through 11, you're probably really excited about the potential of virtualization. And, if you're anything like me, you want to get your hands dirty — you want to *try* virtualization to see how it works.

Never fear. In this chapter and the next two, I give you a guided tour of how you can get started using virtualization. I walk you through installing virtualization software and configuring it so you can actually start using it.

Best of all, I show you how to do it for free. One of the great things about today's software industry is how it's much easier to "try before you buy." Just a few years ago, you had to make a significant financial commitment before you could see how a new technology would work for you. No more! Today, software companies make it easy to gain access to their products so that you can implement and evaluate them. In fact, it's even better than that. The products you look at in these chapters are real products, suitable for real use. No demoware, crippleware, time-bombed evaluation copies here!

In this chapter, I focus on VMware Server.

Understanding VMware Server Architecture: Pros and Cons

VMware Server installs on top of an existing operating system, and virtual machines are then installed on VMware Server — meaning it isn't one of those *bare-metal* virtualization products that you install directly on the server, with no intervening operating system whatsoever. Put another way, the VMware Server architecture means that the virtualization software resides in a layer between the host operating system and one or more guest operating systems.

This approach has pros and cons.

First, the cons:

✔ **The additional layer affects performance.** The machine's own operating system sits between the hardware and the virtualization software; that means there's an additional layer of software between individual virtual machines and the underlying hardware. The result is that a portion of the machine's capability isn't available to your VMware Server because it's devoted to running the underlying operating system.

✔ **The virtualization software contends for hardware resources with other applications on the host system.** The virtualization software has less control over scheduling hardware resources because the underlying operating system controls the overall hardware scheduling, allocating the hardware resources among VMware Server as well as any other applications the underlying operating system is running. In other words, VMware Server is treated like an application, and it gets only a portion of the overall hardware resources.

✔ **It doesn't provide as much functionality as its bare-metal brother.** VMware's ESX Server is the company's flagship product, and as such it provides lots of ways to tweak the virtualization software's configuration and to track the performance of individual virtual machines. It also provides the ability to do virtual machine failover and other higher-level functions. VMware Server is focused on providing basic virtualization functionality on individual machines and therefore doesn't do as much as ESX Server.

Now, the pros:

✔ **You don't need to configure hardware.** Because VMware Server installs on top of the existing operating system, you don't really have to worry about configuring the hardware to work with the virtualization software, which is a big plus.

You can use existing hardware. ESX Server supports only certain hardware products, which might very well mean you need to purchase new hardware to run it. VMware Server imposes no hardware requirements, which means you can use just about any machine as a VMware Server host.

✓ **For typical VMware Server users, the performance hit is irrelevant.** Although you take a small performance hit from the extra layer of software, if you don't really need high levels of performance from the system, that's not much of a sacrifice.

✓ **You get flexibility in your choice of host operating system.** VMware makes versions of VMware Server available to run on either Windows or Linux, so you have a lot of flexibility when it comes to which virtualization path you take.

✓ **Multisystem configurations are welcome here.** VMware Server is ideal for situations in which you need a multisystem configuration — several different virtual machines on a single server. Imagine, if you will, that you need to run a Linux machine running a CRM application, a Windows machine that contains the database the CRM system uses, and a second Windows machine running a Web server to provide access to the CRM system — and you're willing to do all that without getting too worried about performance issues. If that's what you want, then VMware Server is a great choice, because it offers a great foundation for exercising low-load, multisystem configurations. For that reason, the product is often used by software engineers for development and quality assurance purposes because they can easily create complex environments for testing purposes but typically don't put much load on the systems.

✓ **Free:** Did I mention the product is free? That makes up for a lot of drawbacks, doesn't it?

In the remainder of this chapter, I show you how to obtain VMware Server, install it, and install a guest operating system. After I show you how to install a guest operating system, I give you a couple of bonus surprises in the form of other great things you can do with VMware Server.

Getting Your (Free) Copy of VMware Server

VMware has done a great job making it easy to install VMware Server. The product runs on both Windows and Linux operating systems, but for the sake of this discussion, I show you how to install it on a Windows machine.

Acquiring VMware Server

Well, the first step is to get VMware Server itself, right? Fortunately, that's really easy — with one small hitch. Despite VMware Server being a free product, you need a serial number to install it. And how do you get a serial number? I'm glad you asked.

1. **Point your browser to www.vmware.com/download/server, the Download VMware Server page on VMware's Web site.**

2. **Click the Register for Your Free Serial Number(s) link.**

   Doing so takes you to a registration page where you'll fill out information about yourself and your environment.

3. **Answer the questions and click Submit.**

   This step takes you to the aptly named Download VMware Server – Your Registration Has Been Received page that displays your serial number(s).

4. **Print this page.**

   This is your only record of your serial number, and you'll need it later in the install process.

   If you don't have access to a printer, you should write this information down and keep it handy.

5. **Back on the Download VMware Server – Your Registration Has Been Received page, find the Download Now button and click it.**

   An End User License Agreement (EULA) page appears, with Yes and No buttons.

   This is a legally binding agreement, so you should read it in its entirety.

6. **Click the Yes button.**

   You're presented with a page with a number of download options.

7. **Click the very first option — the VMware Server for Windows Operating Systems option — which lets you download a self-extracting, installation-executable file for Windows.**

   Your browser should either download it automatically to your default download location or ask you where you want to download the file. That's it. Now you have the install file for VMware Server on your machine as well as a printed record of your VMware Server serial number(s).

Installing VMware Server

This section leads you through the process of installing VMware Server itself.

1. **Double click the `.exe` file you downloaded to your machine in the preceding step list.**

   The VMware Server installer begins the installation process. You see a welcoming splash screen inviting you to begin installation (see Figure 12-1).

Figure 12-1:
Hi to you,
too!

2. **Click Next to continue.**

   You see another EULA acceptance screen. (You already saw one when you were downloading the `.exe` file.) You might think that a second EULA is redundant, and you'd be right. However, you can't continue the installation without accepting it.

3. **Nod politely to the EULA and click the Accept button.**

   The installation wizard asks whether you want a complete installation or a custom one. If this is your first exposure to VMware Server, I recommend you avoid trying to do any kind of custom installation.

4. **Leave the default Complete radio button selected and click Next.**

   VMware Server depends on a Web server running on the host to enable VMware Management Interface (VMI) access to the virtualization software. If you don't have Internet Information Services (IIS) installed on your Windows host operating system already, you get a message (see Figure 12-2) complaining about the fact that either IIS is not installed or it is misconfigured. Should you choose to, you can always come back and install the VMI at a later time once IIS has been installed and properly configured. Having IIS and VMI installed are not necessary for VMware Server to operate properly, so you can safely ignore the message.

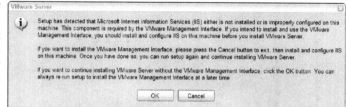

5. **Now you get to choose where to install VMware Server. I recommend you accept the default, as depicted in Figure 12-3, and then click Next.**

   A dialog box appears, noting that you have Autorun enabled for CDs —
   if you have it enabled, of course. If you do see this dialog box, I recommend you disable it. The reason is that the host system and all virtual
   machines will react to a CD being inserted into the machine if Autorun is
   enabled, which will drive you (and the machines) nuts. Better to configure
   the system not to Autorun.

6. **Because you need to deal with CDs to install guest virtual machines, leave
   the default Yes, Disable Autorun check box selected, and click Next.**

   You've now finished the configuration necessary to begin actual installation.
   You get a dialog box asking whether you're ready to begin (see Figure 12-4).

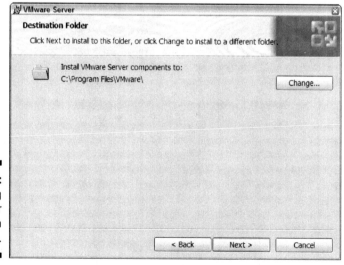

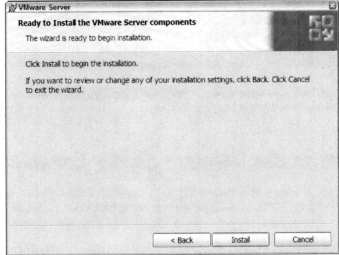

Figure 12-4:
Your
VMware
Installer is
ready to go.

7. **Click the Install button, and you're on your way.**

During the installation, you'll see an Installing VMware Server Components dialog box, along with a progress bar that very nicely shows you how the installation is coming along.

You then see a dialog box indicating successful installation of VMware Server, as shown in Figure 12-5.

8. **Click Finish.**

That's it! You have VMware Server available to run now.

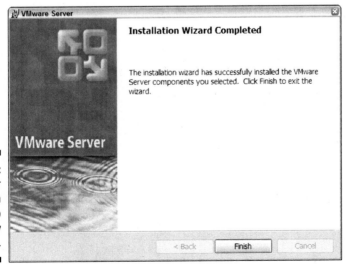

Figure 12-5:
Yet another
installation
job
successfully
completed.

Creating a Guest Virtual Machine

Well, you have VMware Server up and running, but . . . the whole point of running virtualization is to support guest operating systems, right?

That's the task you turn to next. You'll be impressed with how straightforward doing this with VMware Server is.

Starting the VMware Server Console

Everything you do with VMware Server is controlled through the VMware Server Console. Think of it as the main administration mechanism to work with VMware Server and any guest Virtual Machine (VM) systems you've installed.

Getting the VMware Server Console up and running is a piece of cake.

1. **Choose Start⇨Programs⇨VMware⇨VMware Server⇨VMware Server Console.**

   That's it! You're there.

   The first thing you see on the screen is a dialog box asking whether you want to connect to a local or a remote host (see Figure 12-6).

2. **Because your VMware Server is running on this machine, leave the default choice (local) selected and click OK.**

   You're presented with the actual VMware Server Console, as shown in Figure 12-7. This indicates that VMware Server is running and available on the local machine; the VMware Server Console is ready for you to decide what you want to do with VMware Server.

Figure 12-6:
Do you want local or remote? Coffee or tea?

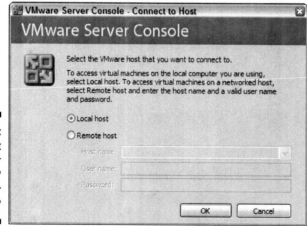

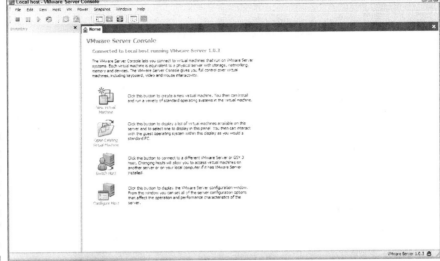

Figure 12-7:
The
VMware
Server
Console
awaits your
command.

Installing a new virtual machine

Your first order of business here is to install a virtual machine. To do that:

1. **With the VMware Server Console open, click the New Virtual Machine icon. (Refer to Figure 12-7.)**

   This starts the New Virtual Machine Wizard, as shown in Figure 12-8.

Figure 12-8:
The New
Virtual
Machine
wizard.

2. **Click Next to kick off the process.**

The next dialog box offers you the choice between a Typical or a Custom configuration. (See Figure 12-9.)

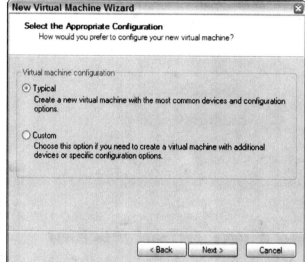

New Virtual Machine Wizard

Select the Appropriate Configuration
How would you prefer to configure your new virtual machine?

Virtual machine configuration

⊙ Typical
Create a new virtual machine with the most common devices and configuration options.

○ Custom
Choose this option if you need to create a virtual machine with additional devices or specific configuration options.

[< Back] [Next >] [Cancel]

Figure 12-9:
Choosing your configur-ation type.

3. **For now, stick with the easiest navigation option; leave the Typical option selected and then click Next.**

The Select a Guest Operating System page of the wizard appears.

I've decided for the sake of this example to install Fedora Core 6, so the next steps deal with that scenario. (If you're feeling adventurous, you can install another OS, but you'd be on your own!)

4. **In the Select a Guest Operating System page, select the Linux option, select Other Linux 2.6.x Kernel from the Version drop-down list, and then click Next. (See Figure 12-10.)**

You're invited to give the new virtual machine a name and a storage location in the next dialog box (see Figure 12-11).

You need to select the Other Linux 2.6.x Kernel option because Fedora isn't one of the default configurations included with VMware Server. Don't worry, it's no big deal.

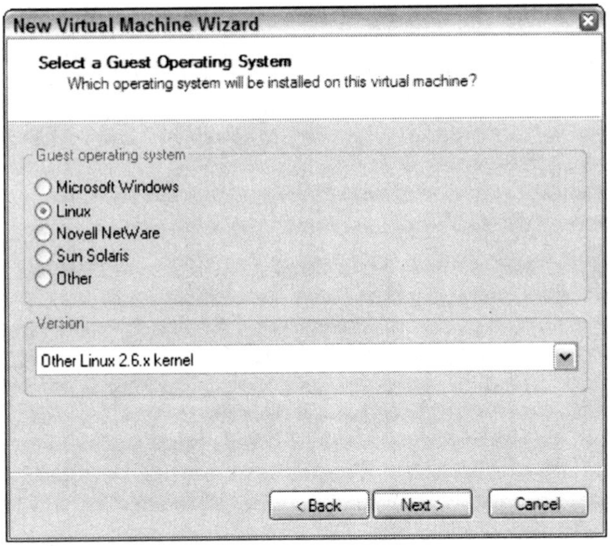

Figure 12-10:
Selecting an
operating
system.

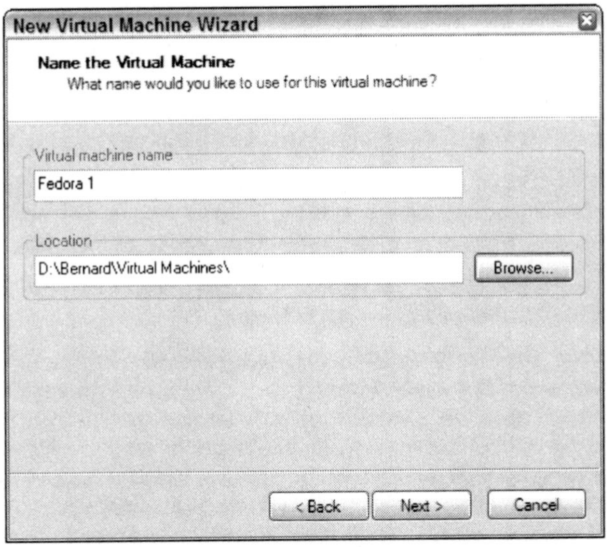

Figure 12-11:
Coming up
with a
name.

5. **Go ahead and cleverly name the new VM** Fedora 1. **(Snappy, eh?)**
   Leave the Location text box set to its default and click Next.

   The next dialog box gives you a number of networking options for your
   new virtual machine. Each of the options uses the networking capabilities
   of VMware Server itself to operate slightly differently. Your choices are:

- *Use Bridged Networking:* This option assigns an IP address based on something external to the VMware Server itself — a hard-coded address that has been physically assigned during guest OS installation, an address that's been set up through the organization's DNS system, or a dynamic address assigned by the organization's DHCP server. In essence, this option makes the virtual machine look like a standard server on the organization's network, and is the easiest to use. I recommend you use this option.

- *Use Network Address Translation (NAT):* This option isolates the VM from the organization network by assigning a private IP address to the virtual machine and translating every communication between the machine and the outside world (outside of VMware Server, that is). This enables the virtual machine to communicate with the organization network (and through it to the rest of the world), but protects the organization network from having any awareness of the machine. This option would be most useful in sophisticated environments, and I recommend you avoid using it for this example.

- *Use Host-Only Networking:* Host-only networking limits the ability of the virtual machine to communicate to only the host OS and other virtual machines running on the host. This capability can be very useful where you want multiple virtual machines to be able to speak to one another, but prohibit the virtual machines from communicating with any other systems. Software engineering and Quality Assurance would be good uses for this networking option; however, since we're experimenting, I recommend you avoid this option.

- *Do Not Use a Network Connection:* This option is appropriate if you truly want a standalone system. I doubt you really want to do that now, so I recommend you avoid this option at this time.

6. **For the purposes of this particular example, select the Use Bridged Networking option and then click Next.**

   The Specify Disk Capacity dialog box appears (see Figure 12-12), inviting you to define just how much space on the local disk you want to allocate for the virtual machine. Depending on what use you'll make of the virtual machine, you might want to make this larger or smaller. For example, if you're setting up VMware Server to perform DNS tasks for your organization, it won't require much disk space, so you could safely reduce the default amount of storage suggested. On the other hand, if you are going to install your company's CRM system on the virtual machine, you might very well need more disk space than the default amount, and you would therefore increase the default amount. If you're just experimenting with VMware Server to see how it works, I recommend you leave the default suggestion as is.

7. **Leave the disk capacity setting at the default: 8GB.**

   This assumes the storage is on the local disk; if you're using networked storage, you'll need to make the same disk size choices, but you'll be locating the machine elsewhere (as you'll see in the next step).

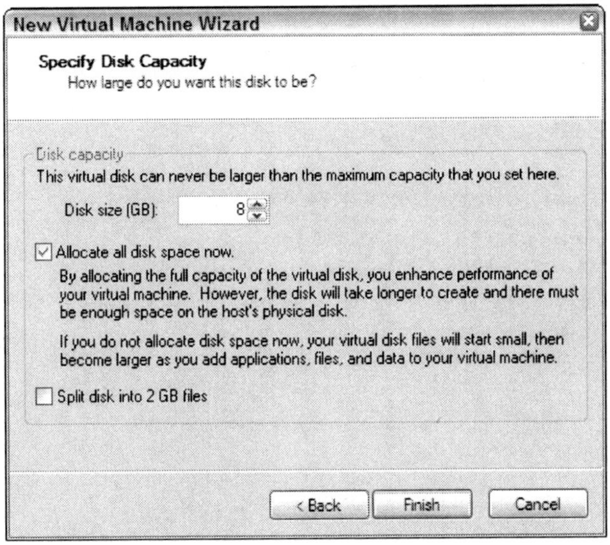

New Virtual Machine Wizard

Specify Disk Capacity
How large do you want this disk to be?

Disk capacity
This virtual disk can never be larger than the maximum capacity that you set here.

Disk size (GB): 8

☑ Allocate all disk space now.
By allocating the full capacity of the virtual disk, you enhance performance of your virtual machine. However, the disk will take longer to create and there must be enough space on the host's physical disk.

If you do not allocate disk space now, your virtual disk files will start small, then become larger as you add applications, files, and data to your virtual machine.

☐ Split disk into 2 GB files

< Back   Finish   Cancel

Figure 12-12:
Specifying disk capacity.

8. **Decide when to allocate disk space.**

   You have two choices for how you'd like to create the disk space.

   - *You can choose to create all the disk space at once.* This ensures that you won't run short of disk space because it's reserved right when you create your virtual machine. As the wizard notes, it might take a while to create the virtual machine, as the space all needs to be allocated and formatted up front. It doesn't take long to allocate 8GB, though, so I recommend you select this option.

   - *You can create the disk space in 2GB chunks as needed.* This solution reduces the time necessary to create the virtual machine, but it poses the problem that later, when you need to allocate more disk space, it won't be available. You might choose this option if you plan to work with the virtual machine files — doing things like burning them to DVD or copying them with Linux utilities. If you're just experimenting and don't plan to do anything fancy with the virtual machine files, you don't need to subdivide the disk space. Also, you won't save much time with this option right now, so I recommend that you avoid it for now.

9. **Click Finish.**

   VMware Server then goes off to create the virtual machine. While it's formatting the disk, go ahead and take a break or get some coffee.

   When this process is complete, the VMware Server Console returns, and you see Fedora 1 listed on the second tab (see Figure 12-13). You've now completed the creation of a virtual machine.

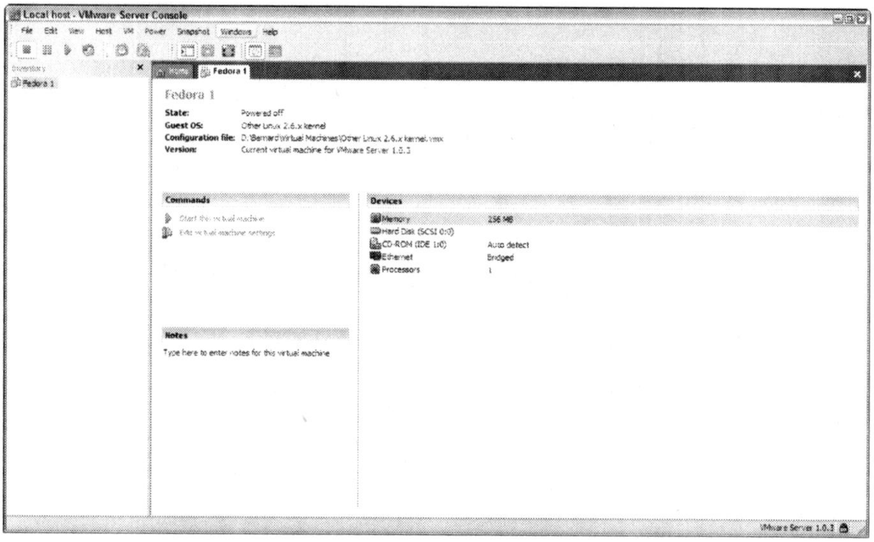

Figure 12-13:
Success! A
spanking
new virtual
machine!

Installing an Operating System

After creating a virtual machine, you have to get an operating system installed. If you peek back at Figure 12-13, the virtual machine's state is currently listed as Powered Off. To install the OS, you need to put an installation CD into the CD drawer of the machine and then click the Start This Virtual Machine link, found under the Commands section on the Fedora 1 tab of the VMware Server Console. You can also install an OS by connecting to an OS installable image (`.iso` format file) or install from an installation CD on a remote machine.

To keep it simple, I'm using the local CD drive, but you can find more information on the other installation options on the VMware Web site.

As shown in Figure 12-14, the information on the tab changes to the standard Fedora installation splash screen. You're now ready to install Fedora. Here are a couple of things to keep in mind:

✔ **You get a cursor within the virtual machine** that you can use to interact with the virtual machine; in this case, your "interaction" involves the Fedora installation process. Keep in mind that the mouse and cursor are shared between the host system and all virtual machines. If you click the mouse within the screen of the new virtual machine, the virtual machine will "capture" the cursor. To release the cursor so that you can interact with the host system, press Ctrl+Alt and the cursor will jump out to the screen of the host system. This might seem complex as a description, but after you do it once or twice it will be second nature.

✔ **You see the standard Fedora message** stating that Fedora will partition the disk during the installation and requesting an OK. This doesn't mean that the installation will format the entire disk of the host system, just that the install program will format the 8GB of disk space you assigned to the virtual machine. So don't worry about this message from the Fedora install program. Click "OK."

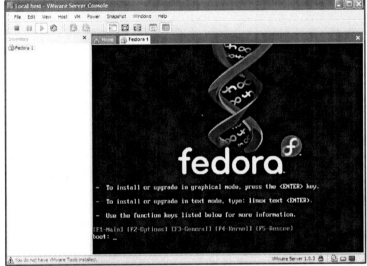

Figure 12-14:
The Fedora
Install
screen
within a
virtual
machine.

To get the installation motor runnin', press Enter. The installation process (in this case, the Fedora installation process) runs through to completion, as shown in Figure 12-15. If this requires multiple CD swaps, your new virtual machine puts up the install splash screen asking you to put in the next CD. The installation takes just about the same amount of time for a virtual machine as it would on a physical server.

When the installation process is complete, the new Fedora virtual machine brings up the standard login panel, as shown in Figure 12-16.

Just to prove it's all working properly, take a look at Figure 12-17. Here's Firefox running inside the new virtual machine, connected to the Internet — when experimenting with VMware, it seemed only natural to make the first Web connection the VMware company Web site.

That's it. You now have a new virtual machine, up and running, ready to take on multiple tasks — surfing the Web, playing Solitaire, downloading music. You name it, the virtual machine can do it.

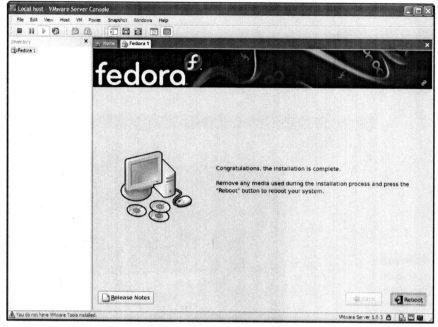

Figure 12-15:
Your virtual
machine
now has an
OS —
called a
Guest OS.

Figure 12-16:
Ready to
log on.

Figure 12-17:
Doing actual
computer-
like stuff on
a virtual
machine.

Can I Skip the Boring OS Installation Process?

The VM installation process has one drawback: You still have to install the guest OS, and if putting it onto a physical server takes an hour, putting it onto a virtual machine will take around an hour.

Wouldn't it be great if you could get a virtual machine OS installed more quickly? In fact, you can. Remember, VMware stores the state of a machine in image files, which are portable. If someone has already made image files of the virtual machine/OS combination you want, you can copy those image files and import them onto your virtualization software and thus bypass the OS installation process.

So, what if you want to create a virtual machine with Fedora installed in it without all that installation hassle? Is that possible? Definitely. Imagine for a moment that you were me, the Virtualization Expert. I'd (you'd) do something like the following.

1. I'd do a search on the Internet for VMware Server Fedora image files and I'd scroll through the results until I found a set available for torrent download.

2. I'd download the files via BitTorrent into a directory on the machine.

If the terms *torrent* and *BitTorrent* are new to you, it's time to do some more research. BitTorrent is a peer-to-peer file-sharing application that works with file formats called *torrents*. Basically, torrents are small files you download to your computer that then enable you to get pieces of a much larger file from bunches of other computers on the Web, and the pieces of files are then reconstructed into one big file on your computer. If you're not familiar with BitTorrent, it's worth your while to get acquainted because it's a widely used way to share files. One way to get acquainted is to check out *BitTorrent For Dummies,* by Susannah Gardner and Kris Krug (Wiley Publishing).

3. In the VMware Server Console, I'd choose File⇨Open. The Open dialog box would give me the opportunity to browse for a .vmx file — the file format used to store VMware Server virtual machine information. I'd of course take advantage of that opportunity to find (and open) the fedora-fc6-i386.vmx file, so that it would appear on a new tab in the VMware Server Console (see Figure 12-18).

4. Because I would be opening an existing image file of which this VMware Server installation had no record, the VMware Server Console would suggest to me that a new UUID be created for the new virtual machine (see Figure 12-19). (UUID stands for universally unique identifier, a unique VMware Server identifier for guest machines; since you're importing a virtual machine, the Server Console can't create a UUID at the time of creation, so it needs to assign one now, thus the suggestion.) I, of course, would willingly click OK.

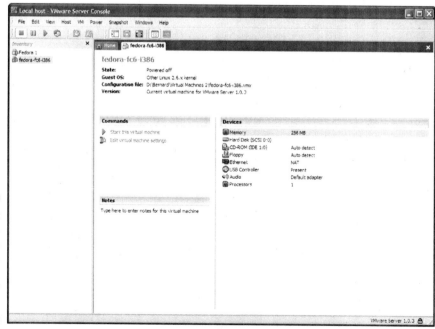

Figure 12-18:
The Fedora image file shows up in the VMware Server Console.

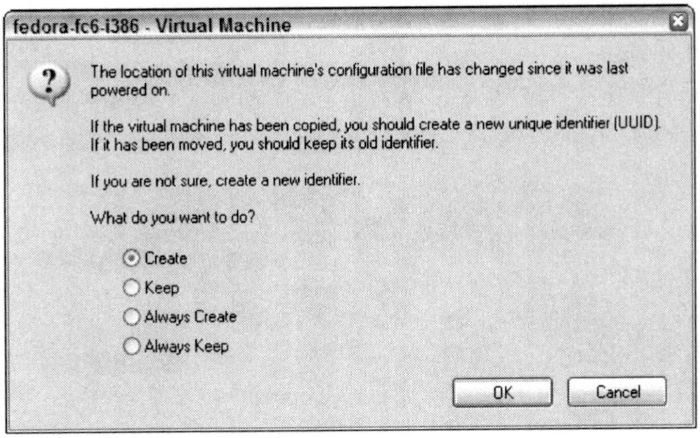

fedora-fc6-i386 - Virtual Machine

? The location of this virtual machine's configuration file has changed since it was last powered on.

If the virtual machine has been copied, you should create a new unique identifier (UUID). If it has been moved, you should keep its old identifier.

If you are not sure, create a new identifier.

What do you want to do?

- ⊙ Create
- ○ Keep
- ○ Always Create
- ○ Always Keep

[OK] [Cancel]

Figure 12-19:
Create a new identifier.

5. Back on the fedor3e-fc6-i386 tab of the VMware Server Console, I'd click the Start This Virtual Machine link right there under the Commands heading, and the virtual machine would immediately start with the operating system already loaded.

That's it. No extended operating system install. Just download the images and then open them with the console as described in such meticulous detail.

After you've installed the images, you might still need to modify the OS because it's probably a vanilla configuration, but that still has to be a lot faster than feeding CDs in, one at a time.

Can I Skip the Boring Application Installation Process?

Okay, you have your OS, and now you're ready to install the application(s) you want on the virtual machine. And, you guessed it, it's back to manual installation and configuration. Sigh. Wouldn't it be great if you could bypass all that installation and configuration work and just get an app installed super fast? In fact, that's a possibility. You might be able to skip all that work by using *virtual appliances* — applications delivered as ready-to-go images that you can just plop into the virtualization software. (Chapter 3 covers virtual appliances in depth.)

In fact, VMware has encouraged people to create software appliances and share them. It even hosts the virtual appliances on the VMware Web site. Just go to www.vmware.com/vmtn/appliances (see Figure 12-20) and check out the links to all the virtual appliances on the site. VMware hosts hundreds of virtual appliances of every different type for you to choose from.

Figure 12-20:
VMware's
Virtual
Appliance
Market-
place.

Imagine this scenario: You want to improve customer service for your company. You've heard about this cool new open source CRM product called SugarCRM, which sounds great, but you've also heard it takes some effort to get installed and configured. But, because you have VMware Server running, you go to the appliance page and search for SugarCRM. As you can see in Figure 12-21, you have perhaps a half-dozen SugarCRM virtual appliances to choose from. Pick one, any one, and get started.

Figure 12-21:
Would you
care for one
SugarCRM
or two?

Because the appliances are in the same image format as the Fedora image discussed in the previous section, you go through the same steps: Download the image from the site and then use the File⇨Open command in the VMware Server Console to open it on its own tab. Click the Start This Virtual Machine link to kickstart the virtual machine, and as Figure 12-22 illustrates, you have SugarCRM up and running. It couldn't be any easier than that, could it?

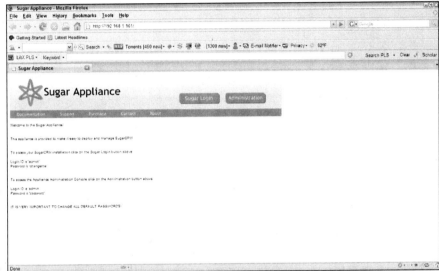

Figure 12-22:
SugarCRM
is running.
Sweet!

If you've worked through this last virtual appliance example, you'll understand why I've been talking about the revolutionary nature of virtualization. The ability to import an image and immediately begin using the SugarCRM application avoided a minimum of two hours of installation work. Not to mention not needing to figure out how to configure all the different software pieces to get the SugarCRM application integrated with the Web server and back-end database. All for a simple demo. Imagine how much heartache this could save you in a production environment? Now you understand why I say (in Chapter 4) that virtualization will transform IT as we know it today.

The image file contains the entire virtual machine, including both the guest OS as well as all software installed on the OS. Think of it as a file that contains the virtual machine and everything in the virtual machine. So, when you import the image file, you need to start the virtual machine; when you do that, all the applications within the virtual machine automatically start as well. Note that the new virtual machine has its own tab in the VMware Server Console; clicking on that tab brings up the virtual machine for you to interact with.

Chapter 13

Implementing Fedora Virtualization

*I*n Chapter 12, I take VMware Server through its paces — definitely a great product. However, you might want to consider another alternative for any number of reasons. Perhaps the fact that VMware Server installs as an application on top of the machine's operating system gives you pause — that solution isn't particularly optimal with regard to performance potential, to be honest. Or perhaps you prefer the Linux operating system and would like to use a virtualization solution integrated with it. Or maybe you just want to experiment with something else to compare it with VMware Server.

Whatever your reason, this chapter is for you. In this chapter, I demonstrate how to use the Xen virtualization technology built into Fedora 7. By the chapter's end, you'll be able to create and run guest virtual machines to your heart's content.

If your company uses Red Hat Enterprise Linux (RHEL), this is a good chapter for you to pay attention to. Features that are going into the next version of RHEL typically first see the light of day in Fedora, where Red Hat can (literally) work the bugs out. The first implementation of Xen in RHEL came in the currently shipping RHEL5. However, the upcoming RHEL5.1 will offer many improvements in virtualization, and most of those improvements are already available in Fedora 7, which is why this chapter uses Fedora 7 as its basis.

So . . . get started!

Obtaining Fedora 7

Unlike VMware Server, which you need to obtain separately from the host operating system, Fedora 7 comes with virtualization built in. So, this means your first task is to get Fedora 7 and install it.

Fedora 7 is Linux, which means it's available as a free download. The following steps walk you through the process:

1. **Point your browser to Fedora's main site at `http://fedora project.org`.**

   The Fedora home page appears on-screen.

2. **Click the Get Fedora link.**

   You see a page with a number of options for obtaining Fedora.

3. **Pick a way to obtain Fedora:**

   - *Download from BitTorrent:* BitTorrent is a peer-to-peer file-sharing mechanism; easy to use, but if you're not familiar with torrents already, this might not be the place to start. If you already have a few BitTorrent downloads under your belt, though, this is often the fastest method of downloading.

   - *Download from Mirrors:* A large number of sites host copies of Fedora and make it available for download. If you choose this option, you're presented with a table containing all the Fedora versions; click Version 7, and the next table down lists all the places that mirror downloads of that version of Fedora.

     When I did my own download, I chose `http://mirror.stanford .edu/fedora/linux/releases/7/Fedora/i386/iso/` because Stanford is just down the road, meaning the data throughput would be good. (Note that on the Fedora page, the link says `mirror. stanford.edu`, but that it actually goes to the longer address.)

   - *Network Install:* The instructions read "recommended for advanced users only," and the Fedora folks know of what they speak. I recommend avoiding this option.

   You also have two alternative options if you don't want to (or can't) download the product:

   - *Purchase media:* This means you pay for someone to place the product on a DVD and send it to you. That way you can avoid all the hassle. Of course, you'll need to pay a fairly small fee to obtain physical media, and you'll have to wait for the disc to arrive.

   - *Free media:* If you can't afford to purchase the media, the Fedora Free Media Program will send you a copy at no cost. You can't get fairer than that, can you?

4. **Do whatever you need to do to get the Fedora 7 files on a DVD.**

If you purchased media or had a free copy sent to you, you already have everything on DVD. If you've downloaded the file, it will be in an .iso format (also known as an optical disc *image* format) that you'll need to burn onto a DVD yourself. But remember that you have to burn it with image-burning software.

A number of good image burners are available at no cost. One that I like is called DeepBurner, which is free and can be downloaded from www.deep burner.com. Of course, if you don't have a DVD burner, all the software in the world won't do you any good. You'll have to go the purchase media/get free copy route to get your own DVD.

When you have your DVD whether burned from a download or sent in the mail — you're ready to move on to installing Fedora and its virtualization capability.

Installing Fedora 7

In this section, I walk you through the process of installing Fedora itself. Linux distributions have improved their installation processes enormously over the past few years, making Linux quite simple to install. If you've installed Windows, you'll be able to follow the Fedora installation quite easily.

The one tricky part about installing the Xen virtualization capability is that it isn't installed by default — you have to choose to install virtualization. But don't worry. The following steps give all the details:

1. **Boot the machine with the Fedora 7 DVD in the CD tray.**

The first thing you see when the installation process starts is a Welcome splash screen.

2. **Use the arrow keys to select the Install or Upgrade an Existing System option and then press Enter.**

The next screen you see indicates that the CD (in your case, the DVD) has been found in the CD tray. The screen also prompts you to test the afore-mentioned media. Testing the media confirms you have an undamaged DVD, but it takes quite a while to run through. I recommend you skip the media test.

3. **Click the Skip button.**

Doing so brings up yet another Welcome screen with pretty graphics, as shown in Figure 13-1.

4. **Click Next in the new Welcome screen.**

A wizard page appears, asking you to select the language you want to use during the installation process.

5. Choose your preferred language and then click Next.

In this example, I chose English as my install language.

Hard on the heels of the Install Language page comes the Keyboard layout page.

Figure 13-1:
Nice
graphics,
Fedora!

6. Make your keyboard choice and then click Next.

I chose U.S. English as my keyboard layout.

7. In the next screen (see Figure 13-2), you should either accept the default partitioning layout or create one of your own; then click Next.

Unless you're experienced with Linux, I recommend you stick with the default offering.

Clicking Next calls up a Warning dialog box stating that you are going to remove existing partitions and data. Don't worry, this is fine.

8. In the Warning dialog box, click the Yes button.

Doing so calls up a Network Devices screen, which lets you define which network interface card (NIC) you want the system to use to talk to the network. You also have the opportunity to choose how to assign an IP address to the system. I recommend you accept the defaults.

9. In the Network Devices screen, accept the defaults and then click Next.

A new screen (see Figure 13-3) appears, allowing you to pick your time zone.

10. **In the time zone page, use the cursor to navigate the world map or use the drop-down menu to choose your time zone and city; then click Next.**

    The next screen asks you to choose a password for the root account.

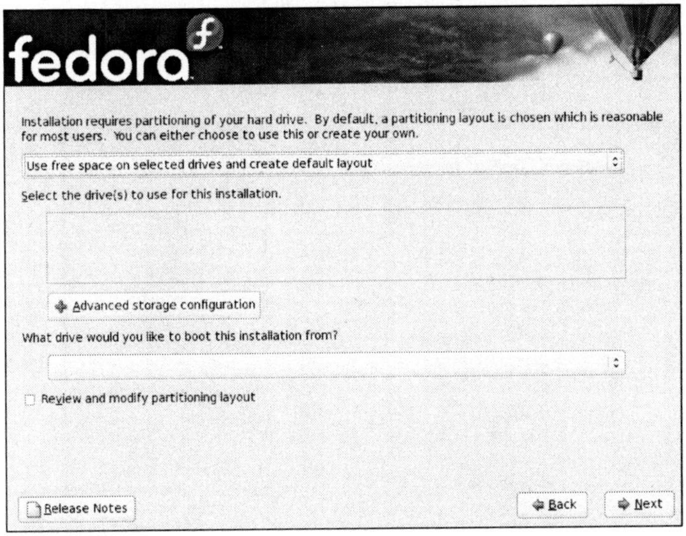

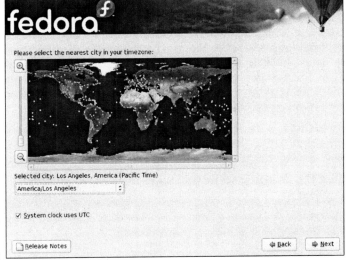

Figure 13-2:
Choosing a
partitioning
layout.

Figure 13-3:
You could
choose
Outer
Mongolia if
you wanted.

11. **Type the password you've selected, reenter it to confirm — as shown in Figure 13-4 — and then click Next.**

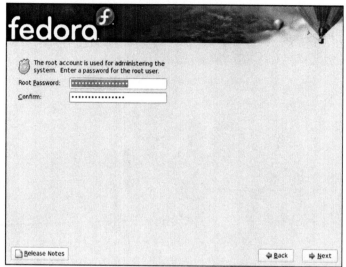

Figure 13-4:
Setting your
root
password.

Don't forget whatever password you choose because otherwise you won't be able to log in after the install is complete! I recommend you write the password down.

The next screen (see Figure 13-5) is the only tricky part of the installation. The default installation of Fedora is pretty bare bones. As you can see from the list near the top, you have a choice of three types of software to install. All three are good, so I recommend you consider installing all three. But the tricky part is represented by the radio button at the bottom, which invites you to customize the install. Seems innocent and not very important, right? Wrong!

If you don't go through the customize workflow, Xen virtualization won't get installed, and you won't be able to use Fedora as a virtualization host. So it's vital you stay awake at this step and customize your install.

12. **Click the Customize Now radio button and then click Next.**

A new screen appears, offering six different aspects of the install you can customize, as shown in Figure 13-6. The important one from a virtualization standpoint is the Base System listing.

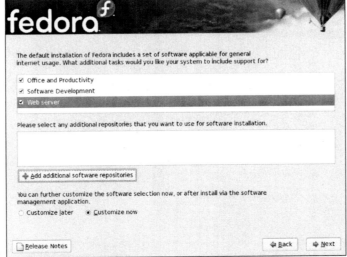

Figure 13-5:
Pay
attention to
the
Customize
Now option.

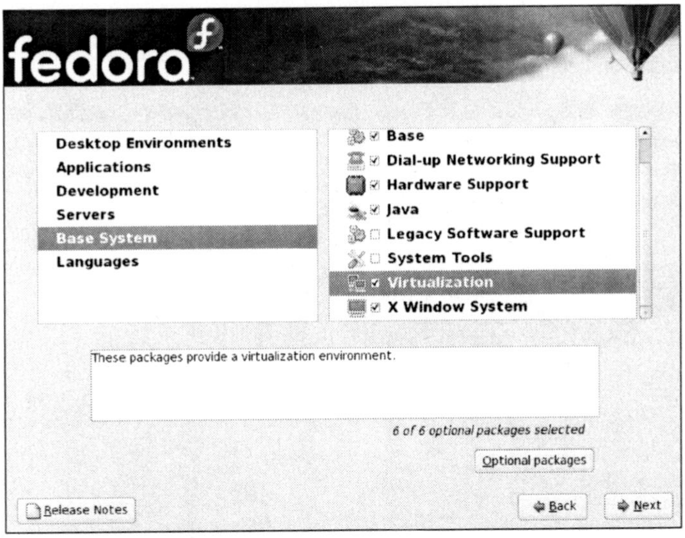

Figure 13-6:
Choosing
the Virtualiz-
ation option.

13. **Highlight the Base System entry in the left box, select the
    Virtualization option in the right box, and then click Next.**

    Okay. You've gotten Xen virtualization set up to install. And, in fact,
    you've completed the entire initial configuration, so a new screen
    appears, informing you that all's ready for the actual installation of the
    software. (See Figure 13-7.)

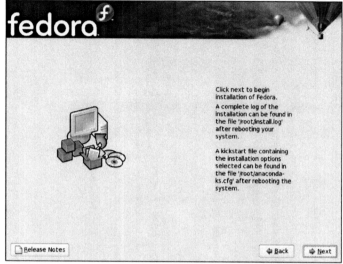

Figure 13-7:
Clicking
Next here
begins
installation
of Fedora.

14. **Click Next.**

With all the preliminaries out of the way, the real work of installation kicks off.

It might take a while for the process to complete — coffee, anyone? — but eventually you get a splash screen congratulating you on completing the configuration process (see Figure 13-8) and inviting you to reboot the operating system.

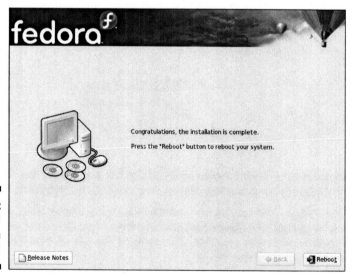

Figure 13-8:
Congrats!
You have
Fedora!

15. **Click the Reboot button in the Congratulations screen.**

    A new screen appears, asking you to begin setting some operational configuration items (see Figure 13-9).

16. **Click Forward in the Setup screen.**

    The next screen presents you with license information about Fedora 7. Assuming the license is okay by you, you can proceed.

17. **Click Forward in the License Information screen.**

    Doing so brings up the Firewall screen, as shown in Figure 13-10. Linux contains firewall software (which, by default, is on) in order to protect the machine. This screen offers you the opportunity to allow certain services to "talk" through the firewall — services like ftp, http (Web server), ssh, and so on. I recommend you enable http and ssh, as they are widely used for remote access and system administration. I also recommend you leave the firewall enabled because it's a good idea to keep the system protected.

18. **Select any services you want to have access through the firewall and then click Forward.**

    The next screen offers you the ability to run SELinux.

19. **Choose either Enabled or Disabled for your SELinux setting and then click Forward.**

    SELinux is a very sophisticated security mechanism, which I recommend you disable — you really won't need the capability for this example.

    The next screen offers you two different options for setting the time on the system you're installing.

Figure 13-9: Booting up brings yet another setup screen.

Welcome
License Information
Firewall
SELinux
Date and Time
Hardware Profile
Create User

🖳 **Welcome**

There are a few more steps to take before your system is ready to use. The Setup Agent will now guide you through some basic configuration. Please click the "Forward" button in the lower right corner to continue.

fedora

⬅ Back   ➡ Forward

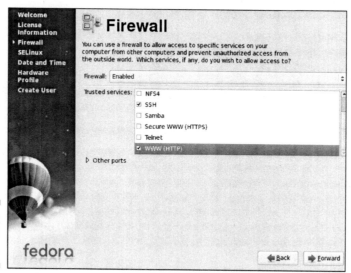

Figure 13-10:
The Firewall
page.

20. **Make your choices in the Date and Time screen and then click Forward.**

I prefer and recommend NTP (Network Time Protocol), which uses a network of extremely accurate time servers that your system can ping to get the exact right time. If you choose this option, your system will ping one of the three sites listed in the NTP Servers box, although you can put your own entries into the box if you prefer to do so.

The next screen offers you the opportunity to provide information about your hardware to the Fedora community, which should enable it to understand its user base better. Depending on your preference, decide whether you'd like to provide your profile.

21. **Click the correct radio button in the Hardware Profile screen and then click Forward.**

The Create User screen appears, as shown in Figure 13-11.

This user is different than the root user and should, generally speaking, be the primary way you interact with the system.

22. **Enter a username in Username field of the Create User screen, fill in the rest of the user information (including password info), and then click Finish.**

Congratulations! You're done!

The system now reboots and then comes up as a finished Fedora 7 system. You'll be offered two versions of Fedora to choose from. Select the Fedora Xen option to ensure the working system is ready to support virtualization.

After you select which version of Fedora that should run, you'll be presented with a login screen, as shown in Figure 3-12. Even though you've just created a user-level username, I suggest you log in as root with the root password (which you remember, right?) because you need to be root to create virtual machines and install guest operating systems.

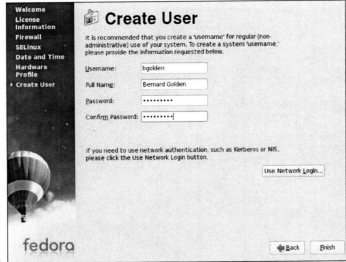

Figure 13-11:
The Create
User
screen.

Figure 13-12:
The
Fedora 7
login
screen.

23. **Log in to your Fedora 7 system as root.**

After you log in, you see the Fedora 7 desktop, ready to begin working on your behalf (see Figure 13-13). I recommend you take a deep breath, get a cup of tea, and relax for a few minutes because you're now ready to begin using Fedora 7 as a virtualization platform.

Figure 13-13:
A new
Fedora 7
desktop.

Creating a Guest Virtual Machine

You have Fedora 7 up and running, including virtualization functionality. Time to install a guest:

1. **With Fedora running, choose Start⇨System⇨Virtual Machine Manager, as shown in Figure 13-14.**

The Virtual Machine Manager appears on-screen.

Fedora relies on the Virtual Machine Manager (VMM) to control all aspects of its virtualization functionality.

2. **Review the current state of the Virtual Machine Manager.**

The Virtual Machine Manger indicates all the virtual systems running on the host, as shown in Figure 13-15.

Wait a sec, you haven't yet installed a virtual machine, but there's already a listing for Domain-0. How did that get there? Remember, Xen works with the concept of a privileged guest that controls all network and storage interaction. Basically, this means that Domain-0 runs as a guest but has privileges that allow it to directly access certain resources on the underlying hardware. Domain-0, then, is a regular operating system (Fedora 7, in this case) that has been modified to work on behalf of a guest operating system (called DomainU in Xen). (For more information on these Xen concepts, see Chapter 3.)

If you take another look at Figure 13-15, you'll notice that Domain-0 currently is allocated all the memory on the system (2GB, in this particular example). Xen doesn't allow the total memory allocated for all guests to be greater than the physical memory present on the system, which means that you'll need to reduce the memory allocated to Domain-0 before you install any other guest virtual machines.

3. **Choose Edit⇨Machine Details from the Virtual Machine Manager's main menu.**

Doing so brings up the Domain-0 Virtual Machine Details screen.

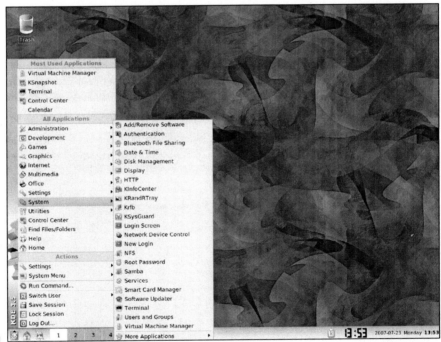

Figure 13-14:
Launching
the Virtual
Machine
Manager.

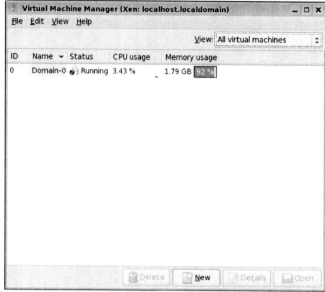

Figure 13-15:
What's what
on your
VMM.

4. **On the Hardware tab of the Domain-0 Virtual Machine Details screen, select Memory from the list on the left, use the Change Allocation spin box to adjust the memory allocated to Domain-0, and then click Apply.**

You're brought back to the main Virtual Machine Manager screen.

I'd say you should adjust Domain-0's memory to 500MB, as shown in Figure 13-16. That should free up enough memory for you to begin the process of installing a new guest virtual machine.

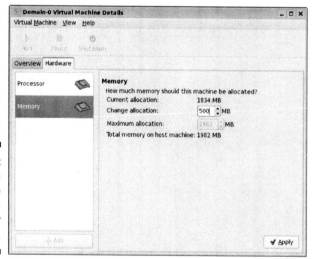

Figure 13-16:
Setting the
memory to
free some
up for
guests.

5. **Click the New button located at the bottom of the Virtual Machine Manager screen. (Refer to Figure 13-15.)**

   The Virtual Machine Manager launches the Create a New Virtual System Wizard with a splash screen explaining what the virtual machine installation process entails, as shown in Figure 13-17.

6. **Click Forward.**

   The Naming Your Virtual System screen appears.

7. **Enter a name for your system in the System Name text box and then click Forward.**

   For this example, you install an Ubuntu Linux Client system, so you should probably name it something wildly improbable — maybe UbuntuClient? (See Figure 13-18.) Of course, you could install a Fedora 7 guest as well. If you decide to do so, you'll follow the same steps up to the point where you begin installing the actual operating system.

   If you're going to be installing a guest OS, you're going to need an OS install disc. If you don't have Ubuntu lying around, you can download all the Ubuntu install files from the Ubuntu site (`www.ubuntu.com`) and then burn the image on a CD — although Ubuntu will kindly send you a CD at no charge, too.

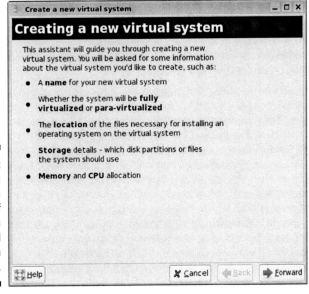

Figure 13-17: The Welcome screen of the Create a New Virtual System Wizard.

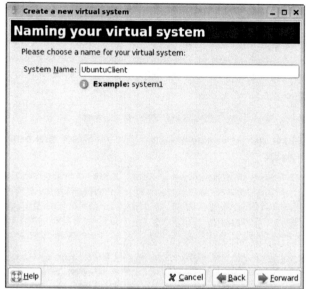

Figure 13-18:
Naming
your new
system.

8. **In the next screen of the wizard, select either Paravirtualized or Fully Virtualized as your virtualization method for your guest virtual machine and then click Forward.**

You see the Fully Virtualized option only if you own a newer model PC with a virtualization-enabled CPU. (See Chapter 8 for more information on virtualization and hardware.) To keep things simple, I'd choose Fully Virtualized, as shown in Figure 13-19.

Paravirtualization refers to virtualization accomplished by modifying the guest operating system so that it can cooperate with the virtualization hypervisor. Paravirtualization offers very good performance, but has the drawback of needing to modify the operating system. With the new generation of virtualization-enabled chips, the Xen hypervisor can support unmodified guest operating systems. This is somewhat confusingly referred to as "full virtualization," but it is still a paravirtualized version of virtualization. It's just that they wanted some way to differentiate between standard paravirtualization, which requires guest operating system modification, and paravirtualization operating on machines with virtualization-enabled chips, which does not require guest operating system modification. Unfortunately, they used the phrase "full virtualization" which seems to be something different than paravirtualization. It's not.

See Chapter 3 for more information on the difference between the two types of virtualization.

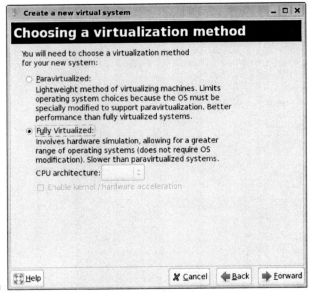

Figure 13-19:
Choosing a
virtualiz-
ation
method.

9. **In the Locating Installation Media screen of the Create a New Virtual System Wizard, choose the CD-ROM or DVD option.**

   This is where that CD install disc I mentioned back in Step 7 comes into play. (By the way, you need to have the disc actually in the drive in order to choose this option, even though the OS installation will happen later in the process.)

10. **In the same screen, use the drop-down menus to specify your OS type as well as your OS variant; then click Forward.**

    Because you're going the Linux route, you should definitely select Linux as your OS type, as shown in Figure 13-20. As for your OS variant, the wizard has a number of preidentified variants it supports, but it turns out Ubuntu isn't one of the defaults, so go ahead and choose the Generic 2.6.x Kernel option.

11. **In the next screen of the Create a New Virtual System Wizard, specify how you'd like to assign storage space on your "real" system for your "virtual" system and then click Forward.**

    The wizard offers you two options: a Linux partition and a regular Linux file. Although a production virtual machine would be better placed in a separate partition, if you're just experimenting you should use the Simple File option.

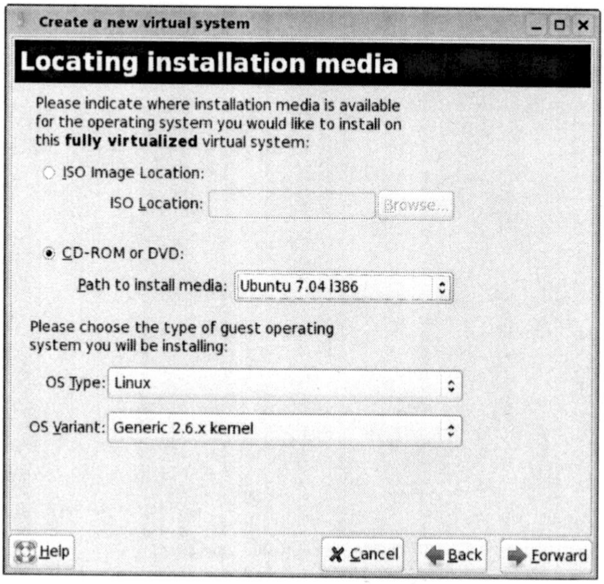

Figure 13-20:
Where did I
put that
disc?

You need to specify a location for the file — using the File Location text box with its accompanying Browse button — and you also need to make sure that the file system has sufficient room for the amount of storage you assign for the virtual machine. The recommended location for simple file images is in the `/var/lib/xen/images` directory, which is where you'll place your virtual machine. Also keep in mind that the virtual machine requires a specific file for the image. I recommend using 0tent with the virtual machine name itself. The default recommendation for file size is 4GB, which you should accept. (See Figure 13-21.)

12. In the next screen of the wizard, specify how you plan to connect to the host network and then click Forward.

The Virtual Network option is useful if you plan to have the machine disconnected from the rest of your network and don't need the virtual machine you're installing to talk to any other applications or systems. However, because you're likely to want to interact with other systems or the Internet, you should select the Shared Physical Device option, as shown in Figure 13-22.

If you have only one network card in your system (which is pretty typical for the type of machine you're likely to be using for this example; production servers, however, usually contain two or more network interface devices), you see only one option for the Device drop-down menu.

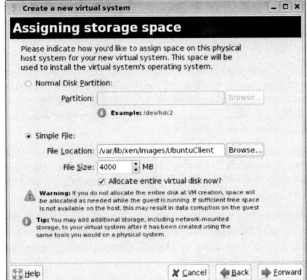

Figure 13-21:
Deciding
where to
store your
new virtual
machine.

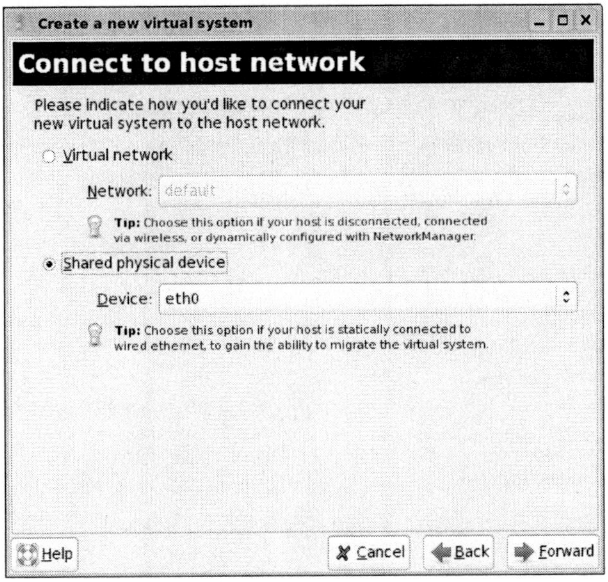

Figure 13-22:
Determining
your virtual
machine's
network
connection.

13. **In the wizard's next screen, use the VM Max Memory spinner box to specify the maximum amount of memory your new virtual machine should be allowed to use, set the number of virtual CPUs you want, and then click Forward.**

   Remember how, in an earlier step, you reduced the amount of memory assigned to Domain-0? In this step of the wizard, you assign some of that reclaimed memory to your new virtual machine. For this example, choose 500MB as the amount of memory assigned to this virtual machine, as shown in Figure 13-23.

   As for how many virtual CPUs you want to assign to this virtual machine, although it's true that Xen can handle multiple virtual CPUs (even more virtual CPUs than physical CPUs exist), for this example, stick with the default suggestion of one virtual CPU.

14. **In the confirmation page that appears (see Figure 13-24), review all the choices you've made during the configuration process to ensure they reflect what you want to install. If what is displayed corresponds with your wishes, click Finish.**

   The Virtual Machine Manager starts creating your new virtual machine. You see a progress page indicating how the creation process is going, as shown in Figure 13-25. When this is complete, you'll have a new virtual machine just waiting for a new OS to be installed.

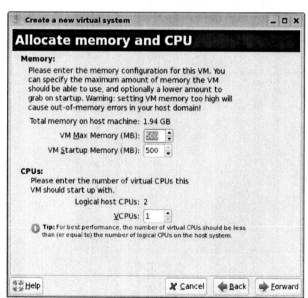

Figure 13-23:
Allocating memory for your virtual machine.

Figure 13-24:
Making
a list,
checking it
twice.

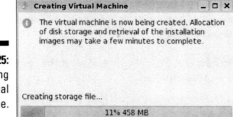

Figure 13-25:
Creating
your virtual
machine.

Installing a Guest Operating System

Okay, you have a brand-new virtual machine, but a machine — whether virtual or physical — won't do you much good without an operating system. Time to get some closure on this process and install the virtual machine's operating system. Luckily for you, the installation media for Ubuntu Client is sitting right there in your CD tray. (Remember placing it there earlier during the virtual machine creation process?)

So you're pretty much ready to go. Your Virtual Machine Manager has successfully created a new virtual machine, and your new machine has automatically powered up and is conveniently displaying the UbuntuClient Virtual Machine Console you see in Figure 13-26.

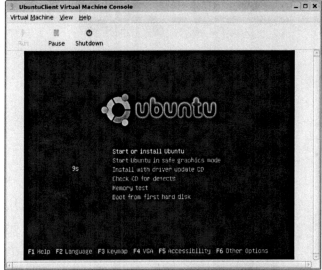

9s

Start or install Ubuntu
Start Ubuntu in safe graphics mode
Install with driver update CD
Check CD for defects
Memory test
Boot from first hard disk

F1 Help F2 Language F3 Keymap F4 VGA F5 Accessibility F6 Other Options

Figure 13-26:
Your virtual machine displaying the first screen of the Ubuntu Client Virtual Machine Console.

Because the Ubuntu Client installation media is in the CD tray, powering up the virtual machine automatically begins the installation process — just as it would if you powered up a physical server with the Ubuntu Client CD in its CD tray. Here's the process in a nutshell:

1. **Using the arrow keys, select the Start or Install Ubuntu option (refer to Figure 13-26) and then press Return.**

   The Ubuntu Client installation process kicks into action just as it would on a physical server, asking you for information on what time zone you're located in, what language you want the OS to use, and so on.

2. **Make your way through the various install screens until you get to the Prepare Disk Space screen. (See Figure 13-27.)**

   An Ubuntu installation is quite similar to the Fedora installation I detail earlier in the chapter, so you can review that discussion if one or two steps don't seem clear.

   One part of the Ubuntu installation process might seem a bit troubling — the aforementioned Prepare Disk Space screen. The screen asks whether you want to partition the entire disk. You might be worried that this is going to wipe out the disk of the host Fedora system and ruin all your work. Don't worry. This is just asking whether you want to partition only that 4GB of disk space you assigned during the virtual machine creation process.

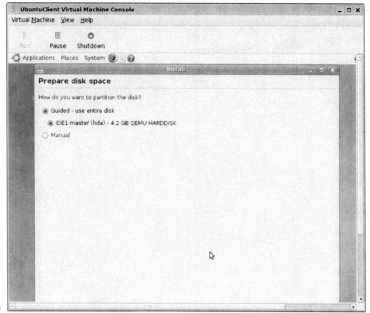

Figure 13-27:
The Prepare Disk Space screen.

3. **Answer Yes in the Prepare Disk Space screen.**

   You might need to scroll down to find the Yes button.

4. **Make your way through the installation process until the wizard completes its work.**

   The installation program reboots the guest, and when it returns, you're greeted by a brand-new Ubuntu desktop, as shown in Figure 13-28. The installation process of the virtual machine operating system is complete. Ubuntu is now up and running in your virtual machine. Good work!

5. **Just to confirm that the new virtual machine is working properly, bring up the Firefox browser, type a URL in the address bar, and then press Enter.**

   For this example, I chose the Fedora 7 Web site (see Figure 13-29), just to show the virtual machine is connected to the Web. Of course, to successfully connect, you would have had to have chosen the right option during the Connect to Host Network step in the Create a New Virtual System Wizard. (That was Step 12 in the list from the previous section in this chapter.)

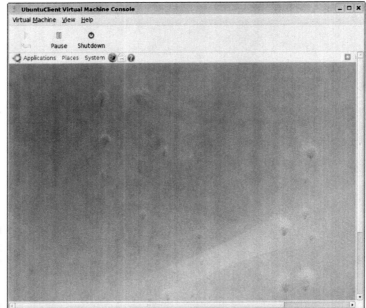

Figure 13-28:
A new
Ubuntu
desktop.

Figure 13-29:
It's alive!

Chapter 14

Implementing XenExpress

*I*f you've made your way through the previous two chapters, you've been exposed to two different flavors of virtualization, both of them completely free. Chapter 12 describes how to use VMware Server, an application-level virtualization product. (By using the phrase *application-level virtualization product,* I clue you in to the fact that VMware Server installs on top of the native operating system on the machine and sits between the native OS and the guest virtual machines the phrase is like a secret handshake welcoming you to the virtualization community, so go ahead and make yourself at home.) VMware Server is available at no cost, and you can certainly obtain commercial support for it, but the folks at VMware don't really position VMware Server as a commercial product for production environments. For production use, VMware would much rather sell you the commercial ESX Server product — and they might be fully justified in doing so because ESX Server really is more appropriate for such an environment

Chapter 13 presents the Xen virtualization that is part of Fedora 7. Xen, as you'll no doubt recall from Chapter 3, is an open source virtualization product bundled with many Linux distributions. In contrast to VMware Server, Xen operates as a *bare-metal* virtualization solution, meaning that it installs directly on the hardware with no native OS residing between it and the physical hardware. Fedora 7 is available at no cost; it's a community distribution associated with the commercial Linux vendor Red Hat. As such, while Fedora 7 is free, it also isn't really focused on being used in real production environments, being aimed more at experimenters and Red Hat users who want to get an early peek at the next version of Red Hat Enterprise Linux (RHEL), because Red Hat usually auditions upcoming RHEL functionality in Fedora.

In this chapter, I focus on a Xen-based virtualization product — XenExpress from XenSource. It's available at no cost but is appropriate for production environments. If that sounds intriguing, this chapter is definitely for you. I walk you through the process of implementing XenSource's version of Xen virtualization. And, in a change from the two examples from the preceding chapters, you'll be installing a Windows client (specifically, Windows XP) to show that virtualization can support more than just Linux virtual machines.

What Is XenSource, Anyway?

Xen, an open source project, is sponsored by a commercial company called XenSource — although Xen, because it's an open source project, has software contributions from people all over the world who work at many different companies (IBM and Red Hat, for example). XenSource distributes a Xen-based product called XenExpress, which is available at no cost. However, unlike my VMware and Fedora 7 examples, where the free product differs from the flagship, production-oriented product, XenExpress is exactly the same code as XenEnterprise, the commercial, production-quality product from XenSource — it is exactly the same code base. The difference between the free and commercial versions is that the commercial versions have additional functionality accessible via input of a software key. In other words, XenSource makes it possible to use production-quality virtualization at no cost.

You might think this sounds too good to be true, and it is true that XenExpress has some limitations. XenExpress is limited to four virtual machines on each system, whereas XenServer and XenEnterprise have no limitations on number of virtual machines. However, as a way to get started with high-performance Xen virtualization with a production-oriented version, XenExpress is hard to beat.

Obtaining XenSource XenExpress

Getting XenExpress couldn't be easier:

1. **Point your browser to XenSource at `http://xensource.com`.**

   The XenSource home page appears on-screen.

2. **Put the cursor over the Products tab and then click the XenExpress link.**

   You're taken to a page with a Download XenExpress for Free link near the bottom.

3. **Click the Download XenExpress for Free link. (You might have to scroll down to find it.)**

   You're taken to a registration page with a number of fields to fill out. XenSource uses this information to get word of updates and the like to you.

4. **Fill out the registration fields and click Submit.**

   You are then redirected to a new Web page, the XenSource Product Download Page, containing product and documentation downloads that are available.

5. **Click the Product CD Image (ISO) link.**

   You'll be taken through several screens, each of which has a link to download the product. Just keep clicking Download XenExpress. Eventually you get a Save As dialog box asking you where you'd like to save the product image.

   I recommend you save the .iso image somewhere on your hard drive so that it's available to you in the future.

6. **To save the .iso image, select a folder to store the image in and click OK.**

   Your download begins. Xen is a very lightweight virtualization product, and the entire XenExpress download is only approximately 200MB, so the download shouldn't take very long.

7. **Do whatever you need to do to get the XenExpress files on a CD or DVD.**

   Unlike the products in the previous two chapters, the XenExpress download is small enough that it can be burned on either a CD or DVD. You should burn to whichever is more convenient for you. Keep in mind that burning images is not like burning music or pictures; you need ISO image-burning capability in your burning software, which means you can't just use the software included with the OS. A number of good image burners are available at no cost. One that I like is called DeepBurner, which is free and can be downloaded from www.deepburner.com.

Installing XenExpress

In this section, I walk you through the process of installing XenExpress. XenExpress installs in two parts: the virtualization hypervisor, which installs on the server, and the management console, which installs on a client machine. This section walks you through installing both. Don't get too concerned, though; the installation process itself is actually not that complex.

1. **Boot the server with the .iso image CD or DVD in the machine's CD tray.**

   The machine starts up and begins the installation process. The initial splash screen displays and welcomes you to the XenExpress installation.

2. **Press Enter to begin installation.**

   The installer displays a Preparing for Installation screen and probes the hardware of the machine as part of its configuration process. It then puts up another screen that asks you to choose a keymap (keyboard layout).

3. **Choose the correct keyboard layout for your machine and then click OK.**

   The installer displays a Welcome to XenServer screen and asks you to select what you want to install.

4. **Choose Install XenServer Host and then click OK.**

   The installer now displays a Welcome to XenServer Setup screen and notes that the installation will overwrite any data on the machine's hard drive.

   Unlike many operating systems, XenExpress and its brethren cannot be installed in a dual-boot mode (that is, with both XenExpress and another operating system installed on the computer's hard drive, with either selected as the working operating system at boot time). XenExpress must be the sole product installed on the system and will overwrite data on the system's hard drive. So only install XenExpress on a machine you're willing to dedicate to running XenExpress on and that has no data you need to keep.

5. **Click OK.**

   The installer now displays an End User License Agreement screen, asking you to agree with XenSource's licensing terms. Read it and decide whether you can continue.

6. **If you agree with the licensing terms, click Accept EULA.**

   The installer now displays a screen asking whether you'd like to install the Linux Pack from a second CD or DVD. Because you're going to be creating a Windows guest virtual machine, this second CD or DVD is unnecessary, so you don't need to install it.

7. **Click No.**

   The installer displays a Verify Installation Source screen. It's always a good idea to make sure your installation source is pristine — just be aware that it will take some time to go through the verification process. This process looks through the installable .iso image to confirm that it has no errors or flaws.

8. **Click OK to start the verification process.**

   When the verification process completes, the installer displays a screen asking you to set the root password for the XenExpress server. Be sure to remember this password, because you'll need it to log on to the XenExpress management console.

9. **Enter your selected password, click OK, enter the password again to verify, and then click OK again.**

The installer now asks you to select your time zone. Actually, this is a two-step process: On the first screen, you enter your continent, and on the second screen, you enter the city you're in (or near) to choose the correct time zone.

10. Select your time zone and click OK.

The installer now asks you to choose how you want to set the system time. You can choose to set it manually, but that seems so . . . manual. Why not use a guaranteed-to-be-accurate online source? Network Time Protocol (NTP) is a service that uses online locations that are synchronized to a government-sponsored atomic clock, which is very cool. I recommend that you go with NTP.

11. Select Network Time Protocol (NTP) as your choice for setting the system time and click OK.

The installer now asks you to enter some NTP sites and offers `pool.ntp.org` as an example. In a production environment, you'd want several sites listed for safety reasons, but using just one for now will suffice for testing purposes.

12. Press the spacebar and enter pool.ntp.org in the Server field; then click OK.

The installer now displays a networking screen and asks you to choose the networking type that you'd like. Automatic Networking Configuration is fine and easiest.

13. Select Automatic Networking Configuration and then click OK.

The installer now wants to know how you'll set the hostname of the machine as well as where your Domain Name Servers (DNS) are. I'll assume that your DNS servers are set automatically, so you don't really need to do anything but accept the suggested defaults. In this screen you'll also be offered the opportunity to set the host name (name of the XenExpress server). The installer offers a default choice as well. Because you're experimenting, I recommend you accept the default choice, although in a production environment you'd probably want to set the name manually.

14. Accept the suggested defaults for your DNS servers and click OK.

You're now done with entering information. The installer displays a Confirm Installation screen, asking you, essentially, one last time, whether all the information you just got done entering is correct. It also reiterates that installing XenExpress will destroy any existing data on the machine's hard drive and asks whether you want to continue.

15. Click Install XenServer.

The installer begins the installation process and displays a progress bar. Go get a cup of tea. Ten minutes later, the basic XenExpress installation is complete. Congratulations, you did it!

Installing XenConsole

XenConsole is the management interface you use to control the XenExpress server along with all virtual machines. If you've read the previous two chapters, XenConsole is equivalent to the VMware Server Console or the Fedora Virtual Machine Manager.

Unlike the management consoles for VMware Server or Fedora Xen, XenConsole must be installed on a separate machine from XenExpress. Note as well that XenConsole must be installed on a Windows machine.

1. **Remove the installation CD or DVD from your server machine (see the preceding step list) and put it into the client machine you'll use to run XenCenter.**

2. **Navigate the tree structure on the CD/DVD to go to the folder named client_install.**

3. **Open the client_install folder and double-click the `XenCenterSetup.exe` file.**

   The Welcome to the XenCenter Setup Wizard splash screen displays, as shown in Figure 14-1.

4. **Click Next.**

   The installer asks you to select the folder you'll install XenCenter into. I recommend you use the default location.

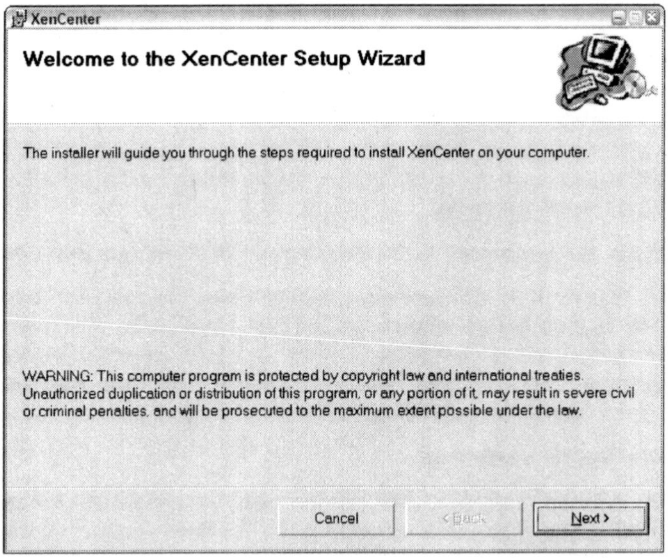

Figure 14-1:
The Welcome to the XenCenter Setup Wizard.

5. **Choose an installation folder and then click Next.**

   That's it. You're ready to install. The installer brings up a Confirm Installation screen. I assume you're ready to go.

6. **Click Next in the Confirm Installation screen.**

   The installer goes off and does its magic. When it's done, it displays an Installation Complete screen, as shown in Figure 14-2.

   Your installation of both the server and console components of XenExpress is complete. You're now ready to begin using XenExpress as a virtualization solution. I'm ready — how about you?

7. **Click Close.**

   Doing so closes the installer and gets you ready to start XenConsole.

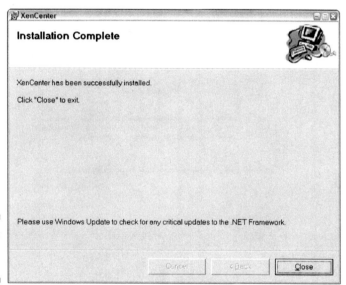

Figure 14-2:
Installation
complete!

Working with XenConsole

To begin working with the XenServer instance you just installed, you need to bring up XenConsole — that other bit of software you just installed. Here's how you do that:

1. **Choose XenConsole from the Start menu of whatever OS you're using.**

   In Windows XP, that would mean Start⇨All Programs⇨XenConsole.

   An introductory screen appears, as shown in Figure 14-3. The screen invites you to add your xenServer (essentially, this means connect to the

XenServer instance you just installed) or learn more about using Xen Server. I'm sure you'll want to get right to work, so go the Add Your XenServer route.

2. **Click the Add Your XenServer button.**

Now you need to select your XenServer. This might seem silly because you've installed just the one server, but the screen is designed to let you select among several XenServer instances. You need to enter either the IP address of the server you installed XenExpress on or the hostname you entered during the XenServer installation process (see Figure 14-4).

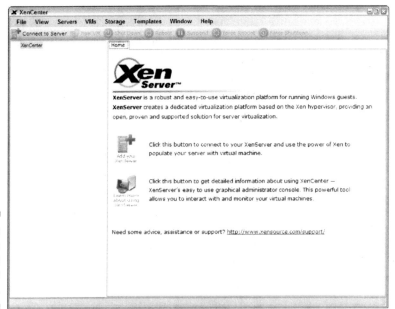

Figure 14-3:
The XenConsole introductory screen.

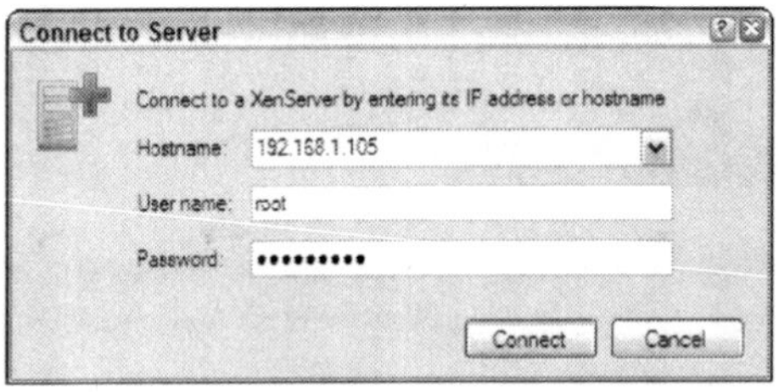

Figure 14-4:
Choosing the right server to connect to.

3. Enter the IP address or hostname and click Connect.

XenConsole is clever. It knows you might want to connect to the same server in the future, so the next dialog box that pops up — the Save Session screen — asks whether you want to save the connection info (see Figure 14-5). I recommend you do so.

Figure 14-5:
Make life
easy; save
your
XenConsole
connection
information.

4. Click OK in the Save Session dialog box.

XenConsole now displays a tree view of all the servers it's connected to in its left pane. (Okay, okay, there's only one, so you won't see much of a display.) The right pane displays the details of the server you just connected to, as shown in Figure 14-6.

Figure 14-6:
Congratu-
lations!
You have
XenConsole
connected to
XenExpress.

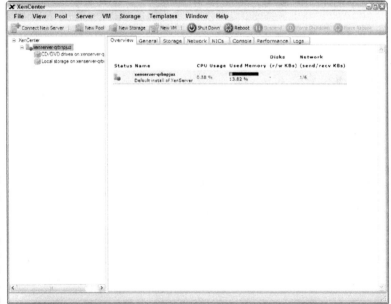

Creating a Guest Virtual Machine

In Chapters 12 and 13, I walk you through the installation of Linux OSes on the virtual machines you create. In this chapter, I take a different tack — you get to install Windows XP. After all, with the previous two examples focusing on installing Linux virtual machines, you might have gotten the impression that virtualization was only meant for Linux. Not so! Windows is an important platform for virtual machines; moreover, XenSource views supporting Windows virtual machines as a key part of its strategy and has done extra work — including coming up with special drivers — to make its virtualization implementation particularly well suited to supporting Windows virtual machines. Don't let my mention of "extra work" worry you, though; I show you how to install those drivers so that you can get the best possible performance from your Windows guests.

If you look at Figure 14-6, the toolbar just below the top of XenConsole has a button labeled New VM. That's where your journey to install a guest virtual machine starts. Ready? Here goes:

1. **With the XenConsole open, click the New VM button on the main toolbar.**

   XenConsole begins the New VM Wizard, as shown in Figure 14-7. As you can see from the figure, a number of templates are available. Because you're going to install Windows XP, you'll use the one labeled Windows XP SP2.

   XenSource supports only Windows XP Service Pack 2 versions of the product. If you don't have a CD with Windows XP SP 2, you need to get one in order to follow this example.

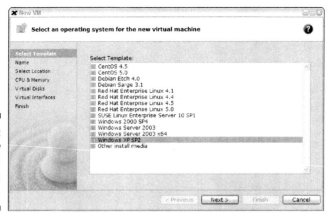

Figure 14-7:
The New
VM Wizard
template
screen.

2. Select Windows XP SP2 and click Next.

The introductory screen of the actual installation process appears. As you'll note, a number of entries are in a panel on the left side of the screen. These are the steps you'll be filling out as you go through the wizard. The main area of the wizard is asking for a name for the virtual machine and a description. The wizard suggests Windows XP SP2 (1) — I suggest you live wildly and change it to Windows XP. For a description, type **Windows XP**. (Figure 14-8 shows the wizard panel with its text fields filled in.)

I suggest using "Windows XP" for this example, which is fine because it's so simple. However, in a production environment, it's important to choose a naming convention and use it consistently. The naming convention should be tied to machine type or workload type, because if you have 40 virtual machines running, each called something like Windows XP N, where N is a sequential number from 1 to 40, well, that's not very informative, is it? You'll go nuts trying to figure out which of the 40 is the one you have DNS running on. It's far better to make the names descriptive, so it's obvious from the virtual machine name what the system does. So, for example, a name like Windows XP 7 DNS Server would be far more informative and much easier to find in a list of 40 different systems.

3. After entering a name and a description for your virtual machine, click Next.

The next screen of the wizard asks you to select a location where the install image for the new virtual machine resides. Because you'll be using a CD or DVD, you don't have to do anything because the wizard has that option as the default.

Figure 14-8:
Beginning
the
installation
wizard.

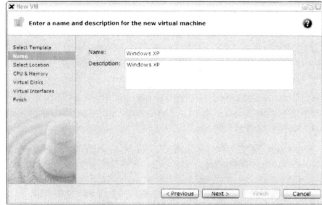

4. **Leave the default setting — Physical DVD drive — and click Next.**

The next screen asks you to select how many virtual CPUs and how much memory you want assigned to this virtual machine. Virtual CPUs are just what they sound like: virtual representations of actual CPUs, which the virtual machine will access for processing.

With regard to how much memory to assign to the virtual machine, the wizard lets you know just how much physical memory is available for assignment. If you worked through Chapter 13 — the one on Fedora virtualization — you'll remember that you had to reduce the amount of memory assigned to Domain-0, which was by default assigned all the memory on the machine. XenExpress has assigned some of the physical memory to this selfsame Domain-0, but left most of it available for virtual machines. This is definitely more convenient. (Domain-0 is the privileged guest that runs on the Xen hypervisor and controls access to networking and storage; it requires some of the memory of the server to fulfill its duties.)

The wizard suggests defaults of one virtual CPU and 256MB of memory.

5. **Leave the virtual CPU default in place, but bump the memory to 900MB and then click Next.**

The amount of memory that the wizard shows as available depends on how much physical memory is installed on the server. Although Windows XP can operate with as little as 256MB of memory, like most operating systems, it performs better with more memory available to it. If you were creating this virtual machine on a production server, you'd have to balance this machine's memory requirements against the other virtual machines, keeping in mind the overall amount of memory available.

6. **In the next screen of the wizard, assign storage for the new virtual machine and then click Next.**

The wizard suggests a default of 8GB located in local storage. If you want a different amount of storage or you want to locate the virtual machine's storage somewhere else besides on the server, you can edit the entry; however, I recommend that, for this example, you stick with the suggested default.

The location and type of storage is one of the most important aspects of successful virtualization and a key factor in your virtualization journey. To learn more about virtualization and storage, see Chapter 11.

After you click Next, the wizard displays a page for adding (or removing) virtual network interfaces. Just like a virtual CPU, a virtual network interface is what the virtual machine interacts with to send and receive network traffic. I recommend that you accept the default.

The Xen hypervisor acts as a traffic cop to send and receive data from the *physical* network interface on the machine, so you're covered there.

7. **Accept the default virtual network interface and then click Next.**

You've now completed all the steps necessary to create a new virtual machine. The wizard displays a final screen (see Figure 14-9), which offers the opportunity to finish creating the virtual machine. Until you signal you're ready to go forward, no actual resources have been committed; when you click Finish, the resources are assigned and the virtual machine created.

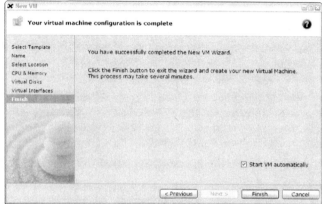

Figure 14-9:
You're done creating a virtual machine. Hurrah!

8. Click Finish in the wizard's final screen.

The installer now exits, and you are returned to XenConsole. Your new virtual machine is listed in the tree view in the left panel, as shown in Figure 14-10.

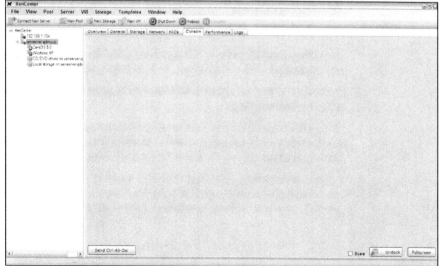

Figure 14-10:
Your new virtual machine shows up in the XenConsole tree structure.

So far, so good. You've got a new virtual machine just waiting for its new operating system. You're going to install from a Windows XP CD, so place it into the client machine's CD tray.

You need to highlight the virtual machine's entry to complete the installation process. To get access to the virtual machine's console, you need to click the Console tab of the right panel.

1. **In XenConsole, click the Windows XP entry in the left panel and open the Console tab in the right panel.**

   The Console controls all the virtual machines on the XenExpress system it's managing. By clicking on the Windows XP entry, the Console identifies that virtual machine as the one you want to work on.

   After you click Windows XP, there are a number of tabs available. To get to the graphic interface of the virtual machine, it's necessary to click the Console tab. After you do so, the console of the new virtual machine appears in XenConsole's right panel.

   You're ready to begin the installation process for Windows XP.

2. **The new virtual machine should start automatically. If for some reason it does not, click Start to start up the new virtual machine.**

   The initial Windows XP install screen appears. It gives you a choice of doing a fresh install, repairing an existing Windows XP installation, or quitting the installation.

3. **Because you're doing an initial installation for this virtual machine, press Enter.**

   The next setup screen offers you several choices of what type of installation to perform. Because all you want to do is install Windows XP, you want the first option.

4. **Press the Enter key to proceed with the installation.**

   The obligatory Microsoft EULA screen appears. If you don't agree, you can't proceed with installation, so I recommend you agree.

5. **Press the F8 key to agree with the EULA agreement — and to proceed with the installation.**

   The next screen lets you decide where to install Windows XP. Because this installation is going to use the storage space you identified earlier when you created the virtual machine, you see only one option.

   It might seem strange for the installer to offer you this screen, because you have only one option, but if several partitions had been available on the disk, you might have wanted to pick a partition.

6. **Press Enter to proceed with the installation.**

   A screen appears informing you that the partition needs to be formatted and offering you several choices, as shown in Figure 14-11.

   I recommend you use an NTFS file format and use the Quick format. This is the default option, so if this is agreeable to you, you're ready to proceed.

7. **Select the file system type and formatting option you want and then press Enter.**

   A new screen appears, showing you the installer's progress in formatting the partition. Depending on which selection you chose and the size of the file system you decided to use, this might take a few minutes or a longer period of time. If the latter, I recommend you take a break while the formatting continues.

   The installer is formatting the storage assigned to this virtual machine, not the entire server.

   After the formatting is complete, the installer copies files needed for the remainder of the installation. This shouldn't take long.

   After the files are copied, the installation of the Windows XP operating system begins, as shown in Figure 14-12. As you can see, the installation switches to a graphical display, indicating you're now in XP territory and that the installer is getting prepared to install Windows.

Figure 14-11:
Choosing
the file
system type
for your
virtual
machine.

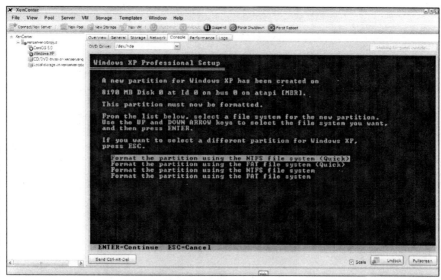

Figure 14-12:
Preparing
for
Windows
installation.

The installer now walks you through a series of OS configuration steps. The initial step (see Figure 14-13) is to ask you to choose your regional and language options — and by implication your keyboard layout type. The installer attempts to discern the proper setup from the computer and will display a default option. This is usually the correct option and doesn't require you to make a selection.

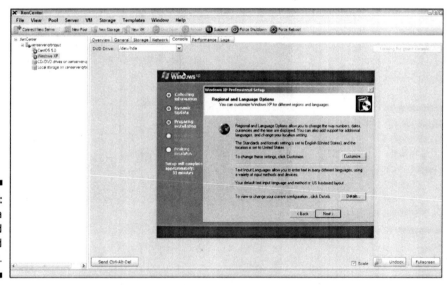

Figure 14-13:
Choosing a
keyboard
and
language.

8. **After verifying your Regional and Language options, click Next.**

   A screen appears, asking for your User and Organization names.

9. **Enter the appropriate information into the text fields and then click Next.**

   The next screen asks you to enter the Product key for your copy of Windows XP. Without a legitimate key number, you can't proceed further with the installation.

10. **Enter the product key for your copy of Windows XP and then click Next.**

    A new screen appears, offering a suggested system name and asking you to enter an administrator password. (See Figure 14-14.) The system name isn't that important, so you can leave the default name in place; however, the administrator's password is critical, so choose one that isn't too obvious (to ensure secure access to the system), but make sure you're not going to forget in an hour or so.

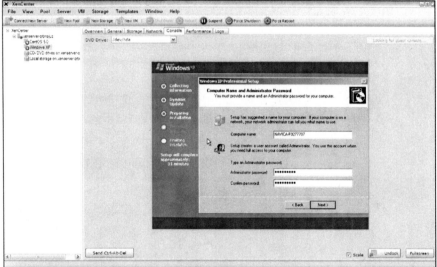

Figure 14-14:
Choosing a system name and an administrator password.

11. **Fill in a computer name, enter the appropriate password, enter the appropriate password again (to confirm), and then click Next.**

    Yet another screen appears, asking you to choose the correct date and time. Typically, the default choice is correct, so you don't have to do anything to give the system the correct information.

12. Confirm that the correct date and time are selected and then click Next.

The next step in the install process is to choose your network settings. The Xen hypervisor takes care of moving network packets from virtual machines through Domain-0 and out to the physical network interface card (NIC), which means that you can use the typical Windows networking choice, as shown in Figure 14-15.

13. Choose the Typical Settings option in the Networking Settings page and then click Next.

You have now completed the configuration steps in the installation, and the installer can begin storing your choices.

Eventually, the registration is complete and the installer is ready to allow you to configure Windows itself (see Figure 14-16).

14. In the Welcome to Microsoft Windows screen, click Next.

Microsoft, like every other operating system vendor, is constantly improving its product by releasing incremental updates, also known as patches. The next screen (shown in Figure 14-17) gives you the option to have these patches automatically installed. I strongly recommend you allow the operating system to do automatic installation because that's the best way to protect yourself from security vulnerabilities.

Figure 14-15:
Selecting the Windows networking option.

Figure 14-16:
Ready to
configure
Windows
XP.

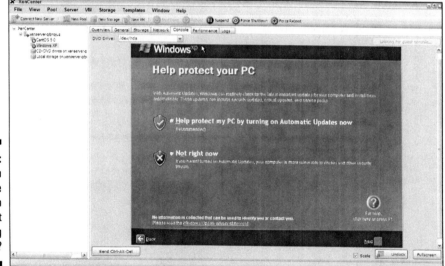

Figure 14-17:
Would you
like
protection
with that
operating
system?

15. **Select the update option you prefer and then click Next.**

    The next screen asks you what kind of connectivity to the Internet this OS will have. Although the installer doesn't understand that this instance of the OS will be a virtual machine, you do; by definition, this means that the virtual machine doesn't connect directly to the Internet, but instead lives on a network, albeit one offered by the hypervisor. Therefore, it's important for you to choose the option indicating that the computer connects through a local area network.

16. **Select the Local Area or Home Network option and then click Next.**

    The installer now displays a screen asking (with an enthusiasm barely held in check) whether you're ready to activate Windows. The screen also informs you that activation involves the installer contacting Microsoft and getting acknowledgement that the copy of Windows you're installing is legitimate. Although this is important (if you don't activate your copy eventually, bad things will happen), it's not critical that it be done now, as the OS will prompt you to activate the Windows instance every day after the install is completed. Therefore, in the interest of completing your virtual machine install, I recommend you skip activation at this time.

17. **Select the No, Remind Me Every Few Days option and then click Next.**

    The installation program now asks you to create one or more user accounts. You need at least one, so you'll need to enter an account name in the initial entry box.

18. **Enter an account name and click Next. (See Figure 14-18.)**

    You're done! Windows now thanks you and congratulates you for successfully installing the product, as shown in Figure 14-19.

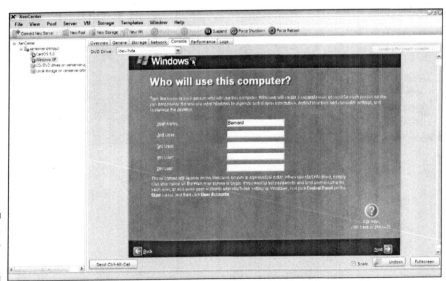

Figure 14-18:
The user
screen.

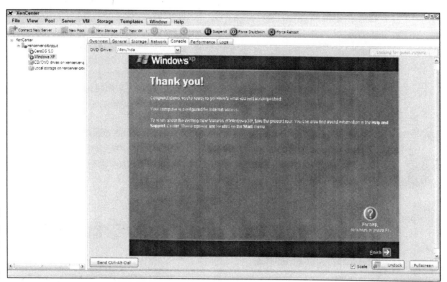

Figure 14-19:
Windows at
last!

Although the Windows installer is finished, you're not. You should take a couple more steps to get the best possible experience and performance from your virtual machine. (Okay, I can tell you right now: You're going to have to install some new drivers and set up a new protocol. I know it sounds complicated, but it really isn't. Don't just take my word for it, though. Read the next two sections and find out for yourself.)

Installing Paravirtualized Drivers

If you cast your mind back to Chapter 3, which described the different types of virtualization technology out there, you'll remember that Xen implements a type of virtualization called *paravirtualization,* which is an unwieldy term indicating that the Xen hypervisor doesn't attempt to emulate a complete hardware environment for the guest virtual machine, but instead acts as a traffic cop to direct traffic to and from individual virtual machines to the native hardware of the server. The drawback this has traditionally imposed is that paravirtualization requires that the kernel of the guest virtual machines be modified in order to interact properly with the Xen hypervisor.

A bit of background, or QEMU who?

With the advent of the new virtualization-enabled chips from Intel and AMD (described in Chapter 8), Xen no longer requires kernel modifications for guest virtual machines. It uses a Linux-based technology called QEMU to allow it to support non-paravirtualized kernels (which are referred to as *fully virtualized,* which I know is confusing, but just accept it as a quirk of the language of Xen). As you can imagine, avoiding kernel modifications is a big win because it simplifies the Xen implementer's experience enormously. (And, no, no one can figure out what QEMU stands for. Fabrice Bellard came up with the software and the name, and he's keeping mum on whether QEMU is an actual acronym or just a bit of nonsense designed to provoke puzzled expressions in people.)

There's another win as well — with full virtualization, Xen can now support Windows, which wasn't possible previously because it was impossible to gain access to Windows source code to implement paravirtualization. A complicated situation, eh?

Baby, you can drive my virtualization environment

Okay, I have to come clean. This whole paravirtualization thing is a bit more complicated than what I describe in the previous section. Although the full virtualization provided by QEMU simplifies the implementer's life, using QEMU imposes a performance hit on the system because now an additional software layer is in the middle of the virtualization software stack.

Is there any way to gain the benefit of being able to operate full virtualization while avoiding the performance penalty of QEMU emulation? Generally speaking, no. But XenSource has a close business relationship with Microsoft and has worked with Microsoft to create paravirtualized drivers (referred to as PV drivers); these drivers enable a Windows guest virtual machine to interact directly with the Xen hypervisor without needing to go through QEMU. These paravirtualized drivers are available for a number of different versions of Windows, including Windows Server and Windows XP.

Naturally, the vanilla Windows installer (for any version of Windows) is not aware of the existence of these paravirtualized drivers, so it's necessary to insert the drivers after the initial installation of Windows (Windows XP, in this example).

That is the next step for you. Fortunately, it is dead simple to install paravirtualized drivers. XenConsole makes it trivially easy by including a set of tools to do the installation. Here's how it's done:

1. **Choose VM⇨Install Tools from XenConsole's main menu option, as shown in Figure 14-20.**

   This step brings up the Xen paravirtualized drivers EULA screen.

2. **Select the Accept check box in the EULA screen and then click Next.**

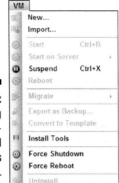

Figure 14-20:
Beginning
the para-
virtualized
drivers
installation.

The next screen prompts you to specify where you want to install the PV drivers on the guest virtual machine. I recommend you accept the default location, as shown in Figure 14-21.

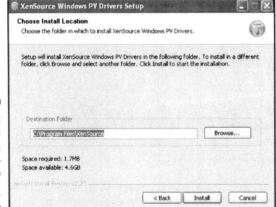

Figure 14-21:
Choosing an
installation
location for
the PV
drivers.

3. **Choose an appropriate installation location and then click Install.**

After the installation of the PV drivers is complete, the XenSource Windows PV Drivers Setup dialog box appears, asking you to reboot the guest virtual machine.

4. **Click Yes in the XenSource Windows PV Drivers Setup dialog box.**

The installation of the PV drivers is now complete and, as you can see from Figure 14-22, you are now given a choice of which version of Windows XP to boot: the slow, fully virtualized one, or the high-performance paravirtualized (PV) one. Although it's good to know that you can always choose which version to install, I recommend you focus on the PV version and select that version to boot.

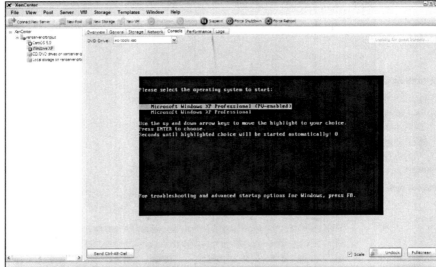

Figure 14-22:
Choosing a
virtualization
type for
Windows
XP boot.

5. **Press Enter to boot the PV-enabled version of Windows XP.**

   That's it. You're now up and running with paravirtualized Windows XP —
   getting better performance from your XenSource virtualization solution.
   See, that wasn't so hard, was it?

Accessing a Windows Guest VM with an RDP Client

If you've come this far, you'll have noticed one thing about interacting with
your Windows XP virtual machine in XenConsole: the cursor is a mite . . .
sluggish. This happens because XenConsole is using VNC (short for Virtual
Network Computing, a remote desktop access application) to access the
Windows XP virtual machine, with some emulation magic in the mix, which
causes the graphical performance of the console to suffer.

A better way to access Windows virtual machines is to use RDP (Remote
Desktop Protocol), which allows you to use a Windows-specific, Windows-
tuned protocol as the communication mechanism.

Fortunately, setting up Windows and XenConsole to use RDP is very straightforward.

The initial step is to configure your Windows XP virtual machine to allow RDP
access. (The configuration for this functionality is located in the Windows

Firewall, which you can access using the Windows XP Control Panel.) Here's how that's done:

1. **Choose Start➪Control Panel➪Windows Firewall.**

   The Windows Firewall dialog box appears. (I suppose Windows Firewall is as good a place as any other to store the controls for RDP.)

2. **Click the Exceptions tab.**

   To no one's surprise, the Exceptions tab of the Windows Firewall dialog box appears on-screen. (See Figure 14-23.)

3. **Select the Remote Desktop check box and then click OK.**

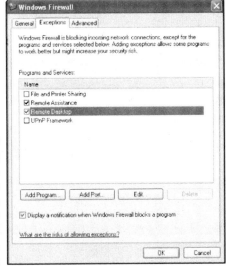

Figure 14-23:
The
Exceptions
tab of the
Windows
Firewall
dialog box.

You might think that, having just enabled Remote Desktop, you might then have remote desktop functionality. You might think that . . . but then of course you would be wrong to think that. We are talking Microsoft here, aren't we? To get remote desktop functionality, you need to enable *remote sharing* in the general computer options. So, get ready for another trip to Control Panel:

1. **Choose Start➪Control Panel➪System Properties.**

   The System Properties dialog box makes an appearance.

2. **Click the Remote tab.**

   You get what you see in Figure 14-24.

3. **Make sure the Allow Users to Connect Remotely to This Computer check box is selected; then click OK.**

   Remote access via RDP is now enabled.

Figure 14-24:
The Remote
tab of the
System
Properties
dialog box.

To actually use RDP as your access protocol, you need to click the Switch to
Remote Desktop button in the upper-right corner of the Windows XP guest
console (see Figure 14-25).

Switch to Remote Desktop button

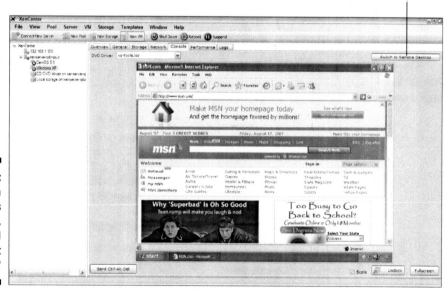

Figure 14-25:
Well, if it's a
Windows
machine,
you should
look at
MSN, right?

After you've done that, you'll be accessing the Windows XP guest virtual machine via RDP and should see better graphical responsiveness from the machine. If you take a look at Figure 14-25, the example installation has now accessed MSN to indicate Internet connectivity.

That's it. You're now running a paravirtualized, graphically responsive Windows XP guest virtual machine in XenSource virtualization. Although it might seem like you have to go through a lot of individual steps, it's very straightforward, methodical, and easy to do. And, best of all, it's free!

Part IV
Implementing Virtualization

The 5th Wave   By Rich Tennant

"So, what's this breakthrough in virtualization you wanted to show me?"

In this part . . .

After reading the previous parts, you're probably chomping at the bit to get going. This part is for you!

I present three different hands-on introductions to virtualization, providing a guided tour of how to install and configure VMware Server, Fedora Xen, and XenSource XenExpress.

Best of all, all three versions of virtualization that I demonstrate are absolutely free! Nothing holds you back from implementing virtualization right along with me. So get ready to download some software and watch the magic of virtualization appear before your eyes!

Chapter 15

Ten Steps to Your First Virtualization Project

*I*f you're raring to go with virtualization but want to approach your first virtualization project methodically, here are ten things to keep in mind as you create your project plan.

Recite After Me: Virtualization Is a Journey, Not a Product

Although it's tempting to jump right into implementation (and it's certainly easy, given that a number of virtualization products are available for free download), it's vital to remember that you're considering changing a part of your production infrastructure. Because critical operations of your company depend on that infrastructure, don't rush headlong into implementation — no matter how tempting it is.

Any significant project requires careful planning and monitoring. You should move through planning, implementation, and operations stages deliberately, with careful project tracking and milestone evaluation.

Virtualization makes the process of project planning even more important because of the fact that many organizations find that their virtualization infra-structure ends up getting modified over time as they realize that they'll get additional benefits if they apply virtualization more widely. In other words, when IT organizations start to reap some of the benefits of moving to a virtu-alized environment, they start to consider whether there are other areas where they could apply virtualization. Truthfully, virtualization can be extremely seductive — once you start to get the hang of it, you look for addi-tional applications of the technology.

What this means is that you need to approach virtualization with a perspec-tive that assumes change in the virtualization infrastructure, which implies that you should plan for a fairly flexible architecture so that you can modify and extend it as you incorporate additional uses of the technology. The remainder of the tips in this chapter relate to how you can take a methodical approach to your virtualization project.

Evaluate Your Use Cases

Because virtualization technology has a number of different uses, you should think through how you're likely to apply it. Earlier chapters of this book (especially Chapters 1 and 3) describe the many applications of virtualization, including server consolidation, failover, high availability, and server pooling. Moreover, some thought should go into how you might use virtualization in the future. This is because the range of products that can be used for virtualization tends to narrow as you move to more complex applications of the technology; consequently, selecting a product that's appropriate for your early application of virtualization, but which doesn't have the ability to offer the additional functionality you'll want later in your journey, is a shortsighted choice, because you'll end up having to replace it. Thinking through your potential future uses of virtualization can help you avoid making a poor decision now.

 You definitely want to avoid a situation in which you purchase a number of licenses for a specific virtualization product, only to find out 18 months later that the product is incapable of meeting your later needs. This can lead to an unfortunate outcome with the organization needing to purchase a whole new set of products, rather than being able to leverage the original product. Even worse, you might end up needing to convert the virtual machines you've cre-ated for your original virtualization product into the image format required by the new virtualization product — clearly a lot of work that could be avoided by upfront planning.

By thoroughly assessing your use cases, you can identify your needs in the here and now as well as your needs that might surface in the future.

What is a use case? Simply put, it's a definition of how you will — or might, in the future — apply virtualization. Where a use case becomes extremely important is in helping you identify virtualization capabilities that you might not need today, but that might become important in the future.

Echoing the "virtualization is a journey, not a product" mantra, be sure to probe (and probe again) during your use case creation about potential uses of the technology. If some group says, "We want to be able to get rid of a bunch of our servers," you can infer that server consolidation is an obvious need. If you left your questioning at that, you'd conclude that any virtualization product that supported moving a number of physical servers onto a single server would do. However, if you asked "Is the downtime of systems a big issue for you?" and got a head nodding up and down vigorously in response, that's a clue that failover or even high availability is perhaps desirable. (This scenario shows why it's important to ask a number of questions and not to be satisfied with the initial answers.)

Another critical step in developing your virtualization use cases is to ask lots of different groups what they're looking for from virtualization. It's a cliché, but people are generally most aware of and vocal about their own problems. Unless you speak to a number of different groups, you run the risk of discovering only a subset of true user needs.

Review Your Operations Organizational Structure

"What's this?" I hear you say. "Why should I look at the organizational structure to help make a technical decision?"

You might be tempted to treat virtualization as a purely technical matter, but that would be a huge mistake. Humans are political (or, at least, social) animals. Decisions, even technology decisions, confront the fact that people have emotional biases that affect their acceptance of new initiatives.

Because you're a savvy operator, you recognize that it's important to make everyone aware of your virtualization project and, if possible, get them to buy in. So canvassing a broad range of individuals within the organization is necessary because it will help you gain acceptance of your virtualization project. Also, talking to a broader range of people will help you flesh out your use cases and avoid the problem of having to discard one virtualization infrastructure because you've moved along with your virtualization needs.

There's a more practical reason to review your organization structure as well. Many IT operations groups are organized along platform lines. In other words, one group manages Windows, and another group manages Linux machines. When it comes time to design your virtualization infrastructure, you should take into account these aspects of your use cases so that you don't try to mix virtual machine types on individual servers. Trying to have two different groups cooperate on administering a single machine is a recipe for problems, if not disaster. Be sure to identify use cases based on a wide variety of perspectives and groups so that you truly identify the needs of the organization today and in the future.

Define Your Virtualization Architecture

Defining your virtualization architecture is a fancy way of saying that you must take your use cases and insights gleaned from your organizational structure and define your virtualization infrastructure design.

For example, suppose you *really, really* need to restart very quickly any virtual machines that have crashed, and you also need virtualization software capable of deciding whether said crashed virtual machine can be successfully restarted on the original server or needs to be restarted on a second machine. In that case, you have a clear need for high availability. This situation implies that you'll need hardware capable of being managed in a more automated fashion so that virtual machines can be automatically migrated. It also implies that you'll need virtualization software that can coordinate multiple machines. Finally, it implies that you might very well need to implement storage virtualization.

As you can see, your use cases and organizational structure can be enormously important in determining your virtualization architecture. So, based on the information you gathered during the first two steps, create a virtualization architecture design.

This design is absolutely critical, and you should definitely review it with all interested parties. The review process serves the following purposes:

✔ First, it ensures that you've captured everyone's needs. If you review the architecture with someone and you hear that the operations groups would like to implement a more automated management capability, that might steer you toward a certain set of products.

✔ Second, and perhaps even more important, the review process will tend to generate awareness and commitment from the different groups for your virtualization project. By building a sense of inevitability, you'll generate momentum for your project, which is important.

Select Your Virtualization Product (s)

After you've defined your virtualization architecture, you can finally select the product or products you'll use in your virtualization project. By this time, this exercise should be relatively straightforward because you've identified what functionality must be present in the virtualization architecture.

You can use Chapter 3 to identify the products available to meet your needs. One thing to keep in mind is that you might need to do some research on the individual products themselves. The fact of the matter is, although the product's Web site might claim that it can do such-and-such a function, the actual implementation of that functionality might only work well enough for the vendor to claim support for it, but not that well in real-world use. You can do this research by reading articles on the product, searching through the product forums, and so on. Often, the forums are available on individual vendor Web sites. For great places to find articles, reviews, and so on, see Chapter 17.

The pilot implementation phase, discussed a little later in this chapter, gives you the chance to truly validate the capability of the products you've selected.

Select Your Virtualization Hardware

Just as your choice of virtualization software is guided by the research you've done, so too will your choice of virtualization hardware be guided. You have lots of choices about what physical infrastructure to run your virtualization architecture upon.

I don't really have enough room here to discuss the different types of hardware currently available, but suffice it to say that you have options well beyond repurposing your existing 32-bit pizza boxes. Chapter 8 goes into great detail about hardware considerations and options for virtualization.

With the rise of 64-bit machines, blade servers, and the like, machines are far more capable of scaling to meet the requirements of heavily virtualized infrastructures. Beyond these options is a whole new generation of virtualization-focused hardware, designed from the ground up to support virtualization. This new generation of systems supports large amounts of physical memory; contains enough slots for redundant storage virtualization hardware; and supports multichip, multicore processors to provide enough raw horsepower for numerous virtual machines.

By mapping your use cases and virtualization architecture onto your existing physical infrastructure, you can determine whether the current infrastructure is sufficient for the final virtualization architecture. And, with that information at hand, you can develop a final virtualization budget to help define your project economics. Don't forget to review the resulting project plan with all important constituencies — having real money at stake gets peoples' attention, which will be necessary for you to get a final approval.

Perform a Pilot Implementation

You should confirm that your project assumptions and choices will actually work in production. Unfortunately, many people wait to find out until they actually go into production with their new system, which is obviously the wrong way to go about things.

By creating a pilot implementation, you have the opportunity to determine whether your virtualization architecture will actually work when you finally go into production.

The goal of a pilot implementation is to replicate on a small scale the final production system you'll run, including hardware, software, applications, and workloads. The closer you come to mirroring your final production environment in miniature, the more likely you'll be able to determine whether everything will work properly when you finally throw the switch and go live.

Implement Your Production Environment

After you've performed your pilot implementation and evaluated its results, you can move forward and build your production environment. In this stage, you order software and hardware; install any necessary data center equipment (for example, power connections); install the virtualization software and hardware; and confirm that you're ready to move forward with migration to your new virtualized architecture.

Although all the work that has gone on before has been interesting and fun, this step has to be executed flawlessly because if the infrastructure's not right, the production systems won't work properly. So install everything, make sure it boots up properly, and do some initial testing to ensure everything is working as it should.

Migrate Your Physical Servers

Migration is perhaps the trickiest stage of your virtualization journey. Making sure that every system gets moved into its own virtual machine and is working properly is a time fraught with danger.

You have two choices for migration:

- ✔ **Automated:** Automated migration software products are available, which are usually called physical-to-virtual migration tools — P2V tools, for short. Depending on what kind of systems you're migrating, an automated migration software package can be a huge help. Unfortunately, the automated packages work best for Windows-based systems and don't always work perfectly for them. Linux automated migration software is much less successful because, in general, Linux systems are much less consistent in terms of setup, which means it's harder to know what to do for all configurations. On the other hand, this is an area with a lot of new products being released all the time, so it pays to do some research before falling back on the manual migration method.

- ✔ **Manual:** Manual migration is just what it sounds like: hands-on work to move systems. It entails installing software in a new virtual machine, backing up the data from the existing physical server, and then recovering that data into the new virtual server. Manual migration is a ton of work and can be error prone. On the other hand, if you do it right, you will come out with perfect virtual machines. Should you decide that manual migration is the right route for you, be prepared for lots of work and the need for painstaking attention to detail.

Manage Your Virtualized Infrastructure

Finally, you've implemented your virtualization infrastructure and gotten your physical servers migrated to it. You've had the party and handed out the T-shirts. Do you think you can rest now?

Not a chance. You need to manage (or, you might say, administer) your new environment. Depending on what vendor you get your hardware from, you might find that they've integrated administering virtual machines into their existing system management tools. However, you might also find the available management tools rather lacking. This is a time to call on your hardware supplier or your operations software provider to see what they have that will help you manage your new virtualized environment.

No matter how you manage your new environment, get ready for new challenges, because the new virtualized infrastructure is definitely different from your old physical infrastructure. I'm willing to bet, though, that after you get used to the new infrastructure, you'll never go back.

Chapter 16

Ten Virtualization Pitfalls to Avoid

*P*eople often say that the best way to learn something is by making mistakes: You learn many lessons about the right way to do something by doing it wrong! I won't necessarily argue with that perspective, but what if you want to smooth the bumpy path to success? Why not learn from *others'* mistakes?

In that spirit, here are ten pitfalls to avoid in your virtualization project. I've drawn them from both personal experience and observation of how other organizations have suffered as they moved forward with virtualization.

Don't Wait for All the Kinks to Be Worked Out

Virtualization has plenty of benefits, and many organizations are finding that they're very happy after moving to a virtualized environment. It must be said, however, that virtualization is a relatively new technology. That means that the field is in a great deal of flux because so many exciting things are going on. Sometimes it seems like a new product or service becomes available every day.

Some people embrace a rapidly changing field because they expect it offers tremendous potential. Others hang back, with the thought that they'll defer taking action until things are more stable.

The reality is that virtualization is a huge technology trend that's going to undergo tremendous change for at least the next five years. Trying to wait until things settle down is pointless. That's a recipe for being left far behind your competitors.

A far better approach is to start small and experiment. You'll learn far more by doing than you will by reading or even talking to others whose organizations have implemented virtualization. Don't wait for all the kinks to be worked out, because kinks are going to be around for the foreseeable future. You need to get on board today.

Don't Skimp on Training

One of the most bewildering things about IT organizations is that they will invest huge sums in new hardware and software but skimp on ensuring that their employees learn how to use their new systems.

Because virtualization is a new technology, you can't count on people already knowing how to use it. It's critical that you understand that there *will* be a learning curve as employees get up to speed on the new infrastructure. Don't compound the challenge by failing to educate employees on how to use and manage the new software.

Most of the virtualization products have an established training program to ensure that people can prepare to use them. Take advantage of these programs and raise the probability of virtualization success in your organization.

Don't Apply Virtualization in Areas That Are Not Appropriate

One of the primary reasons organizations are pursuing virtualization is to use their hardware better. Lightly loaded systems are prime candidates to virtualize. Many important but lightly used systems like DNS and DHCP are good virtualization candidates.

By contrast, systems that already achieve high utilization aren't really good candidates to be virtualized. The perfect example of this is a dedicated database server. Not only are these servers often heavily loaded and using much of the capacity of the hardware they're running on, they're also critical to business operations. Furthermore, they're often tuned to take advantage of the hardware system they're running on. Moving them to a virtual machine forfeits the performance benefits that might have been gained by hardware tuning. For these types of systems, moving to virtualization isn't necessarily a good strategy. This is especially true because, by definition, virtualized machines share resources with other virtual machines. For critical systems, sharing resources might cause them to experience performance issues, which is problematic.

Therefore, don't assume that every system in your environment should be moved to virtualization. Evaluate the load and purpose of systems, and for those systems that are business-critical or already heavily loaded, consider whether it would be better to continue to host them on dedicated hardware.

Don't Imagine That Virtualization Is Static

The global economy is being transformed. No matter what country you live in, your national economy is changing rapidly. Individual businesses find that their business conditions are extremely dynamic, depending on season, market developments, and even merger and acquisition activity.

So don't assume that your virtualization implementation will be static. Far from it.

Not only will your business conditions dictate that you continually evaluate how well your virtualization infrastructure meets current business realities, but virtualization itself is constantly changing. Not only are the virtualization vendors constantly improving their products, but a large number of other companies are creating new products to help IT organizations take advantage of virtualization, all with the goal of helping you run your virtualized data center more effectively. This means that your state-of-the-art virtualization solution implemented 18 months ago might need to be examined in light of new virtualization developments.

Although this might make it sound as if virtualization will be a Sisyphean task, endlessly repeated and never finished, it really means that the field is so rapidly improving that you must assess your current situation to determine whether you can achieve much more.

Therefore, after you make your move to virtualization, be sure to periodically re-examine your current solution in light of what's newly available. And be sure to constantly monitor developments in the field to keep an eye on what the latest trends and products are. If you do this, you'll be able to ensure you're getting the most out of your infrastructure.

Don't Skip the "Boring" Stuff

It's fun to install software and see new things come up and run. It's not nearly as much fun to do all those use case interviews or design reviews. But keep in mind that those "boring" tasks make the fun stuff possible; in fact, without the boring tasks being completed, you probably won't get the go-ahead to move forward with the project and have fun doing the interesting stuff.

So, be sure to review Chapter 15 to ensure you're performing the ten steps to your first virtualization project. There you find an outline of all the necessary steps, both exciting and less-than-exciting, for your virtualization project.

Don't Overlook a Business Case

Although you might read dozens of vendor case studies and even magazine articles about how much money virtualization has saved for different companies, it's important to keep in mind that those *are* different companies.

In these times of short rations for IT organizations, there's no surer way to get your project shot down than by ignoring the business case for it. On the other hand, there's no surer way to ensure your project gains executive support and sails through the approval process than by demonstrating the impressive financial benefits available by moving forward with the project.

This means that you need to evaluate the financial impact of moving to virtualization and present that information as part of the project approval process.

Don't Overlook the Importance of Organization

A sure-fire way of getting your project shot down is to overlook the political implications of implementing it. *Every* change, no matter how small, helps or harms every person in an organization.

Because virtualization affects so many groups, it's important that you work with each of them and convince them that virtualization will make their work lives better and easier.

Furthermore, it's important that you align your virtualization architecture with your company's organizational structure to ensure smooth post-implementation operations.

More projects fail due to people issues than to technical issues. Don't let your virtualization project fail because you don't work on the people issues, too.

Don't Forget to Research Your Software Vendor Support Policies

Because virtualization has caught on so quickly, many technology players are still trying to figure out how to respond to it. This is particularly true of software vendors. More specifically, many software vendors are still trying to work out their policies for supporting their software when it's executing in a virtual machine.

Traditionally, the stance of software companies is to shift the blame for problems to any other plausible party. This often means that, should you experience a problem with two software products interoperating, each vendor will blame the other for the problem.

Because virtualization interposes a software layer between an application and the underlying hardware, some software vendors are reluctant to provide full support for their products when running in a virtual machine.

As you plan your virtualization project, be sure to assess the support policies of each vendor whose products you'd like to migrate to virtual machines. If you find that some of them fail to offer acceptable support, consider leaving those machines as nonvirtualized systems.

Don't Overlook the Importance of Hardware

Virtualization software enables other software resources to take better advantage of underlying hardware. But don't imagine that the hardware itself has no effect on virtualization. Far from it. The type and capability of the hardware you use to host your virtualization solution can dramatically impact the virtualization density you achieve, as well as the performance levels available for your virtual machines. In particular, don't plan on using your existing servers as the foundation for your virtualized infrastructure. Those machines might have been great for working in the "one application, one server" world, but they're woefully inadequate as a platform for running high-density virtualization.

The importance of hardware is only going to increase as new, virtualization-ready hardware comes to market. Hardware manufacturers are cooking up significant virtualization capabilities, so don't overlook the role of hardware in your virtualization infrastructure.

Don't Forget to Have a Project Party

Last, but not least, be sure to celebrate your virtualization success. A party is a traditional way to observe an achievement or a milestone, and I recommend a big one when you finish implementation of your virtualization project. Congratulations, and save a piece of cake for me!

Chapter 17

Ten Great Resources on Virtualization

*W*ell, you have your copy of *Virtualization For Dummies,* but you feel that you need to keep up with the latest news; after all, it's a fast-changing field with new developments all the time. Where can you go for more great information about virtualization?

Maybe your concern is more practical. You want to know how you can get some hands-on experience with virtualization — but you don't want to spend a ton of money? What can you do?

The answer to your questions is right here in this chapter.

Here are ten great resources on virtualization. You can take advantage of them to hone your skills and keep your knowledge up to date.

Get Free Virtualization Software

One of the really great things about virtualization's ever-growing popularity is that you're now at a time and place where you can take advantage of the structural changes in the software industry. Five or ten years ago, to begin using a new type of software, you'd have to buy a copy — and that copy would be expensive enough to dissuade you from buying one just to "experiment."

Today, however, the picture is completely different. Thanks to the assault of open source software, pretty much everyone — even proprietary software vendors — offers free versions of their products. Of course, some of the free products don't offer all the functionality of the for-fee offerings, but they aren't the crippled versions typical of yesteryear's demo offerings, either. No, they're very capable products — so much so, in fact, that many companies use these free versions in production.

Just about every vendor mentioned in this book — companies like VMware, XenSource, SWsoft, and Virtual Iron — has a free offering you can use to experiment, develop, and even deploy. So go ahead, enjoy!

Every vendor prominently features their free products in their product page. Poke around on the vendor Web site and you'll find free products ready for download.

Get Great Content about Virtualization

A great resource with lots of fresh content about virtualization is SearchServerVirtualization, located at `http://searchserver virtualization.techtarget.com`.

This site offers stories about developments in the virtualization market as well as user-experience stories. It also features pieces by virtualization experts discussing technical issues regarding virtualization. (Full disclosure: I occasionally write for the site.) It's well worth checking out.

Get the Latest News about Virtualization

A resource that I take advantage of is the weekly virtualization newsletter published by InfoWorld. Edited by David Marshall (full disclosure again: Dave is the technical editor of this book), it tells you everything that's happened in virtualization over the past week. David also has regular podcasts that are listed in the newsletter, so you can get your virtualization information while on the go. Sign up at the InfoWorld site (www.infoworld.com) on the Newsletters tab.

Read Blogs about Virtualization

What if weekly news isn't quick enough for you? What if you want the latest info as soon as it's ready? Well, then, virtualization blogs are for you. You can track them down on your own to read, or you can get them streamed to you via RSS. If you're looking for an immediate virtualization update, check out these blogs:

- ✔ **Linux virtualization:** http://linuxvirtualization.com
- ✔ **X86 virtualization:** http://x86virtualization.com
- ✔ **Thin client (and more):** www.thincomputing.net
- ✔ **Virtualization for small business:** www.virtualizationdaily.com

And, of course, the vendor blogs:

- ✔ **Microsoft:** http://blogs.technet.com/virtualization
- ✔ **Virtual PC Guy:** http://blogs.msdn.com/virtual_pc_guy/default.aspx (This particular blogger is a program manager in Microsoft's Virtualization group.)
- ✔ **Xen:** http://blogs.xensource.com
- ✔ **VMware:** http://blogs.vmware.com/vmtn/

Keep Up with Hardware Developments Relating to Virtualization

Virtualization is much more than software. (If you're not sure of that, check out Chapter 8.) Hardware is a vital component in virtualization, and hardware vendors are increasingly putting virtualization enhancements into their products.

Sadly, however, hardware vendors have declined to follow the lead of their software brethren by giving away free copies of their products.

Nevertheless, if you want to be on top of what's going on with virtualization, be sure to keep up with what's happening on the hardware side. There's lots of activity in processors, so be sure to follow what AMD and Intel are doing. In addition, the network and storage vendors are moving to integrate virtualization into their products, so companies like Emulex and QLogic are interesting as well. Just about every vendor prominently features virtualization on their Web site home page, with links to technical information, case studies, and product roadmaps.

Find Out More about Virtualization

One of the best ways to learn a subject is from peers. You can get so much from hearing another's challenges in mastering a topic. The same holds true for virtualization. Seek out peer-level events that are focused on virtualization. Several of the virtualization vendors such as VMware have started user groups. Find out whether a user group is meeting near you and get yourself there. VMware's user group listings can be found at `http://vmware.com/resources/communities/usergroup/localgroups.html`.

Another place that you might find virtualization-savvy peers is at a local technology meeting. For example, both Linux and Microsoft often have local user groups that occasionally cover virtualization. Check them out — and if you're brave, volunteer to talk about . . . virtualization!

Attend Virtualization Events

An increasing number of live events and conferences are devoted to virtualization. Attending one of these offers the opportunity to hear about virtualization first-hand. These events typically have both vendors and users as speakers, so you can get the idealized version of the virtualization story (vendors) and the real-life version (users) in one location. Also, other technology conferences have noted virtualization's popularity and have added tracks to their sessions covering the topic. For example, the most recent LinuxWorld had a multiday track devoted to virtualization. I attended most of the sessions and found lots of useful information in them.

It's well worth your time to attend these events. What's even better is that most of them are free to attend, so you can get a concentrated dose of virtualization at low cost.

InfoWorld and TechTarget (parent company of SearchServerVirtualization, discussed above) both put on one-day virtualization events and they're lots of fun to attend — so go!

The largest virtualization-specific event is VMworld, sponsored by VMware — a three day pulsing, noisy circus of virtualization. Moreover, all the other virtualization vendors attend VMworld, so you can see a lot in a little time. (Full disclosure: I was on the product awards committee at the most recent VMworld.)

Take Advantage of Vendor Information

All technology vendors produce a torrent of information: whitepapers, Web sites, podcasts, webinars, on-site seminars. And virtualization vendors are no different. Of course, all vendor information is slanted to make their offering look the best, but you knew that already, right?

So, the right strategy is to skim off the good information and ignore the hype. And there's lots of good information available. Start with the vendor Web sites. Most of them have a signup spot, where you can ask to be informed of new information as it becomes available. Take advantage of all the work vendors are doing to reach you.

Keep Up with Storage Virtualization

If there's one theme in this book I hope you take away, it's that virtualization is a journey. And that journey often makes a stop in Storageville. Every virtualization strategy eventually encompasses storage, so you need to make sure you know what's up with that. Here's a great site to bookmark and keep track of:

```
www.networkworld.com/topics/virtualization.html
```

Get the Latest and Last Word on Virtualization

And, last but not least, one final online site that carries great, up-to-date information on virtualization:

```
www.virtualization.info
```

Part V
The Part of Tens

The 5th Wave   By Rich Tennant

No need to worry. It's just a virtual ravenous anaconda.

In this part . . .

This part lives up to its title. Every *For Dummies* book provides easy-to-follow, useful information in lists of . . . ten! This book lives up to the honorable *For Dummies* tradition by offering pithy guidance in the form of three different lists of ten.

If you want to cut to the chase on starting a virtualization project, there's a list for you. If you want to know what ten things you should avoid when you begin implementing virtualization, there's a list for you. Finally, if you want to pursue virtualization knowledge beyond this book, there are ten great resources for you to check out – every one of them guaranteed to make your virtualization day.

Index

• *N* •

BUSINESS, CAREERS & PERSONAL FINANCE

0-7645-9847-3

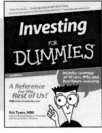
0-7645-2431-3

Also available:
- Business Plans Kit For Dummies
  0-7645-9794-9
- Economics For Dummies
  0-7645-5726-2
- Grant Writing For Dummies
  0-7645-8416-2
- Home Buying For Dummies
  0-7645-5331-3
- Managing For Dummies
  0-7645-1771-6
- Marketing For Dummies
  0-7645-5600-2

- Personal Finance For Dummies
  0-7645-2590-5*
- Resumes For Dummies
  0-7645-5471-9
- Selling For Dummies
  0-7645-5363-1
- Six Sigma For Dummies
  0-7645-6798-5
- Small Business Kit For Dummies
  0-7645-5984-2
- Starting an eBay Business For Dummies
  0-7645-6924-4
- Your Dream Career For Dummies
  0-7645-9795-7

HOME & BUSINESS COMPUTER BASICS

0-470-05432-8

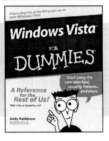
0-471-75421-8

Also available:
- Cleaning Windows Vista For Dummies
  0-471-78293-9
- Excel 2007 For Dummies
  0-470-03737-7
- Mac OS X Tiger For Dummies
  0-7645-7675-5
- MacBook For Dummies
  0-470-04859-X
- Macs For Dummies
  0-470-04849-2
- Office 2007 For Dummies
  0-470-00923-3

- Outlook 2007 For Dummies
  0-470-03830-6
- PCs For Dummies
  0-7645-8958-X
- Salesforce.com For Dummies
  0-470-04893-X
- Upgrading & Fixing Laptops For Dummies
  0-7645-8959-8
- Word 2007 For Dummies
  0-470-03658-3
- Quicken 2007 For Dummies
  0-470-04600-7

FOOD, HOME, GARDEN, HOBBIES, MUSIC & PETS

0-7645-8404-9

0-7645-9904-6

Also available:
- Candy Making For Dummies
  0-7645-9734-5
- Card Games For Dummies
  0-7645-9910-0
- Crocheting For Dummies
  0-7645-4151-X
- Dog Training For Dummies
  0-7645-8418-9
- Healthy Carb Cookbook For Dummies
  0-7645-8476-6
- Home Maintenance For Dummies
  0-7645-5215-5

- Horses For Dummies
  0-7645-9797-3
- Jewelry Making & Beading For Dummies
  0-7645-2571-9
- Orchids For Dummies
  0-7645-6759-4
- Puppies For Dummies
  0-7645-5255-4
- Rock Guitar For Dummies
  0-7645-5356-9
- Sewing For Dummies
  0-7645-6847-7
- Singing For Dummies
  0-7645-2475-5

INTERNET & DIGITAL MEDIA

0-470-04529-9

0-470-04894-8

Also available:
- Blogging For Dummies
  0-471-77084-1
- Digital Photography For Dummies
  0-7645-9802-3
- Digital Photography All-in-One Desk Reference For Dummies
  0-470-03743-1
- Digital SLR Cameras and Photography For Dummies
  0-7645-9803-1
- eBay Business All-in-One Desk Reference For Dummies
  0-7645-8438-3
- HDTV For Dummies
  0-470-09673-X

- Home Entertainment PCs For Dummies
  0-470-05523-5
- MySpace For Dummies
  0-470-09529-6
- Search Engine Optimization For Dummies
  0-471-97998-8
- Skype For Dummies
  0-470-04891-3
- The Internet For Dummies
  0-7645-8996-2
- Wiring Your Digital Home For Dummies
  0-471-91830-X

* Separate Canadian edition also available
† Separate U.K. edition also available

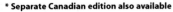

Available wherever books are sold. For more information or to order direct: U.S. customers visit www.dummies.com or call 1-877-762-2974.
U.K. customers visit www.wileyeurope.com or call 0800 243407. Canadian customers visit www.wiley.ca or call 1-800-567-4797.

WILEY

SPORTS, FITNESS, PARENTING, RELIGION & SPIRITUALITY

0-471-76871-5

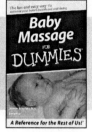

0-7645-7841-3

Also available:

- Catholicism For Dummies
  0-7645-5391-7
- Exercise Balls For Dummies
  0-7645-5623-1
- Fitness For Dummies
  0-7645-7851-0
- Football For Dummies
  0-7645-3936-1
- Judaism For Dummies
  0-7645-5299-6
- Potty Training For Dummies
  0-7645-5417-4
- Buddhism For Dummies
  0-7645-5359-3

- Pregnancy For Dummies
  0-7645-4483-7 †
- Ten Minute Tone-Ups For Dummies
  0-7645-7207-5
- NASCAR For Dummies
  0-7645-7681-X
- Religion For Dummies
  0-7645-5264-3
- Soccer For Dummies
  0-7645-5229-5
- Women in the Bible For Dummies
  0-7645-8475-8

TRAVEL

0-7645-7749-2

0-7645-6945-7

Also available:

- Alaska For Dummies
  0-7645-7746-8
- Cruise Vacations For Dummies
  0-7645-6941-4
- England For Dummies
  0-7645-4276-1
- Europe For Dummies
  0-7645-7529-5
- Germany For Dummies
  0-7645-7823-5
- Hawaii For Dummies
  0-7645-7402-7

- Italy For Dummies
  0-7645-7386-1
- Las Vegas For Dummies
  0-7645-7382-9
- London For Dummies
  0-7645-4277-X
- Paris For Dummies
  0-7645-7630-5
- RV Vacations For Dummies
  0-7645-4442-X
- Walt Disney World & Orlando
  For Dummies
  0-7645-9660-8

GRAPHICS, DESIGN & WEB DEVELOPMENT

0-7645-8815-X

0-7645-9571-7

Also available:

- 3D Game Animation For Dummies
  0-7645-8789-7
- AutoCAD 2006 For Dummies
  0-7645-8925-3
- Building a Web Site For Dummies
  0-7645-7144-3
- Creating Web Pages For Dummies
  0-470-08030-2
- Creating Web Pages All-in-One Desk
  Reference For Dummies
  0-7645-4345-8
- Dreamweaver 8 For Dummies
  0-7645-9649-7

- InDesign CS2 For Dummies
  0-7645-9572-5
- Macromedia Flash 8 For Dummies
  0-7645-9691-8
- Photoshop CS2 and Digital
  Photography For Dummies
  0-7645-9580-6
- Photoshop Elements 4 For Dummies
  0-471-77483-9
- Syndicating Web Sites with RSS Feeds
  For Dummies
  0-7645-8848-6
- Yahoo! SiteBuilder For Dummies
  0-7645-9800-7

NETWORKING, SECURITY, PROGRAMMING & DATABASES

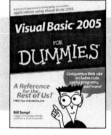

0-7645-7728-X

0-471-74940-0

Also available:

- Access 2007 For Dummies
  0-470-04612-0
- ASP.NET 2 For Dummies
  0-7645-7907-X
- C# 2005 For Dummies
  0-7645-9704-3
- Hacking For Dummies
  0-470-05235-X
- Hacking Wireless Networks
  For Dummies
  0-7645-9730-2
- Java For Dummies
  0-470-08716-1

- Microsoft SQL Server 2005 For Dummies
  0-7645-7755-7
- Networking All-in-One Desk Reference
  For Dummies
  0-7645-9939-9
- Preventing Identity Theft For Dummies
  0-7645-7336-5
- Telecom For Dummies
  0-471-77085-X
- Visual Studio 2005 All-in-One Desk
  Reference For Dummies
  0-7645-9775-2
- XML For Dummies
  0-7645-8845-1

HEALTH & SELF-HELP

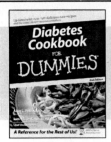

0-7645-8450-2

0-7645-4149-8

Also available:

Bipolar Disorder For Dummies
0-7645-8451-0

Chemotherapy and Radiation
For Dummies
0-7645-7832-4

Controlling Cholesterol For Dummies
0-7645-5440-9

Diabetes For Dummies
0-7645-6820-5* †

Divorce For Dummies
0-7645-8417-0 †

Fibromyalgia For Dummies
0-7645-5441-7

Low-Calorie Dieting For Dummies
0-7645-9905-4

Meditation For Dummies
0-471-77774-9

Osteoporosis For Dummies
0-7645-7621-6

Overcoming Anxiety For Dummies
0-7645-5447-6

Reiki For Dummies
0-7645-9907-0

Stress Management For Dummies
0-7645-5144-2

EDUCATION, HISTORY, REFERENCE & TEST PREPARATION

0-7645-8381-6

0-7645-9554-7

Also available:

The ACT For Dummies
0-7645-9652-7

Algebra For Dummies
0-7645-5325-9

Algebra Workbook For Dummies
0-7645-8467-7

Astronomy For Dummies
0-7645-8465-0

Calculus For Dummies
0-7645-2498-4

Chemistry For Dummies
0-7645-5430-1

Forensics For Dummies
0-7645-5580-4

Freemasons For Dummies
0-7645-9796-5

French For Dummies
0-7645-5193-0

Geometry For Dummies
0-7645-5324-0

Organic Chemistry I For Dummies
0-7645-6902-3

The SAT I For Dummies
0-7645-7193-1

Spanish For Dummies
0-7645-5194-9

Statistics For Dummies
0-7645-5423-9

Get smart @ dummies.com®

- **Find a full list of Dummies titles**
- **Look into loads of FREE on-site articles**
- **Sign up for FREE eTips e-mailed to you weekly**
- **See what other products carry the Dummies name**
- **Shop directly from the Dummies bookstore**
- **Enter to win new prizes every month!**

* Separate Canadian edition also available
† Separate U.K. edition also available

Available wherever books are sold. For more information or to order direct: U.S. customers visit www.dummies.com or call 1-877-762-2974.
U.K. customers visit www.wileyeurope.com or call 0800 243407. Canadian customers visit www.wiley.ca or call 1-800-567-4797.

CPSIA information can be obtained at www.ICGtesting.com
Printed in the USA
BVOW02n0741170714

359505BV00003B/7/P